A ransom for many

A ransom for many

Mark's Gospel simply explained

Steve Wilmshurst

 BOOKS

EP Books
Faverdale North, Darlington, DL3 0PH, England
e-mail: sales@epbooks.org
web: www.epbooks.org

EP Books USA
P. O. Box 614, Carlisle, PA 17013, USA
e-mail: usasales@epbooks.org
web: www.epbooks.us

First published 2011

British Library Cataloguing in Publication Data available

ISBN 13 978 085234 744 7   ISBN 0 85234 744 8

Printed and bound in the UK by Charlesworth, Wakefield, West Yorkshire

Contents

Preface

This book is based on a series of sermons preached at Kensington Baptist Church in Bristol, a series I began a few weeks after concluding the series on Revelation which subsequently became a previous book, *The Final Word* (also in the Welwyn Commentary Series). I have loved preaching through Mark. Increasingly, and beyond my expectations, I have been drawn in by the sheer power of the storytelling. Grasping something of the skilled and beautiful construction of the Gospel has frequently shed fresh light on familiar passages; recognizing the half-concealed links to the Old Testament prophets has opened up new understanding of the mission of the Lord Jesus.

I would like to thank many people who have helped and guided me with thoughts about Mark's Gospel, beginning with Craig Smith, formerly of Trinity College, Bristol, who has been a model of the godly scholar combining academic integrity with spiritual insight and the 'real world' of Christian ministry. Chris Kelly's article in *Foundations* provided very valuable help with the structure of Mark. I greatly appreciate the support of my ministry colleagues, my family and those others who have encouraged me in this preaching series in particular — they know who they are!

Mark's Gospel focuses on the Lord Jesus as the crucified Christ; as his followers we are called to take up our cross and follow him who gave his life as a ransom for many. If this book encourages you in this path of discipleship, it will have achieved its purpose.

Steve Wilmshurst
July 2011

Introduction to Mark's Gospel

What is a Gospel?

We are all used to having four Gospels; most of us probably grew up knowing many of the Gospel stories. But what *is* a Gospel? Is a Gospel just a straightforward biography of the life of Jesus, or is it something else? The vital clue is in the name. The English word 'gospel' is our translation of the Greek word *euangelion* — sometimes in English we still use the word *evangel*. It means an announcement of good news. A gospel, an evangel, is a proclamation: originally, something that was *announced*. The Gospels, like the rest of the New Testament, were written in the days of the Roman Empire. In Rome, when a new emperor was enthroned, or if the emperor's wife gave birth to a son, it would be announced through an *evangel*, good news. In Jewish tradition, an evangel meant good news especially about God's coming kingdom.

This helps us to understand what kind of documents our four Gospels are: they are making announcements of good news. They are not simply dispassionate, factual biographies of the Lord Jesus, but were written to bear witness to his life and ministry, both for Christians to learn about their Lord and for unbelievers to be challenged to accept the good news. So we should not think of the Gospels as simply stories written down by people who had nothing better to do! Each was put together, under the inspiration of the Holy

Spirit, for a specific reason. They all have a theological purpose in mind, and by reading each Gospel carefully we can understand something of what that purpose is. It is important that we let each Gospel speak for itself. You do sometimes hear preachers, for instance, preaching on some Gospel narrative and constantly cross-referencing to the parallel accounts in the other Gospels — as if the Holy Spirit would have done better to produce just one Gospel story, with all the differences of emphasis and selection of story ironed out. But the Holy Spirit did not do that, and I think we need to let each account stand on its own with its own integrity. Sometimes there is much to learn by comparing them, but we should remember that, under divine inspiration, Mark chose what to include, what to leave out and how to express what he wanted to say.

Introductory issues about Mark

Author

Although the Gospel itself nowhere says so, there is an unbroken tradition from the earliest days that the author is the John Mark we know from Acts. It is quite likely that Mark is the young man we meet briefly in chapter 14, running away from the scene of Jesus' arrest. We know that Mark lived in Jerusalem, where his mother hosted one of the first house churches (Acts 12:12). Peter goes there when an angel rescues him from jail; Mark will no doubt have been present at the time. A few years later we meet him again: in Acts 13 Paul takes him along on his first missionary journey together with Mark's cousin Barnabas. At this point, Mark is what we would call a ministry assistant, or an apprentice. He doesn't do too well; a few weeks into the mission he gives up and goes home (Acts 13:13). Paul is not impressed. When

Paul and Barnabas launch out on their second missionary journey, they have a blazing row which ends with Barnabas taking Mark with him and Paul going elsewhere (Acts 15:36-40). But Mark turns out well in the end. At the end of 2 Timothy, his very last letter, Paul writes, 'Only Luke is with me. Get Mark and bring him with you, because he is helpful to me in my ministry' (2 Tim. 4:11). Interestingly, this verse also suggests that Mark and Luke spent time together in Rome, in which case they would surely have discussed the Gospels they were both about to write. When Peter writes his own letter from Rome, he describes Mark as his son (1 Peter 5:13). So Mark is someone greatly beloved by both Peter and Paul.

Date and relationship to other Gospels

We can't be sure, because of course none of the Bible books comes with a date attached, but tradition tells us that Mark was especially closely associated with Peter, that his Gospel is based very closely on what Peter told him, and that he wrote his Gospel either just before or soon after Peter died. That was almost certainly during the reign of Nero and the persecution of Christians in Rome around AD 65. As we read through Mark, it is easy to imagine the voice of Peter recalling the times he spent with the Lord Jesus thirty years before.

Obviously, the Gospels have much in common, especially Matthew, Mark and Luke, which are known as the Synoptic Gospels. Over the years, there has been much discussion about how the three Synoptic Gospels are related, and which was written first. There is certainly not time to go into the arguments here; it is enough to say there are good reasons for believing that Mark was the first of the Gospels to be written and that both Matthew and Luke had a copy of Mark's Gospel in front of them as they wrote soon afterwards.

Target audience

There are a number of clues in the book that it was written not for Jews, but for Gentiles. For instance, in 7:3-4 Mark takes the trouble to explain about Jewish ceremonial washing. No one in Israel would need that explanation, but it would certainly be helpful to Gentiles living elsewhere. Mark 12:42 uses the Greek form of the Latin word *quadrans* to explain the value of the widow's gift, but the quadrans was used only in the *western* empire, not in places like Israel. There are also clues that Mark was writing to believers who were persecuted; there is an emphasis on suffering throughout his Gospel, as we shall see shortly. All this fits the idea that Mark was writing for the Christians in Rome in the later years of Emperor Nero.

Style and structure

The Greek of Mark's Gospel is plain, even rough; it is different from the more correct and polished Greek of Luke, for instance. Many things seem to happen 'quickly', 'suddenly' — this is one of Mark's favourite words (Greek *euthus*). The most obvious difference from the other Gospels is that it is far shorter: there are no birth narratives, unlike Matthew and Luke, no extended accounts of Jesus' appearances after his resurrection, and whole blocks of material that Matthew and Luke include about his ministry are absent. With Mark, a larger proportion of the Gospel is concerned with the passion of Christ; in this Gospel, it is even more obvious that the death and resurrection of Jesus are central to the whole story, with six out of sixteen chapters devoted to the closing events of Jesus' earthly life.

Mark's key aims are to show us who Jesus Christ is and what he came to do. He structures his Gospel in a way which will serve those aims. Various ways have been found of dividing it into sections, some more helpful than others, but everyone agrees that the vital turning point of the Gospel is at the end of chapter 8. In the first half of the Gospel, we follow the disciples as they spend time with Jesus, seeing him work miracles, teach in parables, heal people, face opposition, and so on; and through all these events it gradually becomes clear who Jesus is. The disciples see and hear many amazing things, but only very slowly do they begin to understand. Thus the first half of the Gospel is about answering the question, 'Who is Jesus?'

Peter's confession of Christ in 8:27-30 — the moment when he grasps that Jesus is in fact the longed-for Christ — is the hinge-point on which the whole Gospel turns. It is immediately followed by Jesus' first prediction of his death. There will be two more of those predictions before they arrive in Jerusalem, but here for the first time Jesus says, 'This is what I have come to do, and this is also a model for everyone who wants to follow me.' At this point, then, the focus changes from who Jesus *is* to what he has come to *do*. The whole Gospel is built around this central point, as Jesus' identity and mission are revealed, stage by stage. My suggested outline structure, dividing by themes rather than the geographical movements which some prefer, is as follows.[1] After the prologue, the sections are all defined by what are called *inclusios* — where the section is bracketed by a theme or motif which is found at both the beginning and the end of the passage. This structure is memorable and also, I believe, convincing.

1:1-13	*Prologue*
1:14 – 6:30	*Authority and opposition.* This section begins and ends with John's imprisonment. This section and the following one are both concerned with 'Who is Jesus?'

6:31 – 8:21   *From Israel to the nations.* This section is
                  bracketed by the two great feeding miracles:
                  in 6:30-44, the feeding of the five thousand
                  — a story which has a very Jewish feel —
                  and in 8:1-21, the feeding of the four thou-
                  sand — with no Jewish feel. Thus this section
                  moves from providing for Israel to providing
                  for the whole world.

8:22 – 10:52   *Jesus shows that he must suffer.* This section
                  is bracketed by two stories about opening the
                  eyes of a blind man — the only such stories
                  Mark includes.

11:1 – 13:37   *Jesus declares judgement.* This section is
                  bracketed by stories about Jesus and the
                  temple. At the start, he enters Jerusalem and
                  then condemns what is going on in the temple,
                  declaring its failure. At the end, he prophesies
                  the destruction of the temple and the end of
                  the age.

14:1 – 16:8   *Jesus' passion and vindication.* This section
                  is bracketed by stories of Jesus being
                  anointed. In 14:1-11 he is anointed for his
                  burial by the woman at the dinner party; in
                  chapter 16, the women come to the tomb, the
                  place of burial, with the intention of anointing
                  him — but they cannot, because he has risen!

Mark's presentation of Jesus

Mark's Christology — the way he presents Christ — is 'a
story of a crucified Messiah'.[2] Mark's Gospel begins with
'the gospel of Jesus Christ, the Son of God' (1:1, ESV), a
truth testified to by God on two occasions (1:11; 9:7). We
have already seen that the Gospel centres around the question

in 8:29: 'But who do you say that I am?'(ESV). Having identified Jesus as the Messiah, the Christ, the rest of the Gospel is devoted to exploring what that means. Three times in chapters 8-10, Jesus explains that his suffering is essential and inevitable. Mark tells us that while the miracles show that the kingdom of God is arriving, knowing Jesus as a miracle-worker alone is not enough. At the heart of the kingdom is the truth that Jesus must die as the crucified Messiah: this is his mission, expressed supremely in 10:45 — he is the 'ransom for many'.

Key themes in Mark

Following closely on from Mark's presentation of Christ, he focuses especially on three intertwined themes, all of which relate very closely to the cross.

Discipleship: carrying the cross

The key passage here is 8:34-38, where Peter has just declared in verse 29, 'You are the Christ,' and Jesus begins to explain what that will mean for him. Then from verse 34 we discover that coming after Jesus, being a disciple, means denying yourself, taking up your own cross and following him. The last thing any follower of Jesus will be found doing is boasting about himself and his achievements, because to follow Jesus means to deny yourself and place him at the centre. Following Jesus means taking up the cross. Jesus himself will have to do that literally; as his disciples, we must be prepared to follow our Master on the path of suffering, and if we are called on, we too must be willing to die. In verses 35-37 Jesus expands and reinforces the message. Of the four Gospels, Mark gives the starkest and, in a sense, the bleakest picture of discipleship.

Opposition: the reproach of the cross

Over and over again throughout his ministry, Jesus faces relentless opposition — and not just from the people we might expect. If Jesus the Master faces such opposition, then his followers must expect to face it too. First, there is a block of five stories, collected together in 2:1 – 3:6, where opposition comes from the teachers of the law, the Pharisees and others. In 3:20-35 we find opposition from two different sources; it is interesting to see how Mark arranges the story. At the beginning and end of this passage, you have Jesus' family — they are actually going to come and take him away because they think he has gone mad (3:21). In the middle, the religious authorities appear again, this time accusing him of driving out demons by the power of Beelzebul. Then in 6:1-6 we find Jesus rejected in his own home town. In 7:1-23 we have another round of opposition from the Pharisees and teachers of the law. They are criticizing him once more for not doing the proper religious things; he in turn criticizes them because their religious rules have missed the point of following God. Finally, in the closing week of his life, in the approach to the cross, there is another series of opposition stories. By now the authorities have decided that Jesus has to die, and they are just looking for the right opportunity. So from the middle of chapter 11 onwards comes attempt after attempt to catch Jesus in his words, to trap him into saying something dangerous. If we are misunderstood, or if we find that people who should be on our side turn against us, we are in good company: it is exactly what happened to the Lord Jesus.

Suffering — the pattern of the cross

Immediately after Peter's confession in chapter 8, Jesus begins to talk about how he must suffer. Three times he does this; three times they misunderstand him; and three times he has to correct them. We can set out the pattern like this:

Passion prediction	*Misunderstanding*	*Corrective teaching*
8:31	8:32-33	8:34 – 9:1
9:31	9:33-34	9:35-37
10:32-34	10:35-41	10:42-45

The threefold repetition emphasizes that the cross was at the heart of God's plan. This is exactly what the Lord Jesus came to do — to face the cross, to face rejection and suffering and die in our place. If our Master suffered, then we shall face suffering too. We can expect to be persecuted.

Mark places greater emphasis on persecution than any of the other Gospels. The first example is in 1:12-13. Mark's account of the temptations is very short, but he alone includes the note that Jesus 'was with the wild animals'. The reason, presumably, is that Mark's readers are facing persecution. In Rome, the Emperor Nero is arresting Christians and making them fight wild beasts in the arena. In 9:47-49, Jesus is talking about how terrible it is to lead other people into sin, but in verse 49 he adds this strange note about fire — it's quite difficult to understand until we realize that Jesus is referring to persecution. Again, only Mark includes this. Salt was added to sacrifices in Old Testament times; it was part of making the sacrifice acceptable to God. Jesus says, 'Your sacrifice to God is going to be made acceptable through the fiery trials which you will face.' In 10:28-31, Peter reminds Jesus that the disciples have abandoned everything in order to follow him. Jesus promises them a recompense, but at the end of this list Mark alone has included 'and with them, persecutions'.

For further reading

Mark's Gospel is well served by longer, more technical commentaries. Some valuable recent works are Robert Gundry's *Mark: A commentary on his apology for the cross*, which emphasizes the clarity and straightforwardness of the Gospel as against the claims scholars sometimes make for hidden meanings or codes. Dick France's *Mark*, in the NIGTC series, is very good, although, like many, I differ sharply from his view of chapter 13. Alan Cole's *Mark*, in the TNTC series, is a good shorter commentary, at least in the revised edition. My favourite commentary, however, is William Lane's *The Gospel of Mark*, in the NICNT series, which I have found unfailingly helpful and illuminating, even where I have not followed his line. I have also found fresh and useful Richard Hays' *The moral vision of the New Testament*.

Part I
Prologue (1:1-13)

1.
The good news begins

Please read Mark 1:1-13

He seems to have appeared from nowhere. One day, there was nothing; the next, there he was, out in the desert, the dry wilderness area away to the east, across the river. A strange character, they say — wild-looking, with a strange light in his eyes. He looks like one of those prophets from long ago, those wandering holy men who used to live in strange places and eat strange food. They call him John, and out in the desert is where he lives. He wears the *clothes* of the desert, rough-woven from the hair of camels, the animals of the desert. He eats the *food* of the desert — locusts, grasshoppers and the honey from swarms of wild bees. If he invites you to dinner, you had better think twice before accepting the invitation! They call him John the Baptizer, because that is what he does. Down by the River Jordan, the people come out to him in their droves and he leads them out into the water and dips them under. Strange! A strange man, apparently *from* nowhere, in the middle of nowhere — John the Baptizer. Thus Mark begins his story (1:2-6).

This is Mark's '**gospel**' (1:1) — good news as told by Mark. But who decides whether the news is good or not? In Rome, where Mark is writing, this word *evangel*, good news, is a proclamation throughout the empire: for instance, that a

new emperor has taken power. Good news! Or is it? That
would all depend on where you stand. If you don't like this
emperor, if you are his enemy, you may not think it is good
news at all. Clearly, Mark thinks what he is about to tell is
good news — but it can only be good news if you are going
to be a friend of the new emperor, this new King.

John the Baptizer appears

So when this mysterious character called John the Baptizer
appears in the desert, it is not necessarily good news that he
brings. Look at what he says and does (1:4-5). If you know
your Bible, this should remind you of something. Here are
crowds of people, thousands of them, streaming out from all
the places where they live, from town and country, going out
into the desert. Notice the word **'out'**. They go *out* into the
desert, called there to meet with God. When they get there,
they have to pass through *water* in order to encounter him. If
you know the Old Testament, this will remind you of the
story of the Exodus, when God brings his people out of the
land of Egypt into the desert and meets with them in a
decisive way. Time and again in the Bible, the desert is
where God takes people to meet with him. He takes them
away from the places where they are comfortable, the busy
situations they are embroiled in, out where there are no
distractions and they can hear him speaking. It's a biblical
pattern, and here it happens again. Even today, the Lord so
often takes us to a place where we have no resources of our
own, a place that feels dead and dry, so that we can hear his
voice without distraction. Have you been there?

In verses 2-3 Mark has quoted the prophecies of Isaiah
40:3 and Malachi 3:1. Those prophets, hundreds of years
earlier, look forward to a day when God is going to do
something new; this is all in God's plan. **'Prepare the way**

for the Lord,' he says. God is doing something new. This time it is not just another prophet who will come; it is the Lord God *himself* who is coming into the world. God is coming in human form in the person of Jesus Christ, God's final word to humanity.

Is this good news? That depends on what people do with the one who is coming. John calls people out into the desert to repent (1:4), to recognize that they are guilty and they need to change. Then, as these thousands of people swarm out to meet with John, and they *do* want to repent and confess their sins to God (1:5), he gives them a message of hope. Running through the dry, brown desert there is a river, with a narrow green strip of living vegetation on either side, an avenue of hope in the wasteland. And there, near the point where the River Jordan runs into the Dead Sea,[1] he baptizes them and tells them their sins can be forgiven.

The one who is coming

By being baptized, these people are saying that they are ready for a new start. They are ready for God to do something new. But this is just the beginning, because John goes on to say that someone else is coming who will do far more than dip them under some water. John cannot forgive their sins; only God can do that. See how he announces this in verses 7-8. In those times in Israel, untying someone's sandals was the most menial task you could undertake. It wasn't just that people's feet got very dirty and smelly; this was simply a job for the lowest of the low. Jewish slaves didn't have to do it at all. Now John says of the one who is coming, 'It's not just that I am low enough to undo his shoes: compared to him, to his greatness, I am even lower than that. There is simply no comparison between him and me: I'm just the messenger boy. He's the real news! He won't just

dip you under this water; he will baptize you in the Holy
Spirit — in other words, he will immerse you in the very
presence of God. He will bring God himself into your life. I
can do nothing like that,' he says, 'but the one who is coming
can, and he will.'

The *Da Vinci Code* is popular for many reasons. It's not
just that it is a clever story and offers to explode a conspir-
acy. It's also because it seems at the end of the quest to offer
a spirituality that costs nothing. The book ends with a man
falling to his knees in front of — nothing, really: a myth that
will cost him nothing and demands nothing from him. People
love that — just one more idea to put into their heads, like
one more wristband or bracelet to wear, a mystical book to
read, some cards or crystals to play with, costing them
nothing. So many people are reaching out for something and
clutching at emptiness. But here is the good news — if it
really is good news — a message that will cost you, not
nothing, but everything. John's message was simple, straight,
uncompromising: 'Repent. Turn round and let Jesus bring
God himself into your life.' Good news? That depends on
our response!

The trailblazer arrives

In the world we know, heroes do not shun the limelight.
They will not avoid the glare of publicity. This world's
heroes want to be known; they need to be admired; the last
description they would want is 'anonymous'. Yet when
Mark introduces us to his main character, his hero, it seems
that anonymity is exactly what he is aiming for. When Jesus
makes his appearance, he does so as an unidentifiable figure
in a great crowd. The crowds are still coming out to John, out
from Judea and Jerusalem to be dipped under the water, and
hidden somewhere among those crowds is the man John has

been talking about (1:9). He simply appears. He doesn't even have the cachet of coming from the capital; he is from Nazareth, the original one-horse town, right out in the sticks of Galilee — for Jewish purists, a dodgy area. He turns up with the crowd, stands in line with the others, wades out into mid-stream and comes face to face with John to be baptized. What kind of a grand entrance is *this*? But Mark's brief account of the baptismal scene and what follows is packed with clues to Jesus' identity and mission.

The unexpected baptism

If Jesus is the hero of Mark's story, it is surprising enough that he appears in the way that he does, as just one of the crowd. But it is even more surprising that he appears *where* he does. Imagine that you have to take an exam in the coming week. There, as you make your nervous way into the examination room, you see your lecturer, or your teacher, coming in with you, and he is not there as examiner — he sits down at the table next to you, gets his pen out of his pocket and starts working his way through the exam paper. That would be unexpected, to say the least! Jesus' appearance here is just as unexpected. John has been telling people to come out to him, to turn away from their sins, and be baptized in water to show their clean break with their past. But why should *Jesus* need to do that? Why does *he* need a baptism of repentance? Mark points it up for us: if you put verse 5 and verse 9 side by side, you can see how pointed he makes it. Only the mention of 'confessing their sins' is missing from the second verse, for Jesus has no sins to confess. This is the perfect man. We have already had strong hints about this. In verse 3, the message was: 'Prepare the way for the *Lord*' — this is no ordinary man; this is God himself in human flesh.

Whether they understand it fully or not, the crowds are there with John to acknowledge that they have done wrong and that they are under God's judgement. Jesus joins them, not because he has sins to confess, but because he wants to identify with them. That is his mission. He is here to place *himself* deliberately under the judgement and condemnation of God. The sinless one is standing with the sinners; he is going through the water with the sinners: as Isaiah put it long ago, he is here to be 'numbered with the transgressors' (Isa. 53:12). All of this points ahead to the day when Jesus will take that judgement on himself even though he deserves none of it, when the *one* who has come from Nazareth will take the place of the *many* by suffering God's punishment on the cross and, crucified between two criminals, he will again be numbered with the transgressors.

Ahead of him and behind him in that line stand men and women with the guilt of their sins hanging round their necks — sins that fully deserve God's condemnation. Only he stands there as the one who can take that condemnation, that judgement, on himself, in place of them, can forgive their sins and bring them freely to God. So he takes his turn and is immersed in the water that means sins are washed away, blazing the trail for us, opening up the pathway for men and women to come back to God.

The unique qualification

But what makes it possible for Jesus to perform this mission? How can this apparently anonymous figure attempt such a task? Look at verses 10-11. As Jesus emerges from the river, with the water still streaming off him, something amazing happens. As he looks up, he can see what seems like a tear in the fabric of the sky and, descending from above, the shape of a dove, flying down and alighting on him; at the same time he hears a voice that speaks to him words of assurance and affirmation. However anonymous Jesus may appear in the surging crowds around the river, however little they may recognize his real identity, with God there is no doubt. Far from it! This is an apocalyptic moment — heaven is opened to show that God is breaking through, intervening in human history in a new way.

This scene is full of echoes from the distant past — echoes of creation itself, when God spoke the word and brought the universe into being, and we read that the Spirit of God was moving over the formless waters. Here, once more, God speaks and the Spirit descends from heaven and moves over the waters, to show that, in his Son Jesus Christ, he is beginning his *new* creation, the new people he will call to himself. Once again Father, Son and Holy Spirit are here together to fulfil their unique roles.

There are further echoes in the words Jesus now hears his Father speak: **'You are my Son, whom I love; with you I am well pleased'** — echoes, among others, of Isaiah's words about the Servant whom God is sending into the world (Isa. 42:1) That passage goes on to explain how this Servant will bring hope even to the islands at the ends of the earth; he will be a light for the Gentiles; he will open blind eyes and set captives free. All this Jesus has come to do, not just as a Servant, but as the unique, beloved Son of the Father. The hopes and longings of the centuries are focused and fulfilled in Jesus Christ.

So, with the Spirit descending from heaven and with the words that he speaks, God the Father publicly sets the seal on the mission of his Son. He smiles down at the Son he has sent into the world out of his love to save it. Jesus himself knows his unique qualification for his mission. Looking back, we too can understand and know. This is the Lord Jesus, who is both God and man so that he is able to stand in the gap that separates us from God: the man who can identify with us in our weaknesses, who feels the cold as he stands on the riverbank and the wind dries him off; but who is also God the Son, with the authority and power of God, the authority that will be seen throughout his ministry as he heals diseases and drives out demons with a word — the one who is qualified and able to save us.

The unavoidable encounter

Now Jesus comes up from the River Jordan, commissioned by his Father, equipped and prepared for his ministry. We might expect that he will immediately swing into action — a preaching tour, some healings to prove to everyone who he is. But not yet: his mission has to begin in a much more remote and lonely place (1:12-13). The Holy Spirit *drives him out* into the desert (the same word is used regularly for driving out demons — the sense is that this is an absolutely inevitable part of Jesus' divine mission) and there he comes face to face with the greatest enemy of all. His name is Satan, the evil power that the Bible calls 'the god of this age' (2 Cor. 4:4). Jesus has now come into the world, and Satan sees his chance to attack and to destroy his mission. Jesus opens the conflict by taking on Satan himself, alone in the desert, in forty intense days. Unlike Matthew and Luke, Mark doesn't name the specific temptations; he wants us to see that the whole of Jesus' ministry is one long battle against Satan and his servants. Mark will show us that much of his time is spent dealing with demons, freeing people from Satan's control. This battle will not reach its climax until Jesus finally defeats Satan at the cross.

The fight takes place far from where people can see it. It lasts **'forty days'** — a time that links Jesus directly with the prophets Moses and Elijah, both of whom spent forty-day periods out in the desert at key points in their ministry. Yes,

Jesus will be like Moses and Elijah in their ministry of speaking God's words faithfully to the people. And yet he will be so much more. Only he can take on Satan directly and win the decisive victory which will set people free.

Mark adds something that none of the other Gospels tells us: **'He was with the wild animals'** (1:13). For modern city-dwellers, perhaps, that sounds quite appealing! But if we take off our urban spectacles we will see it differently. The desert is a place of danger. Wild beasts can kill unwary travellers; Jesus has both spiritual and physical danger to face. But there is more to it than that. Mark is probably writing from Rome during Nero's violent attacks on the church which followed the great fire in AD 64. Christians in Rome were likely to face persecution, vicious persecution — and for some of them that would mean that they were sent to the arena to be torn apart by wild animals. We have vivid contemporary accounts of how this was done. The event that was supremely likely to make you a target for official perse-cution was *baptism*, when Christian believers took a clear, public stand and declared that Christ was their Lord and King. In some cases they might go straight from the baptis-mal water to face the wild beasts. Now Mark writes to tell them that their Saviour faced that too. The message for his readers is this: 'The Lord Jesus has been there before you. He has blazed the trail for you. If you face the ultimate test in the arena, be assured of this: he knows what you are facing, and you too will receive God's help so you can stand firm in the trial. There, in the place of terrible danger, where the temptation to give up, to abandon your faith, is at its most acute — he will be there with you, and he will send his angels to look after you. Not that you will escape from the trial — the trials are unavoidable — but he will keep you safe through it, and, if the end is death, even that is not to be feared when Jesus is waiting for you on the other side of it.'

Perhaps you know what it means to face the 'wild beasts' of persecution. For Christians in so many countries around the world today, persecution is very real. Today Christians are facing physical attack, imprisonment, torture, deprivation, hunger and even death because they will not abandon their Lord and Saviour Jesus. There are others who face pressure of a quieter kind, from family or friends, at work or in their community. All that is normal. The normal Christian life involves being persecuted. It happened to Jesus; it happened to the early church; it will happen to us. God will send his angels to protect and defend us too. Take courage; be strong; he has not forgotten you or abandoned you. Nothing can separate you from his love.

Part II.
Authority and opposition (1:14 – 6:30)

2.
The mission is launched

Please read Mark 1:14-45

Authority is an unfashionable concept today. The whole idea that one person should have power over someone else is deeply unpopular. But, to put it bluntly, that's what authority is — the right to be in control, to tell other people what they can or cannot do. So, in sport, a football referee can control the game by blowing the whistle, awarding free kicks, or sending players off. A cricket umpire can turn the whole game by raising one finger at a particular moment. If you take part in a sport, you have to acknowledge that authority. In the army, a commanding officer has every right to order his subordinates into action, whether they feel like it or not. In fact, someone once used that very illustration when speaking to Jesus.

If some law or contract — or, indeed, the rules of the game — gives you authority, then you have it, and it is up to you to wield it properly. Jesus came into the world with authority from his Father God — an authority that did not extend over a mere sporting arena, or an army, or even over a country, but over the entire world. Jesus came into this world with authority to rule, to establish what he called **'the kingdom of God'** — the space where God's sovereign authority is recognized and accepted. At this point in Mark's account we see the first beginnings of that kingdom, as Jesus launches his mission.

John the Baptizer has raised the spiritual temperature of the nation, ready for Jesus to step forward. In verses 14-15 we see that John has been imprisoned because his message about repenting of your sins has not gone down well with Herod, the local despot (though Mark does not give us this explanation until 6:17-18).[1] Now Jesus appears publicly, back in his home region of Galilee, and he comes proclaiming the **'good news'**, *the gospel*, which, as we have seen, means a big announcement of a world-changing event. **'The time has come'**, or, 'has been completed'. It's *now* that this is happening: **'The kingdom of God is near.'** The Jews knew what that meant. Their prophets had spoken about it centuries before: the arrival of the kingdom of God means that God comes to assert his authority, publicly and openly, here on earth. At last God would break into history and establish his everlasting kingdom. The Jews had many wrong ideas about the kingdom and the kind of freedom it would bring, but they were right about that much. Jesus says, '*I* am here to bring it in.' He says, in effect, 'It's me! I am the good news! So repent: turn away from your past life and get ready for God to act.'

The call you can't resist

In verses 16-28 we meet three groups who come face to face with the authority of Jesus.

First we meet *the fishermen*. Jesus is walking beside the Sea of Galilee. **'Sea'** is rather a grand name for a freshwater lake that is only about six miles from side to side and less than twelve from end to end. But it had a very successful fishing industry and, as Jesus walks along, it is these fishermen that he encounters (1:16). Now if we know this story

well, we need to draw back a little in order to see these
characters properly. As with the shepherds in the Christmas
story, we tend to romanticize the Galilean fishermen, but
these were the ordinary industrial workers of their day.
Fishing was hard, physical work, extremely smelly work,
carried out on a notoriously stormy lake.

Jesus calls them (1:17). The reference to **'fishers of men'**
is not just a play on words, but an Old Testament expression
about God gathering people for judgement.[2] Jesus is saying,
'Now that I am here, it's decision time. People must repent
of their sins and turn to God, or else they will face God's
judgement. I am bringing in God's kingdom, and I am
calling people into it, and everyone will end up on the inside
or the outside. You unpromising-looking fishermen are
going to join me in my mission.' Five minutes later he says
the same thing to James and John, busy on the fiddly task of
net repair (1:19-20). He calls them — Simon and Andrew,
James and John, impetuous, stormy, given to fits of rage,
lacking confidence; they offer a wide range of flawed per-
sonalities and a complete absence of academic qualifications,
but Jesus says, **'Follow me.'** The cost will be very high: they
must abandon their sole means of livelihood and the only
way of life they have ever known. Unless this wandering
beachcomber is someone extremely special, what they are
being asked to do is crazy. Yet when he speaks, they recognize the voice of authority, and they cannot resist the call
(1:18,20).

Jesus takes them on to his next destination (1:21). Capernaum is on the north shore of the lake; it may have been the
home of the four fishermen. It's a sizeable village, and Jesus
makes it his base for operations around Galilee. The **'synagogue'** would have been the most prominent building in the
village, probably the only one of any size. On the Sabbath,
Jesus, along with the rest of the community, would be there,
and it was not unusual for a visitor to be asked to speak at the

appropriate point of the service, following the prayers and
the readings from the Law and the Prophets. Mark doesn't
tell us exactly what Jesus says, but there can be little doubt
that he speaks about the kingdom of God. Luke describes a
very similar occasion in Nazareth when Jesus reads from the
prophet Isaiah and calmly tells the people, 'This is happening
now — because I am here' (see Luke 4:16-30).

Jesus certainly gets a reaction (1:22 and again, with a
different word, in 1:27). The **'teachers of the law'**, or
scribes, were the ordained religious professionals; they will
feature prominently in Mark's account, especially when we
reach chapter 12, where Jesus faces them in the temple.
Originally, these men were simply copyists. Their job, long
before the age of printing, was to write out the words of
Scripture, creating new manuscripts to replace the ones
which wore out — hence the name 'scribe'. The only qualifications they needed were an eye for detail and clear hand-
writing. But as time went by, members of this profession
became specialists in the law itself. They didn't just write it
out; they studied and learned it, and by the time of Jesus they
were the acknowledged experts. That is why the NIV trans-
lates the word for 'scribe' as 'teacher of the law'. Teaching
was their job — and how they taught! Their technique with
any question was to go back and quote the experts, and the
way the experts had quoted other experts: 'Rabbi Yohanan
said that; Rabbi Eliezer said so-and-so; but Rabbi Yehuda's
opinion, according to Rabbi Ben-Ammi, was this...' — until
in the end, a couple of centuries later, all this opinion-
quoting was gathered into a shelf-full of huge books called
the Talmud (if you ever have the chance to see a copy, or to
read it online, you will see what I mean!). What they did *not*
have was authority. Then one day Jesus gets up and says,
'The kingdom of God is here, and it's all about *me*!'

It doesn't take long for the people to notice the difference.
This reaction is very interesting. They don't say, 'This man

is crazy, or insufferably arrogant.' They are **'amazed'** (1:22).
The word carries the sense of being overwhelmed with
wonder; they are disturbed by what he says. This is the
second group who encounter Jesus' authority. Many of them
never fully understand who Jesus is, but they clearly see that
he is different. He demands their attention.

Sitting among the people is someone who certainly does
recognize who Jesus is — a third 'group' if we can call it
that (1:23-24). This man is under the controlling authority of
'an evil spirit' — literally, an 'unclean' spirit, a demon.
Some people try to explain away stories like this one. They
are the product of primitive cultures, they say, and we have
moved beyond such naïve beliefs. The truth is that in most
parts of the world people understand only too well that the
spirit world is real. If you go to Africa, or to large parts of
Asia or South America, you will find that people have no
doubt about the reality of evil spirits. Muslims rightly understand the existence of demons, or 'jinns' as they call them;
they are a feature of everyday life. It is only in the sophisticated West that we are stupid enough to stop believing in
evil powers that can control people's lives. Such fools we are
— even some Christians — that we think we know better
than the Bible! The spiritual world is as real as anything you
can touch, see or hear, and demons are the most pure and
naked forms of evil that we will ever meet.

We have seen that Jesus began his ministry by going out
to confront Satan, the controlling power behind all demons.
Now the confrontation continues. His presence flushes them
out of hiding; here, in the synagogue, he has not gone looking for a demon, but his presence has forced the demon to
show itself. As far as we can tell, this man has been peacefully attending the synagogue all his life — which probably
says something about the level of spiritual life in the synagogue. While the people sitting around may not be too clear
who this new teacher is, the demon has no doubt at all.

'Jesus of Nazareth' — there is nothing remarkable about his knowing Jesus' home town, but probably the use of his name represents a futile attempt to control him — **'Have you come to destroy us?'** That may well in fact be a statement: 'You *have* come to destroy us.' The demon correctly identifies Jesus as God's unique representative, **'holy'** — set apart, the antithesis of all evil — and recognizes that his coming spells the end, not just for one demon that Saturday morning, but ultimately for all the powers of evil, because Jesus has come bearing all the authority of God.

How is it that a demon can recognize the Son of God for who he is, while the people, by and large, do not? The answer is that Satan blinds people to Jesus' true identity (2 Cor. 4:4). The demons are perfectly clear about who Jesus is, though the knowledge does them no good. Now, in verses 25-26, comes the moment of truth. Literally, Jesus says, 'Be silenced.' 'Be muzzled', says Jesus, as if he was dealing with a little, yapping dog. **'Come out ...!'** And, with a convulsion and a yell, the spirit is gone. There will be no more anonymity after this! (1:27-28).

In Capernaum the people are astounded to see evil spirits banished with a word. This shows more clearly and dramatically than anything that Jesus is creating a space on earth where only *God's* authority is recognized, only *his* writ runs. That is the kingdom. The driving out of demons is a foretaste of the cross, where Jesus will achieve his decisive victory over Satan as his death sets people free from the power of sin and hell, breaks Satan's power and establishes the kingdom. Still today, the kingdom is spreading and growing. The life and activity of each local church is a small sign of God's kingdom on earth — a place where we acknowledge God's right to rule, where we say, 'Jesus is King.'

The 'call you can't resist' forms the strange link between the disciples and the demons. For the first disciples, it is a call to *follow*; for the demons, a call to *be gone*. In both cases, they recognize the authority of Jesus and they cannot resist the call.

This is why he has come

That Saturday evening, Jesus finds himself surrounded by intense excitement. The next stage of the story (1:29-39) contains two major surprises. The synagogue service is over and the people spill out, full of excitement with their news. But Jesus and his group of four go home with Simon and Andrew — very likely we are still in Capernaum — and in what follows we can hear Simon Peter's voice as he sits down years later and recalls it all for Mark. This is clearly his own, eyewitness account: 'We went back to my place, the five of us. My mother-in-law was sick; she had had this fever for weeks. Normally she was so active, but she was just flat out. Well, of course we told Jesus — and you know what he did? He simply walked into the room, took hold of her hand and hoisted her to her feet! And that was that! The fever was gone! No trace of weakness — she insisted on sorting out the meal for us all then and there.'

So Peter's mother-in-law is healed (1:30-31). But Jesus does not have peace for long after his lunch. As soon as the sun goes down and the Sabbath is over, the crowd starts to gather. There has been just long enough for everyone in Capernaum and the surrounding area to hear what happened in the synagogue this morning; it's not hard to guess that in a densely packed village like Capernaum, news of the healing in the house has got around too. I doubt that there is an orderly queue outside Simon Peter's house in Capernaum that night. There are at least dozens — scores — of sick, injured and demonized people outside the door. Some have brought themselves; others have been cajoled, carried or dragged here by their families. No matter — Jesus heals them all (1:32-34). There is no illness, no condition that he cannot tackle. There is no demon that can resist his command. Such is his divine power; such is his authority.

Finally the crowd clears, the last straggler has gone and Jesus can rest. It has been dark for hours by this time. Surely he will need a good rest, but apparently that is not his priority (1:35). Again we hear Simon Peter's voice behind Mark's narrative: 'It was just getting light when we got up. We looked round for Jesus, but he was *gone!*' So they go looking, and somehow they find him. Jesus is out praying in '**a solitary place**'. Literally, Mark tells us that it was a *'desert* place'. That is odd, because the whole area was in fact thickly populated, with well-cultivated farmland among the towns and villages. But, as we saw in verses 3-4, the *desert* is the place where people go in order to meet with God, to see spiritual realities more clearly.

Jesus has come out here to some quiet hillside to find solitude with God, that union with his Father that matters even more than catching up on his sleep. *This* is where he finds renewal and refocuses his vision after the clamour of the crowds. The divine Son of God is also the fragile man who needs to do that. Simon and company find him — and they are not impressed. It's morning now: '**Everyone is looking for you!**' (1:36-37). But Jesus does *not* go back to Capernaum that day. Instead he moves on. There are other places, lots of them, that need to hear (1:38). The word here for '**villages**' suggests, not the tiny hamlets like Nazareth, but bigger places, small market towns. The episode concludes with the picture of Jesus pursuing this strategy, travelling between these centres, preaching in the synagogues and driving out demons (1:39).

But now for the surprises. The first comes in verse 34: '... **he would not let the demons speak because they knew who he was.**' Now, we could understand it if Mark had written, 'He would not let the demons speak because they were telling *lies* about him.' After all, Satan is called the 'father of lies'; falsehood is his speciality. But in the presence of Jesus' authority, the demons do not lie; like the one in the synagogue, they will blurt out his true identity as they depart the scene. Of all those who hear him, they know Jesus' identity more accurately than anyone. So doesn't he want to be known for who he truly is? Yes, of course, but not like this, not with the terrified squeaks of an enemy. Jesus' mission is not simply to get people to realize who he is, as if this were some kind of cosmic identity parade. His mission is to confront people with the decision they have to make: to recognize him, yes; but then to decide for him, follow him, love him. Without that, the most complete knowledge about Jesus is useless. So he silences the demons, proving again, just by the way, that he has total power over the forces of evil.

The demons' theology is excellent. They know who their enemy is; they know he is going to win. When they see Jesus appear on the earth, the Son of God, they recognize him as the one who will finally defeat them. They have only the haziest notion about *how* that will happen, and they don't understand about the cross, but they do know that Jesus' arrival spells their final defeat. They have a superb grasp of biblical theology. But do they have faith in Christ? Of course not. The demons, in fact, are a perfect illustration of the fact that simply believing in God is no good to anybody (James 2:19). We should never think that just because someone can say, 'I believe in God', they are thereby close to faith in Christ. The brutal truth is that unless you *know* Jesus Christ, unless you embrace him and follow him, you are no better off than these demons. They know all about God, but in the face of Jesus all they can do is scream and disappear for ever. Plenty of people say they believe in 'God', but only real, living Christians start with Jesus and being united with him.

Surprise number two comes in verse 38. Simon Peter and friends go out in the gloom of early morning to hunt Jesus down — that is what the word means. 'Everyone is looking for you!', they say. In other words, 'What on earth are you doing here? Look, you have drawn a crowd. Why are you hiding yourself away out here?' Jesus says, 'Let's go somewhere else'! Something has started to happen in Capernaum, but instead of returning to build on his success, Jesus says, **'Let us go somewhere else ... so that I can preach there also. That is why I have come.'** Yes, the crowds in Capernaum are very excited, but they haven't grasped who Jesus is. Jesus is not here to put on a show, or simply give people what they want — a bit of free health care, a few problems straightened out, a flurry of excitement. He is here to preach the kingdom of God.

Remember the message from verse 15. All the exorcisms and healings, dramatic as they are, are simply signs that the kingdom is breaking in, that evil will be driven out, Satan will be defeated and broken humanity will be restored. Those are just the signs — signposts. The idea of signposts is not that you stand and admire them, but that you go where they point. 'Don't look at the signs,' Jesus says. 'Look at me.' People get terribly confused about this even today. There are churches where you can hear Jesus portrayed as a sort of free health service — only with no waiting lists or prescription charges — combined with a jackpot-winning lottery ticket. People like that idea — Jesus as my heavenly therapist. It fits so well with the spirit of the age. Yes, there are still healings today in Jesus' name (as well as many imitations); demons are still driven out in Jesus' name; and for the people involved it is extremely significant — but even for them it is still not the main point. Even when Jesus healed an entire crowd, without exception and flawlessly, that was not the main point. Jesus is not our passport to health, wealth and an easy life.

The real Jesus came to proclaim a kingdom — a kingdom that would begin with a cross, where the King poured out his own life for the sake of his subjects, the cross that rightfully became the symbol of this kingdom and is the pattern for the whole Christian life. When we accept Jesus Christ, we don't take him on as our therapist; we bow to his mastery and then set out to follow him as Lord and King. The first step is not to queue up to have our aches and pains fixed, but to repent.

Bringing in the outcast

Only once in my life have I met a man with leprosy. I had an uncle, Paul Brand, who was a leprosy surgeon, and he devoted the best years of his life to working in a remote corner of India devising ways to reverse the worst ravages of the disease and helping his patients to return to a normal life. I knew about leprosy: how it works by destroying nerves, killing feeling and sensation. I knew the stories about how leprosy patients are outcast and rejected by their families and in their villages. I knew too what my uncle wrote in one of his books: 'Of all the gifts we can give a leprosy patient, the one he values most is the gift of being handled and touched. We don't shrink from him. We love him with our skin, by touch.' I knew all this, but I had never *met* anyone with leprosy until I visited Tibet a few years ago. That was when the stories came to life.

There was a beggar on the street, and as I looked at him it was painfully obvious why he was there. This man had leprosy, and begging was how he survived. I think he was elderly, but it was very hard to be sure. His face was so stricken and wasted I couldn't really guess his age. There wasn't a great deal I could do for him. I didn't know a soul in the city and I couldn't speak his language. I did speak to him; I did pray for him; and I did put money in his bowl. But

I knew there was something very simple I needed to do. I grasped what little remained of his two hands in mine and looked him full in the face as I talked to him and tried to imagine the depth of his suffering. That was it — not much, really. But at least I had given him what I can almost guarantee no one else ever did — a caring touch for the outcast.

Jesus came to this earth to bring in the outcast. That's what the story in verses 40-45 is about. We find him doing what he has just said he must do: touring the area of Galilee, preaching in the synagogues, driving out demons. In one of these places a man with leprosy begs him, **'If you are willing, you can make me clean'** (1:40). **'Leprosy'** in the Bible does not mean exactly what it does today. It's probable that our 'leprosy', Hansen's disease as it's also known, spread into the land of Israel from the east a few centuries before the time of Christ. But in those times they did not have the benefit of precise medical terminology, and the expression 'leprosy' covered a number of different conditions, including other conditions with visible effects on the skin. Unlike the leprosy we know, some of these conditions would be highly contagious. The whole range of infectious skin diseases were covered in the Jewish law by very detailed regulations (Lev. 13 – 14). Leprosy created two problems. The first is the obvious one: it was a disease that disfigured you, damaged your body and made people afraid of you — the kind of fear that today accompanies AIDS. The second problem is that leprosy also made you ritually unclean, excluded from God's people. You could not go to worship; you could not share in the sacrifices; you were effectively cut off. If you did recover, only the priests could declare that you were 'clean' once more. There were detailed rules for that as well, including sacrifices that had to be offered.

All of this meant that life for the leprosy sufferer was very grim. Although in theory they were allowed to live anywhere except inside a walled city, in practice they lived away from everyday society, quite literally out of touch. To make matters even worse, the religious authorities in typical style had added to the original rules a whole tranche of legislation about exactly how clean people might be made unclean. See if you can make sense of this, for example: 'If an unclean man stands under a tree and a clean man passes by, the latter becomes unclean. If a clean man stands under a tree and an unclean man passes by, the former remains clean. If the latter stands still, the former becomes unclean.' All this would make normal people more wary than ever about contact with the disease. This was one set of regulations the people of Israel observed very strictly. Even Uzziah, one of their greatest kings, when struck with leprosy was shut away in a house by himself for the rest of his life — a king, yet an outcast (2 Chr. 26:16-21). The rabbis believed that it was as difficult to cleanse a leprosy sufferer as it was to raise the dead, which was not exactly encouraging. The Old Testament records only two cases of leprosy being healed, both by divine intervention: one was Miriam, the sister of Moses, and the other was Naaman, the Syrian general.

So here comes this man, carrying all that weight of exclusion on his shoulders. Think how he must have felt! Knowing the hopelessness of his situation, the scale of the barriers which divide him from his fellow man, we can understand why he goes down on his knees! He has clearly heard about Jesus; perhaps from a distance he has watched him in action. In any case, he seems to have no doubts: **'You can make me clean.'** The only question in his mind is whether Jesus is *willing* to do so. Jesus at once speaks and acts (1:41). Moved with deep compassion, he stretches out his hand and, breaking all those barriers, he *touches* the man. By that action, the rules say, Jesus himself becomes ritually unclean — by the touch that the man has not felt perhaps for many years. **'Be clean!'**, he says. In verse 42 the original word is not literally **'cured'**, but *made clean*.

A diseased man has been healed — healing that is immediate and 100% successful. But, more than that, the barriers
have been broken down; the outcast is brought back in and
restored. Now Jesus sends him off to the priest (1:44). That
is what the law says: the priest is the only one qualified to
check you over and declare that you are clean. The custom is
that you visit the local priest and then go on to the authorities
in Jerusalem. Then there are special ceremonies to perform,
partly to act out your freedom, and partly to give thanks to
God, and you will be certified free of disease and fit to rejoin
society again. At last, this man can now look forward to
normal life — back to the family, back to work, back to self-
respect.

It sounds like such a happy ending, a wonderful story: the
ravages of disease are undone; the pain of separation is
reversed. Yet there is a tragic twist to this incident, and it is
vital that we understand it. This man with leprosy, like so
many others, has missed the point. He comes to the healer; he
is healed; he is thrilled with it; he is overjoyed. But, even so,
he has missed the point. How do we know? Verses 43-44 tell
us. The word for **'strong warning'** is *very* strong: 'You are
absolutely not to go spreading this around!' Why? Because
the man has seen only the healer, not the King. He is to tell
only the priests: they, as the religious professionals, should at
least be able to recognize the evidence of their eyes. If, as
they believe, it's as hard to heal from leprosy as to raise
someone from the dead, surely they will see that God must be
in this. If they don't, what Jesus probably means is that it will
be evidence against them that they have refused to recognize
the true messenger of God. But the man does the exact
opposite of what Jesus has insisted on — he goes and tells
everybody he can find. It's hardly likely that he tells them
God's promised kingdom has arrived and that he has met the
King. If nothing else, the fact that he directly disobeys Jesus'
clear instructions proves that he has not recognized him as the

King. The outcome is that he succeeds in derailing Jesus' whole strategy (1:45). He no longer enters the towns: instead, the people come out to *him*.

Jesus did not come to give people *normal* life; he came to give people *eternal* life! This is what the healings point to. For a start, Jesus' actions show that the ceremonial rules about 'clean and unclean' and 'touching and not touching' are finished with. He is not concerned to obey those rules any more. But, more than that, as Jesus touches the man, he takes on his uncleanness so that the man can be made clean and the barrier which excludes the outcast is broken down. In a sense Jesus *becomes* the outcast, so that the outcast can be brought home. Jesus has come into the world to do just that on a grand scale. Leprosy was a terrible curse: it ruined normal life and brought pain and ugliness into human life. Jesus healed people from it — such was his compassion — but, wonderful as that was, it points ahead to the healing of the far greater curse of *sin*, which, even more than leprosy, ruins normal life, destroys relationships and brings pain and ugliness into human life. Jesus came to provide *cleanness* from sin, the disease, the curse that affects us all because we have all broken God's law. Under the curse, we are all outcasts, cut off from God by the barrier of sin. But, as Galatians 3:13 puts it, 'Christ redeemed us from the curse of the law by becoming a curse for us.' When Jesus the King went to the cross, he *became* the curse for us, dying under the weight of it and bringing in the outcasts. Life can begin anew — not just a normal life regained, like the one this man knew when he was healed, but far more: eternal life. This is what the kingdom of God is all about. The one thing that can keep you an outcast from God is exactly the same disease that we all start with — our sin. If you have been to the cross and seen Jesus made a curse for you, there is nothing at all that can ever separate you from his love. ' "I am willing," he said. "Be clean!" '

3.
Who does he think he is?

Please read Mark 2:1 – 3:6

Imagine that you are inside your local prison. You have just been sent down for a long sentence, the gates have clanged shut behind you, and it dawns on you that you will have many years to get used to these walls and bars, to this dreary routine. If only there was some way out! Time passes, and then one day you are told you have an unidentified visitor. 'Another do-gooder come to tell me to mend my ways,' you think gloomily as you slouch along behind the warder to the visiting room.

Your visitor seems glad to see you. As you sit down with him, he smiles and hands you a very official-looking document. 'Whatever is this?', you ask him. 'Look at it', he says. 'It's what you have longed for — it's a full and complete pardon for all your crimes. You are free to go!'

Well, this seems like good news, but surely it's a bit too good to be true! You study the document more carefully. 'Hold on, whose signature is this at the bottom?' 'Oh', says the visitor, 'That's mine. I'm pardoning you; you're free to go.'

Now, your visitor has no identification — no badge, no uniform — apparently he is just a member of the public. What are you going to say? Who is this strange man who can wander in and claim to tell you that you are free to leave, simply on his say-so? Who does he think he is?

That is exactly what happens at the beginning of Mark 2 when Jesus looks at a man lying paralysed on a mattress and tells him, 'Your sins are forgiven. You're free!' Who does he think he is, to dare to claim that *he* can forgive people their sins? And that is just the first of this series of five stories, concluding in 3:6, which are linked together by the theme of opposition to Jesus and his ministry. Jesus' opponents are challenging his *authority*: first to forgive sins, then to break the traditional religious rituals, and finally to redefine the Jewish Sabbath. Mark is particularly concerned with the opposition Jesus faces: he emphasizes it as part of his very stark portrayal of the challenges which Jesus' followers can expect to face. In 11:27 – 12:40 we will find that just before Jesus' death he faces another round of opposition on much the same ground.

Who is he to forgive sins?

The first story, in 2:1-12, takes place in Capernaum by the Lake of Galilee. Jesus has been touring the region, moving from place to place, but has now decided to come home for a while. Probably he has entered quietly, under cover of darkness, and is once more based at the house of Andrew and Simon Peter where he stayed before. But his presence cannot be long concealed (2:1). Word soon gets out, and once more the crowds gather. After all, it is only a few weeks since he was last here, that Saturday night when it seemed the whole village assembled outside the house and everyone who was sick or controlled by an evil spirit was healed on the spot (1:33-34). Very soon, there is Jesus inside, with the house full of people and crowds around the door and at every window, so that no one else can even get near (2:2).

Jesus is not actually healing today. Time and again he makes it clear that his priority is to declare this message: the kingdom of God is near. But now here come some new arrivals: a group of five men, four of them struggling along supporting the four corners of a simple mattress on which lies their paralysed friend. Maybe they missed their chance when Jesus was here before, or maybe his disease is very recent, but they are not going to miss him again. They haul their friend up the steps onto the flat roof and then they begin to dismantle the roof of the house — which probably consists of wooden rafters, straw and clay — with their bare hands. Imagine how you would feel if you had a house full of visitors, and suddenly there was a noise overhead, a few lumps of plaster came crashing down and, the next you knew, a cheery face were to appear through a fresh hole in the ceiling! I think you would remember the day! In all likelihood, this is Simon Peter's own house and this is his own eyewitness account.

Fortunately for them, the four friends have chosen just the right spot at which to dig, because now here comes the man on his mattress dangling and swaying until he lands right in front of Jesus (2:3-4). It is fortunate because there are some people in the room who certainly wouldn't be impressed if a loaded mattress were to land in their laps! These men are the teachers of the law (2:6), the scribes who first appeared in 1:22. They are the professionals — legal experts, theologically trained to sniff out error. They are not here by accident. It seems that they are on a fact-finding mission, a commission of inquiry sent down from religious headquarters in Jerusalem to track down the rumours about a man called Jesus who is operating around Galilee. Undoubtedly, as they sit there like judges, they are very suspicious.

So the mat reaches the floor. The crowded room falls silent. The man lies rigid; he can't move. The law teachers pick crumbs of clay off their white robes. Four faces peer expectantly down from above. What will Jesus say? **'Son, your sins are forgiven'**! (2:5). If it was quiet before, you could hear a pin drop now. The shock arises not for the reason we might have thought: *we* might be surprised because we would think a paralysed man needs *healing*, not forgiving. But these people understand that there could be a link between the sin in someone's life and his physical condition. They understand what many do not — that sin means rebellion against God, and only God can set us free from the prison it creates by forgiving us. Nothing can be more urgent than that. It's not the idea of forgiveness that shocks them, but the fact that Jesus claims to be handing it out in his own right. They know there is only *one* who can forgive sins — God himself.

Thus far at least, the law teachers are right to think as they do (2:7). The Jews were very clear on this: one God; one authority; one place to deal with sins — the judgement seat of God. They were right. What Jesus has just said is blasphemy: he is claiming to hold the authority of God. They don't say it aloud, but Jesus knows, and perhaps that fact should have suggested something (2:8-9). Notice *how* Jesus says this. He does not condemn the teachers. Their point is a fair one. Any of us who believe in God ought to ask the same question. So in verse 9 Jesus comes back with a question of his own, a technique he often uses. What is the answer? Obviously, it is easy to say words. The question is really: 'Which of these is easier to *do* — to forgive, or to heal an incurable illness with a simple word?' The answer, of course, is that neither is easier, because both are impossible — for a man on his own. Both are impossible, and this is indeed blasphemy, unless Jesus himself carries the very authority of God.

At this point in Mark's narrative, a tricky question of interpretation arises. To whom is Jesus speaking in the first part of verse 10? **'Son of Man'** is a title that Jesus adopts for himself. It originates with the vision in Daniel 7:13-14, where Daniel sees 'one like a son of man' coming into the presence of God and being given authority, power and an everlasting kingdom. Understood in that way, the title therefore carries great weight and implies great claims, but on the other hand, the phrase 'Son of Man' actually *means* no more than 'member of the human race'. So it is really a rather ambiguous expression, well suited to Jesus, who is being so cautious about revealing his identity. The tricky question here in verse 10, therefore, is this: would Jesus, at this point in his ministry, make such an open declaration of his own authority — especially in front of his opponents? Even as late as a few days before his death, Jesus refuses to be so open with them (11:33). It seems much more likely, and it makes better sense of the broken sentence structure which comes over even in the English translation, that the first part of verse 10 is an 'aside' by Mark, addressed to his own readers, pointing out to them that the Jesus they follow does indeed possess the authority to forgive. Then in the second part of the verse the story itself resumes.[1]

In front of the whole crowd, in the face of the lawyers lined up by the wall, and without even a touch from the hand of Jesus, the paralysed man rises to his feet, bends down again, rolls up his mattress, puts it over his shoulder and makes his way out through the throng (2:11-12). So which is easier? The point is that the healing proves that Jesus is genuine. Although the Old Testament prophets occasionally healed people, no real prophet ever claimed to forgive sins. But Jesus does! Now it is up to the crowd and the teachers of the law to draw the correct conclusions. The fact that Jesus has healed the man with a word excludes the possibility that he is a harmless madman. The fact that he lives a humble life and accepts the rejects of society excludes the possibility that he is an evil tyrant (for even Hitler spoke with authority). The only option left is the hardest one of all — that he is actually who he claims to be; he is what the Bible points us to: he is the man who is God.

What, then, is the reaction on the day, as the crowd find their voice, as the teachers sit there in judgement, as the man walks away and his friends celebrate on what is left of the roof? The law teachers will soon be back. In this story, they have merely grumbled quietly, but the accusation of blasphemy will not go away. Even when they see the evidence with their own eyes, as they do here, most of the religious leaders will never accept the verdict. To them Jesus is dangerous, subversive, a threat to their own position. In the end he simply has to go. This cycle of five stories sees the intensity of opposition steadily mounting; eventually it will lead to Jesus' crucifixion.

The crowd's reaction is described in verse 12. They have seen the healings before, though this is probably the most spectacular yet. They have heard Jesus teach before. What is new is the pointer to who Jesus really is. They praise God because they now see his hand clearly at work and they begin to glimpse that Jesus is something more than a prophet and healer. But do they really make the connection? Sadly, from what follows, it seems that most of them do not.

What does he think he is doing?

How would you feel if your name became a byword for betrayal? In the years before the Second World War, Vidkun Quisling was a gifted Norwegian diplomat, army officer and politician. But in 1933 he founded the Norwegian Nazi party, and when Nazi Germany invaded his country in April 1940, Quisling attempted to seize power. He betrayed his own people, urging them not to resist the invasion, and managed to delay the mobilization of the army. Later the Germans made him head of state of occupied Norway. Not surprisingly, at the end of the war he was tried and executed for high treason. And now in the dictionary a 'quisling' is defined as a traitor who serves the enemy occupying his country. When Jesus was on earth, there was a group of professionals who fitted the word 'quisling' perfectly. At a time when their country was occupied by Rome, and the area of Galilee where they lived was under the control of a puppet government, these men made their living by exploiting their own people and helping the occupiers to do their dirty work. Not surprisingly, they were detested. These lowest of the low were the 'tax collectors', and in verses 13-17 Jesus meets one of them.

We have seen Jesus meeting outcasts before. At the end of chapter 1, he meets a man with leprosy; he reaches out across the barriers to touch the man and bring the outcast in. We saw that Jesus is not bothered about the barriers that cut people off — not in the least. But now the picture is worse. In this story, Jesus meets a tax collector named Levi and, astonishingly, he holds out his hand to him as well. Elsewhere (see Matt. 9:9-13), Levi is known as Matthew. That is not a mistake; it simply reflects the fact that people often had more than one name, even in those days — in fact we have examples from inscriptions which list both first names and surnames. Whereas the man in the earlier story had no choice about his leprosy — it was hardly *his* decision to become an outcast — Levi has made exactly that choice for himself. He has volunteered to do the dirty work, knowing full well what the consequences will be.

We need to see this from the point of view of an ordinary Jew in Galilee. Levi is in the pay of Herod Antipas, who rules Galilee under Rome's overlordship. So, unlike Zacchaeus, that other famous tax collector down south in Jericho (see Luke 19:1-10), Levi does not work *directly* for the Romans. Most likely, Jesus encounters him on the edge of Capernaum, on the northern shore of the Lake of Galilee, at the point where people coming in from the neighbouring territory enter Antipas' realm. There they will come across Levi collecting customs duties on whatever they are carrying. Now that may sound innocent enough, until you realize how these tax collectors actually operated. Levi will have paid a fixed fee to buy the tax franchise for that spot. It was a bit like paying to run a burger stand at a festival — only rather more sinister, because he was now free to charge people whatever he could screw out of them in order to increase his profits.

For our ordinary first-century Jew, then, tax collectors were offensive in at least three ways. Firstly and most obviously, they were notoriously dishonest and corrupt. Secondly, they were objectionable because their job brought them into constant contact with Gentiles, who were regarded as unclean; that meant the tax collectors were likely to be permanently unclean as well. The Talmud, that great multi-volume compendium of rules and commentary, lists tax collectors along with murderers and robbers and disqualifies them as witnesses in court. Thirdly, they were quislings, working for the establishment, for the Herods, who were known as a gang of criminals and were only puppets of the Roman overlords. So anyone with an ounce of patriotism, even if he had no time for religious rules, was still going to hate these people.

This is the man Jesus meets as he makes his way from the side of the lake back home to Capernaum, no doubt still followed by a considerable throng (2:13-14). Levi sits there by the road ready to demand payment from any likely-looking victims; we can imagine everyone shuffling past on the other side of the street. But Jesus is different. He walks up to Levi, this quisling, and says, **'Follow me'**! You can almost hear the sound of jaws dropping. And Levi actually gets to his feet and goes with Jesus. Much remains unsaid. We don't know what runs through Levi's mind. We don't know what else is said. But we do know that Jesus has called and Levi has responded.

In the next scene, here is Jesus having dinner at Levi's house. It seems likely that he has thrown a party for his colleagues and associates to come and meet this amazing man who has broken through the triple barrier of religious prejudice, politics and morality and has asked for his company (2:15-16). There are spies at the party — Pharisees. If anyone is going to object to Jesus' consorting with undesirables, it will be the Pharisees, who now make their first appearance in Mark's Gospel. They represent the party who are the most passionate about following the Jewish law and all the extra regulations that tradition has added to it. Within that Pharisee group, their legal professionals — **'the teachers of the law'** — are the ones who actually make the rules. **'Sinners'** is what they call anyone who does not take the rules as seriously as they do. They are watching Jesus closely and, frankly, they don't like what they see. No true Jew, still less anyone who claims to be a teacher, a rabbi, should have anything to do with these common people, these 'people of the land' (in Hebrew, the *am ha'aretz*), as they dismissively title them, let alone these tax collectors, who are corrupt, unclean and serving the enemy.

But now Jesus lays his cards on the table: **'It is not the healthy who need a doctor, but the sick. I have not come to call the righteous, but sinners'** (2:17). Clearly, Jesus is not saying that there is nothing wrong with the Pharisees. In other places (such as 7:6-13) he makes it abundantly clear that the Pharisees' religion is *very* sick. Jesus is adopting their own language, which divides people into 'righteous' and 'sinners', 'OK' and 'not OK'. In other words, 'If you think you are fine, if you think you are so healthy, all right — but kindly let *me* get on with looking after the sick.' Jesus has come for those who *know* they need him. Most of the people at the party may not feel that, but Levi certainly does.

He knows he is a sinner, and Jesus has come and found him. The Pharisees have missed the point. They think they are simply dealing with someone who is breaking their rules. In fact, Jesus is doing far more than that. This meal with Levi points to something much greater.

Look closely at verse 15, and you will see that it is Jesus, not Levi, who is the focus, even the host, of the party, and here are the ordinary people of the land, the undesirables, the rejects, gathered together to celebrate his coming. There is a strong hint here of something the Old Testament prophets look forward to: in the future time when God breaks into history and establishes his kingdom on earth, one way in which it is described is as a banquet, a party which God will throw for his people — the 'messianic banquet', as it was known. You find this theme in various places in the prophecy of Isaiah, especially in Isaiah 25:6-8. This is one of many occasions when Mark's narrative alludes to Old Testament themes without saying so explicitly. In this he is unlike Matthew, who usually points out to us the ways in which Jesus is fulfilling the prophecies.

So here is the Messiah, hosting a party not for the elite, but for all comers — the sign that God is breaking in, that his kingdom is coming to earth, and we have just a foretaste of the golden age which is still to come. The Pharisees don't see that; they don't see that they themselves are just as much sinners as the people they despise; they simply see a list of rules which Jesus is shredding. But Jesus has come to make strangers into friends, to build bridges instead of barriers as people join his kingdom.

The story which immediately follows (2:18-22) simply hammers that message home. Verse 18 gives us the challenge. The rules about fasting are a good example of what the Pharisees have done to the law God gave in the first place. The law lays down only one day a year for fasting — the Day of Atonement. But by the time of Jesus, pious Jews are fasting two full days *every week* — Mondays and Thursdays. In their minds, therefore, Jesus should take the lead and do the same.

Jesus' answer is interesting. He doesn't say, 'Wait! You have gone a bit too far. I think you should tone it down a bit.' We find his answer in verses 19-20. Fasting in the Bible is generally connected with mourning, or deliberately humbling yourself before God, or else it is a response to disaster. Jesus is saying, 'Why should my friends fast *at all* while I am here? That would be like starving at a wedding!' At the same time, by using this illustration of himself as the bridegroom, Jesus is dropping another hint about his true identity. Yes, the time will come when Jesus is taken away — first when he dies; then when he ascends to the Father — and *that* will be a time for sadness. Fast then, by all means. The kingdom of God is breaking in, but the time for the real party, the never-ending party, still lies in the future. Until then, there will still be times of sadness and pain — time for struggle, time when fasting is absolutely right — not because it's Thursday, but because sometimes it's a helpful thing to do. 'But for now,' says Jesus, 'my friends have got me here. It's all about me! Don't you understand — this is not about keeping your beloved rules, as if God were more impressed with you when you're hungry?'

Jesus makes the point even clearer with the little parables in verses 21-22 about patching clothes and storing wine. In those days, people might own two sets of clothes at most; if one of them went into holes it was a calamity. Knowing how to patch those holes was vital. You didn't take your worn old coat and patch it with a brand-new piece of cloth that hadn't been shrunk. If you did, you would end up with a bigger hole than you had before. It was the same with the leather bags that wine was kept in — again, not a luxury item, but something you needed in a situation where drinkable water was often hard to find. Suppose you get some new wine, still fermenting, with the gas bubbling out of it. What do you keep it in? Not the stiff, unyielding old wineskins that are on the point of cracking. All you will end up with if you do is a flood on the floor.

Obviously, Jesus is not giving us his top ten household tips here! He is saying you can't fit him into your religious box. He doesn't match up to your old, rule-bound religion. You need a new set of clothes, a new set of wineskins to put the new wine in. The Pharisees simply failed to see that Jesus' arrival changed everything. They saw him as just another teacher who was a bit out of line. Plenty of people today look at Jesus and that is all they see. He breaks a few taboos, offers us some positive values — well, add him to the mix, put him in there with Gandhi and Mohammed, and perhaps a guru, or maybe just some wise words from your friend down at the pub, because everyone has useful things to say. As Jesus makes crystal clear, that is not his way. His coming changed everything. He is unique.

The natural way that people think is to live by a set of rules. If they have some sense of God — and nearly everyone does — they feel that if they can keep these rules then God will be pleased. This is a comfortable way to think because it means you know what is expected of you. That is what the Pharisees were doing in Jesus' time. They had their rules — they were all in the book — and they devoted their lives to keeping them. They knew where they stood and it made them feel healthy. Today there are millions who do much the same. In Islam, it's a question of performing five key actions. Say the right words, give away some money, pray five times a day, fast one month per year, go on a pilgrimage at least once in your life — do all that and God will be pleased with you. It's a comfort zone. But people in churches do this too. Go to mass, go to communion, be respectable, say the right words, sponsor charities, keep lots of external rules, and you will be OK.

The story of Levi points in exactly the opposite direction. If ever you want proof that God doesn't choose people because they are good, here it is. Here is an outcast, a collaborator, and Jesus says to him, 'Follow me.' A hundred years later, opponents of the Christian faith were still trying to discredit Jesus because he had associated with people like Levi. But Levi the traitor — Matthew — becomes one of his closest followers, one of the Twelve. His name goes down in history as the writer of one of the four Gospels. Jesus came for the sinners, not the self-styled righteous.

Why is he breaking the rules?

Humans, as well as dead animals, can become fossilized! A fossil can look so lifelike that you would think it could walk or swim away at any moment, but in reality it is long dead, hardened, totally incapable of moving, or responding, or of any kind of life. It takes hundreds, or even thousands, of years for dead animals to become fossils. But people are very often fossilized when they are still alive! Not their bodies; it is their spirits that are fossilized — what the Bible calls a hardened heart. What could be worse than being fossilized while your body is still alive? But without Jesus in our lives, that is what we are. These five opposition stories are about people who are fossilized, people Jesus meets who simply will not respond to his love and grace, even when they see him in the flesh.

The last two stories in this group (2:23 – 3:6) are about Jesus and the Sabbath, and again we find people accusing him: 'Why is he breaking the rules?' The hearts of these accusers are fossilized; they will not see or recognize who Jesus is. This passage contains a strong warning for people like that.

Both stories take place on the Sabbath day — that is, Saturday, which was the Jewish day of rest. Look at verses 23-24. Now this incident seems innocent enough, so what is the problem? The law decreed that on the Sabbath no work should be done. That rule made sure that no one could force you to work on the day, and everyone, even including the animals, had a complete day off every week. But the tradition has added to that a whole superstructure of additional regulations. The religious experts have 'helped' by dividing 'work' into thirty-nine major categories, just so that everyone can be sure what they are not allowed to do. Category number three involves *reaping*. In fact, to a really sharp legal mind, the disciples are breaking three Sabbath regulations in verses 23-28. By picking off heads of corn, rolling them in their fingers and then chewing them, they are (a) reaping, (b) threshing and (c) preparing food on the Sabbath day! And the Pharisees spot them.

What, we may well ask, are the Pharisees doing out for a walk on the Sabbath? Almost certainly, they are there to spy on what Jesus and his company are up to. By the way, in case you are wondering what kind of high-powered binoculars the Pharisees are using, remember that these fields would be very small, unlike the huge prairies we know today, so it would be easy to stand at the edge of the field and see what is going on. For the Pharisees, the most legally-minded of all the Jews, this presents another great opportunity to attack Jesus, because obviously if his disciples are cheerfully breaking all these rules, that does not reflect very well on their leader. That is why they address *Jesus*, not the disciples.

Jesus responds in verses 25-26 with a question of his own, which may sound strange to us and to which we will return in a moment. But, first, we need to deal with an apparent problem in verse 26. Abiathar was not actually high priest at the time of the story. It was his father Ahimelech that David spoke to. Abiathar became high priest soon afterwards and was much better known than his father. The most likely solution to the problem is that the Greek construction used here can perfectly well mean 'in the section of the story relating to Abiathar the high priest', instead of literally 'in the time when Abiathar *was* the high priest'.

Let us return to the story itself. How does it relate to the issue of Jesus and the Sabbath? The story comes from 1 Samuel 21:1-6. David is on the run; he goes to the priests and he persuades one of them to give him and his companions the special bread from the altar of God, which only the priests are supposed to eat. Jesus says, 'Look, one of your biggest heroes, David, who became the great king, did something much worse than this, and no one condemned *him*.' In fact, even what David did was a very minor breach of the law: the priest freely gave him the bread, after all. The point is that meeting human need is more important than keeping every letter of the law, and, once again, the Pharisees cannot see that. They are blind, hardened.

Behind that there is a bigger point. These religious experts have made the Sabbath an intolerable burden on ordinary people. The Sabbath was a gift from God. It was important, yes — keeping it special is one of the Ten Commandments. It was the world's first law on workers' rights and it has protected untold millions of people from exploitation down through three and a half thousand years. God *gave* us the Sabbath because he knows how easily people exploit one another and he knows we need guaranteed rest. We work best in that seven-day rhythm. In Western society today, and especially in Britain in the last twenty years, that protection is being removed in the name of freedom. It is actually rank stupidity. We all need one day a week that is set apart and completely different from the others; for most of us that ought to be Sunday, but if it can't be Sunday it should be another day. If we are Christians, we should reject the notion that every day is the same — that is simply not how God has made us. His gift of the Sabbath proves it.

This is what Jesus means by verse 27. But for the Pharisees, the Sabbath is not a gift; it's a blank space just waiting for more rules to define it — rules that go well beyond any need or common sense. They have forgotten that it's a sign of God's grace, his kindness. The same stubbornness, the same hardness, prevents them from seeing Jesus for who he really is. Jesus' conclusion comes in verse 28. Yes, he is **'Lord'**: he has authority, even over applying one of the Ten Commandments. That implies that he is far more than the Pharisees bargained for, and much more than they want to hear; so they set up a trap. All through these five stories there is a gradual ramping up of the opposition, starting from quiet questioning, running through open accusation and, eventually, as we shall now see, culminating in a murder plot.

In this last story (3:1-6) we find Jesus in the synagogue on another Sabbath day. Probably this is in Capernaum, though we can't be sure. In the congregation, before the service starts, sits a man who has lost the use of one hand through some kind of wasting disease: it is useless now, and it probably prevents him from earning his living effectively. But it seems that he is here for a reason (3:1-2). Have his enemies *planted* the man, knowing that Jesus will be here today? If so, they have chosen him carefully. He will make a good test case. Their rules are clear: you can work on the Sabbath in an emergency, if there is an immediate risk to life. Healing definitely counts as work in their eyes, but there is no emergency here. Why, this man can easily come back tomorrow to be healed! Once again, they are spying, making an injured man the bait for their trap.

Jesus' response will be forthright (3:3). For the man, perhaps, this is embarrassing, but Jesus is taking his opponents on directly, and it is necessary that everyone should be able to see what is going on. Moreover, if the man wants to be healed, it's important that he should be willing to stand up and show his faith in Jesus publicly. The tension mounts as the man makes his way out to the middle of the crowded room. Everyone's eyes are fixed on the scene being played out. Jesus knows exactly what is at stake here: he knows what they are waiting for and what is likely to follow. Once again he asks a question — a dual question (3:4). The Pharisees can't really answer, because, in their hardened minds, a healing today would be an evil, not a good thing. And a 'killing' is just the idea that is starting to form in their minds. So they say nothing, and keep watching as Jesus heals the man (3:5). For the first time in many years, perhaps, he is able to straighten that useless hand, and as he does so, it is instantly restored to full health. A man is set free from a condition that has devastated his life; it has happened publicly, in the middle of a crowded synagogue. It's wonderful and, to the Pharisees' disgust, it has happened on the Sabbath day — and that is all that matters.

The Pharisees are, in fact, so appalled that Jesus is breaking their Sabbath rules that they are even prepared to kill him. They immediately begin to make plans with their temporary political allies, the supporters of Herod, to kill Jesus (3:6). The *Pharisees* are worried that their religion is being subverted. The *Herodians* (whom we will meet and discuss further in chapter 12) are worried that Jesus will start a revolt and the Romans will come and crush it, along with everything else in their path. Neither group is bothered about the true identity of the man they so easily condemn. The reason, as verse 5 clearly states, is the stubborn hardness of their hearts. Their religion of rules and respectability has taken the place of a living faith in God.

Jesus' response to that unbelief is a model for his people today. Look again at verse 5. His enemies have been looking at Jesus, studying his every move. But now he returns the compliment and, as he gazes around the room, he is filled with two emotions: he is *angry*, and he is filled with *grief* at their hard hearts. When our friends reject what we tell them about Jesus, over and over again, how does it make us feel? We live in a world where everyone's opinion is said to count for the same. 'If it works for you, that's fine, but don't push your ideas onto me.' That is what we are told. Jesus would not accept that attitude. When he meets such hardness, he responds with both anger and grief — anger that people can be so hard, so indifferent to God's grace, so closed to his love; and deep distress at what this hardness is going to do to them. Do we feel pain that so many are rejecting our Saviour, or have we believers become a little hard-hearted ourselves, so that nothing really upsets us any more?

There is also a powerful warning in these stories for those who are still spiritually fossilized. Whatever their appearance — however long they may go on coming to church, meeting with Christians just as if they too were genuine believers — the day is coming when every one of us will stand before Jesus Christ and our genuineness or deadness will be clearly exposed. Revelation 20:11-15 speaks of a great white throne and one sitting on it, and all the dead, great and small, standing before the throne to be judged. Long ago, on that day in the synagogue, Jesus looked round at the people with hardened hearts, the ones who were rejecting him, and he was *angry*. How will he look at you, then, on that great day? The good news is that Jesus can bring even a fossilized, stone-dead heart to beating life.

4.
Wanted: genuine followers

Please read Mark 3:7-35

In 1859 the great circus performer and tightrope walker Blondin — real name Jean François Gravelet — came to Niagara Falls. I don't know how he managed this, but he set up a rope 350 metres (1,150 feet) long that stretched right across the top of the falls. Using a long balancing pole for assistance, he proceeded to walk across. That amazing act would have sufficed for most people, but not so for Blondin. Over the next year or so he undertook the crossing about a dozen more times under the gaze of ever-vaster crowds. It is said that hundreds of thousands of people watched him as he walked across: blindfold, then pushing a wheelbarrow, and then with a stove, stopping in the middle to cook an omelette. As more and more people heard about these spectacular performances, the crowds continued to come from far and wide.

There is a further story about Blondin which is often told, although, to be honest, I am not convinced that it is true! After one of these crossings someone is said to have called out to Blondin, 'You are the greatest tightrope walker in the world!' Blondin called back, 'Do you believe I could take a man across those falls in a wheelbarrow?' 'Yes, of course', the man said. 'Well then, in you get', Blondin replied. 'Prove your faith in me.' Of course, when the man was called on to convert his admiration into faith, he simply wouldn't do it.

However, we do know that on 19 August 1859 Blondin *did* carry a man across the falls — not in a wheelbarrow, but on his back. It was his manager, Harry Colcord, who, not surprisingly, described it as one of the most terrifying experiences of his life — especially when one of the guy ropes broke and the tightrope itself swayed wildly from side to side fifty metres above certain death. Colcord was willing to place his life quite literally in the hands of the man he admired.

When people in Galilee heard about Jesus and his spectacular miracles, the crowds continued to grow. They came from far and wide. Many enjoyed watching; many came along for the thrill; but far fewer were willing to step out of the crowd. Even today, all sorts of people hear about Jesus and are impressed. But only a small number of them are willing to hear his call and place their lives in his hands.

Wanted: a crowd or a call?

Moving on from the five stories of mounting opposition, we now find Jesus deliberately withdrawing from the towns where the opposition has been concentrated. He cannot spend his whole time dealing with them. Mark's geographical notes are usually significant; here he is telling us that, by leaving his enemies behind, Jesus is symbolically breaking with the old established religion. He takes himself off to the familiar territory of the lakeshore (3:7). The local crowd come with him, but is it really a crowd that Jesus wants? In verses 7-19 we see the difference between a *crowd* and a *call*. Once again the spotlight will shine on us, the readers: what is our response to Jesus? Are we only to be admiring onlookers, or are we going to hear the call and place our lives in his hands?

The crowd

In verses 7-12 we see the crowd. News has spread fast. Although Jesus has told people not to go spreading stories about him, he has not been obeyed (1:45). As a result, Jesus is faced by huge crowds wherever he goes, many of whom are little more than sensation-seekers. The places listed in verse 8 cover almost every point of the compass and include Gentile areas as well as Jewish. There are Judea and its capital Jerusalem to the south; Tyre and Sidon to the north; the Transjordanian lands (such as the Decapolis mentioned in 7:31) to the east; and Idumea, or Edom, to the south-east. Jesus will later visit most of them in person. These places are far away — at least in times when nearly everyone has to travel on foot — and clearly all this doesn't happen on a single day. These verses describe developments which probably take place over several weeks.

Down by the lakeshore they find Jesus *healing* (3:10); the picture is that of a dense scrum, as people struggle to get close enough to touch him so that they will be healed. They find him *driving out demons* (3:11). Sceptics think that all this talk of demons is just some primitive description of mental illness: these simple first-century types didn't understand about schizophrenia or epilepsy, they say, and so they put it all down to demons. But we read here that the demons speak *articulate words* as Jesus drives them out. And these are not just *any* words — no, it is only the demons at this point who have an accurate view of Jesus' identity (see 1:34). Jesus refuses to accept their testimony, not because it is inaccurate, but because the only confession *he* wants is from the mouth of someone who understands and who submits to his authority with delight, not terror. So Jesus is healing and driving out demons, but above all he wants to speak. We know from chapter 1 that this is his top priority, and we know it here because of verse 9. Why does Jesus need to have a boat on standby? Clearly, not so that he can heal; he usually heals through touch. Not so that he can drive out demons, either; he does that from close up. The only reason he could need a boat is to speak without constant interruption. From a boat a few yards out on the lake he can probably get better acoustics, and he can certainly pull back from the scrum. Jesus' priority is to teach people about the kingdom of God. He drives out demons to prove that the kingdom is here, but nothing will make sense to people unless they can hear and understand what it is all about. We are not told that on this occasion he actually uses the boat, but when we come to chapter 4 and the parable of the sower we will see that he does.

So much for the crowd. They have come from far and near, converging on the figure standing at the lakeside. The crowd is drawn by the headline-grabbing healings and exorcisms and, sadly, their testimony about Jesus is not much more helpful than that of the demons. The crowds in Galilee always *like* Jesus, but for most of them it never goes much beyond that. They remain outsiders.

The call

Now for the call. Look at verse 13. Mark tells us that Jesus calls the ones *he* wants to come up to him. In the Greek there is a very strong emphasis on the word **'he'**. The crowd may want Jesus for all sorts of reasons, but overwhelmingly it is for what they can get. But Jesus calls for the people *he* wants.

He chooses **'twelve'**. Why twelve? He has just broken with the leaders of the old religion, which is based on the nation of Israel. Israel had twelve founding fathers, and now

Jesus begins to create his *new* people, 'the Israel of God' (Gal. 6:16), also with twelve founding fathers. This is the beginning of the church. On that Galilean mountainside the church of Christ appears in embryo, and this is its very first meeting.

Verses 14-15 explain why they are called. First, they are to **'be with him'** — they are to spend time with Jesus, getting to know him for himself, learning all that he has to teach them, seeing how he lives right up close. They will know him as those crowds never will. Secondly, they will be sent out to **'preach'** about him, to announce that the kingdom of God has come. Their job will be to cover the ground in a way in which no single individual, no matter how powerful and persuasive, could ever do. They will multiply the presence of Jesus twelvefold and in their turn bring others to know him too. Thirdly, they will take his **'authority'** to drive out demons.

This is the beginning of the church. When Jesus calls people today, he calls them into the same mission. People sometimes ask if he has given us the same authority, even over demons, that he gave the disciples. Demons figure prominently in Jesus' ministry because it was his unique mission to confront Satan and defeat him; Jesus' appearance on earth seems to have drawn out demonic opposition on a massive scale that has never been seen before or since. Yet demons still exist today. We don't expect to meet them very often, but we should not be shocked when we do. If we belong to this new people, the church, then we too have the authority of Jesus over the spiritual powers — including Satan himself when he tempts us or tells us we are useless. Although the first disciples' position was unique, there is a sense in which *every* Christian is part of the Twelve.

Now let's take a closer look at the twelve Jesus calls at first (see 3:16-19). Even Judas has his part to play in God's purposes. Some of them have extra names, nicknames, and

they are very significant. This is not a gallery of heroes —
not yet, at least. Simon is called **'Peter'**, meaning 'the rock'.
Jesus calls him that because he is going to be the strong
foundation of the new people, the church — one day! For
now, though, the name 'rock' is, shall we say, ironic — Peter
is one of the most unstable people you will meet. The brothers James and John are nicknamed **'Sons of Thunder'** —
explosive hotheads who can create a violent argument out of
thin air. The other Simon is a **'Zealot'**; the 'zealots' later
become an organized extremist group, who in forty years'
time will lead the revolt against the Romans, a sort of first-
century Hezbollah whose tactics include mingling with the
crowds, sidling up to suspected collaborators and sticking
daggers in their backs. That organized violence still lies in
the future, but it shows where Simon's sympathies lie. Simon
now finds himself in the same group as Matthew, or Levi,
the former tax collector and collaborator. To put it mildly,
the Twelve are a motley crew — unqualified, untravelled,
untrained, yet called by Jesus to be the founding fathers of
the church. And with them he will turn the world upside
down.

Today, many who admire Jesus are content to remain in
the crowd. They never do hear the call and climb the mountainside. The crowd is a comfortable place to be. You don't
have to commit yourself to anything in the crowd. You can
turn up in Galilee to watch Jesus do his thing, and then you
can walk away. We need to show people that it's not enough
to be part of the crowd. We have to come on *his* terms, in *his*
way, when we hear him call. Unlike the man watching
Blondin at Niagara Falls, we have to turn our admiration into
faith. If we have heard the call and responded to it, verses
13-18 remind us what we are called to: to be 'with him' —
not as nodding acquaintances, but to *know* him. And we are
called to *ministry* — just like the Twelve.

Wanted: a new family

Perhaps, like me, you have squirmed your way through
watching the film comedy *Meet the Parents*. It tells the story
of Greg, a young man in love who goes to stay with his
girlfriend's parents so that he can ask her father for permission to marry her. From the moment he arrives, however,
everything begins to go wrong. As Greg struggles to ingrati-
ate himself with his prospective father-in-law, Jack, the plot
lurches from one disaster to another. As he desperately tries
to get inside this family's strange traditions and relate to their
way of thinking, so that he can break into what Jack calls the
'circle of trust', he only succeeds in getting himself deeper
and deeper into trouble. If you are engaged, or even thinking
about it, this is definitely not a film you should see! The
reason the film works so well is that anyone who has ever
had trouble with their in-laws — in fact everyone who has
had any kind of family problems — has at least a little flash
of recognition. The message is: 'Families are trouble.' Of
course, it's all very well to laugh about family troubles.
There are plenty of family problems that no one would want
to laugh at. There are all too many families where the problem is bigger than dad's eccentricities or mum's obsession
with the pets! Maybe when you think of *your* family — past
or present — you don't smile at all.

   In Mark 3:20-35 we are introduced directly to the family
of Jesus — the new family that he came to establish, that we
become part of when we follow him. Having called the
Twelve to him, Jesus now returns to town (3:20). Probably
he is back at his Capernaum base, and maybe this is once
more the house we have been in before, first in chapter 1 and
then again in chapter 2. Not surprisingly, he will have to face
his opponents again as well as the crowds. The fact that
opposition now also comes from his own human family must
have hurt. It is against this background of false accusations,

of blindness and hostility towards Jesus, that he shows us his *true* family.

The story focuses around two ideas about Jesus — the first from Jesus' physical family, who think he is mad, and the second from the religious authorities, who think he is possessed by evil. Jesus and his team are so busy that they don't have time for a lunch-break (3:20). It is quite possible to read the report in verse 21 as, '*People were saying*, "He is out of his mind."' In other words, a *rumour* is doing the rounds that Jesus is mad. Alternatively, it could mean (as the NIV translators have assumed) that the family themselves have come to that conclusion. Either way, it is the family who feel that they have no choice but to come and take him away. Yes, Jesus is a thirty-year-old man who is living an independent life, but in a culture where the honour of the family is so vital, they simply have to follow up on stories like this. It is a question of honour or shame, just as it is in the Middle East even today. Presumably it is what Jesus has been saying, the claims he has been making, that has led people to say that he is mad. After all, he has been claiming to forgive people's sins in his own name! (2:5). He has been announcing that, now he has arrived, God is in action again, doing new things — in fact, God's longed-for kingdom is here.

Interestingly, it seems that the final straw is the report that Jesus isn't getting regular meals. Like many mothers, Mary is probably most concerned that her eldest son should be *eating* properly! So the family set off, and they will appear again shortly.[1]

Meanwhile, the religious leaders are getting in on the act (3:22). We have seen before that Jesus' opponents have watched him closely, even setting traps for him (3:1-6), but here it is absolutely clear that he is faced by a special commission of inquiry sent down from headquarters in Jerusalem. Rumours haven't only reached his family; the news about Jesus' activities is now seriously worrying the temple authorities. They have a policy in their files for dealing with cases like this. So, according to their clear procedures, they now send this commission up north to Capernaum, about eighty miles away. Possibly they are enquiring whether the whole town needs to be declared apostate — that is, rejecting God — but certainly they are given the task of drawing a clear conclusion about Jesus himself. Now, probably after spending some weeks in the area, they have reached their conclusion. **'Beelzebub'**, literally 'Beelzebul', is based on an Old Testament name for one of the ancient false gods of the region, now long-forgotten; but the name has hung on and is here being applied to Satan and his demons.[2] Whereas the family and others have concluded that Jesus is mad, these religious experts declare him to be possessed and inspired by evil. That, they claim, is how he is driving out demons.

Notice that no one doubts the reality of what Jesus is doing. No one who is actually on the spot suggests that Jesus is using trickery, or faking the miracles. Still less is anyone coming up with the ridiculous idea that Jesus is nothing but a good man who is being misunderstood. No, the miracles are real; the exorcisms are real; what the experts lack is an explanation. They need to put something in their report! So because it is unthinkable that Jesus can be wielding the power of God, they are forced to attribute his power to the only other possible source — the chief demon himself, Satan.

Now it's not very difficult to show that this idea is absurd, and in verses 23-27 Jesus proceeds to do just that. He sets up a public confrontation to face the experts with the truth: 'You say I'm possessed by an evil power? Very well, let me prove that's wrong. Here are a couple of simple illustrations. What you're implying is that there is civil war in Satan's kingdom, and in that case, he's finished. What would be the point of that? It would be absurd!'

Yes, the accusation is absurd. But worse than that, it is unforgivable (3:28-30). Jesus is not bandying abstract ideas here, you see. What the religious experts have done is to label the work of God in Jesus Christ as demonic, as coming straight from the pit. They have decided that the spiritual power behind all of Jesus' works is not God's Holy Spirit, but Satan. This is not some idle, throwaway remark; it is their careful and settled conclusion. Jesus responds, 'If you say that, you are placing yourself right outside the scope of God's forgiveness.' That is what the blasphemy against the Holy Spirit is — a settled attitude of deliberate hostility against the work of God. Occasionally today you will meet Christians who are worried that they have committed this sin — either unintentionally, by making some rash remark, or deliberately before they knew Christ — and that therefore God can never forgive them. We can reassure anyone who thinks that: 'If you are worried about it, you haven't done it.' This is a warning against setting yourself deliberately to reject Christ when you have all the evidence before your eyes that he is real and true.

So the family think Jesus is mad; the delegation think he is inspired by evil — and there aren't many other options left, not for people who really know about him. Jesus himself tells us what he is all about right here in verse 27. It's another little parable. The strong man is Satan; the one breaking in is Jesus himself. This is precisely his mission: to break into Satan's territory, to tie Satan down and to steal his possessions. He is not mad; he is not evil. And this is no civil war; this is an invasion of enemy territory. Satan's possessions are the people of this world who are in his grip, even though they don't know it. Jesus came to set those people free. Most people don't want to be told they are helplessly held by Satan, but it is true even so, and the Bible confirms it in other places — you are either a member of the kingdom of God, or else of the domain of Satan. But the message of

Mark's Gospel — indeed of the whole of Scripture — is that Jesus Christ is more powerful than Satan. Driving out the demons proves that, and here he is on his way to the great battle, the battle of the cross. Satan's power over us, his claim on us, is that we are sinners, offenders against God. But when Jesus Christ went to the cross he dealt with our sin and reconciled us to God. The sins are forgiven; the broken relationship is restored; and Satan's claim on us is gone. So Jesus' death on the cross defeats Satan, the strong man, and Jesus comes in and rescues from Satan's house everyone who will follow him out of the prison. And so (3:28) all our sins will be forgiven.

Now it is time to meet the family (3:31). They have been on their way, and now they turn up — Mary and her other sons. Presumably they know where to find him because this is his regular base. They wrongly assume that if they send a messenger into the house, then Jesus will immediately drop whatever he is doing and emerge. That is what the culture assumes. Inside, the house is crowded as usual; the message is passed along until it reaches him, and soon everyone knows that the family is waiting outside (3:32).

Jesus responds with a distinctly odd question (3:33). Then he looks around. Now the house *is* crowded, but of course this is not the heaving crowd of thousands that we see with Jesus by the lakeside. This is a house in a fishing village; at most a few dozen people are within earshot and these are not the sensation-seekers. These are people who want to sit and listen to his words — a group that consists of his core team of twelve with a wider group of others. In verses 34-35 Jesus gives his verdict. He looks at the group gathered round him on the floor. Then he looks at the messenger at the door and speaks through him to the family gathered outside, and he says, 'You say they are outside looking for me? No, my true family have already *found* me. My true family are *here*, on the inside.' It's not so much that he is rejecting his human family — though we should note that there is no special place given to Mary, his mother, here. But this is one more way that Jesus is overturning people's assumptions, redrawing the boundaries. He is speaking to a nation who believe that family is everything. These people live and die by genealogies. They think God will accept them simply because two thousand years ago they had an ancestor called Abraham.

But, says Jesus, 'my true people' (and therefore God's true people) 'are these: the ones who know me, who listen to me, who do the will of God' — the God who is creating a new people that doesn't depend on physical family ties, or on the nation you were born into, but only on belonging to Jesus. It's a family that will extend right round the world, into every country and across every boundary. It doesn't divide people by their background, or their colour or race.

In every local church we have a small fragment of that big family. It's not perfect, because it's full of people who still get things wrong. Sometimes bad things happen in this family. But the good news is that the head of this family is perfect. The day will finally come when we are too; we will see Jesus face to face, and he will look at us and say, 'Yes, you are my brother, my sister.' In this family, we are united by ties much stronger, far deeper, than those of even the closest human family. These ties are stronger than genetics, stronger than marriage, stronger than human love. They are ties based on blood, but not ours. The life of this family begins with the blood of Jesus.

5.
Wanted: ears that can hear

Please read Mark 4:1-34

Imagine you have brought home a rather tricky piece of self-assembly furniture. You dig out the instructions and start leafing through. First you find the diagrams. 'Yes,' you think, I can see roughly what's going on, but — hang on, what on earth is that telling me? I had better find the text that goes with it — where are the words? … Hmm, German, French — I can't *really* understand that… Danish, Finnish, Lithuanian — this is getting worse… Arabic — can't even read the *script*. Where's the English? There's no English.' Suddenly you realize that you can't follow these instructions at all. You thought the instructions would make it easy, but in fact it's as though someone is deliberately making it as difficult as possible for you to understand. You now have a choice. You can try with just the pictures, but they don't look as if they will get you very far; you could just give it up as a bad job; or you could go back and ask for advice, find someone who will actually give you some instructions and explain these mysterious pictures!

When Jesus taught the crowds in parables, he didn't make it easy. What he gave the people were *pictures*, but without an explanation. The pictures were intriguing, but they were hard to understand. He put his listeners in the situation where they had to decide what to do with the pictures. They could do nothing, or they could come back and ask what it all meant. But, of course, when Jesus spoke there was more at stake than putting together a TV cabinet or a folding table. These picture stories, these parables, are about whether or not we are going to be part of God's kingdom. They are about joining up with Jesus, and thus belonging to God, or being left outside in the cold. That makes it essential that we understand the instruction book, that we listen very carefully to the story behind the pictures. Or, to put it in the way Jesus himself puts it here, we must have *ears that can hear*.

Jesus has once again left the town, and he is back in one of his favourite haunts — on the shore of Lake Galilee (4:1). Once again the huge crowds have gathered. Previously (3:9) we saw that he asked his team to have a boat ready for him to speak from, because the crush was so intense. This time he actually gets into it; they anchor the boat a few yards out, and from that vantage point Jesus can address the crowd in peace. It's as if to tell us, 'This is the big one. This message is so crucial that it has to be heard properly.' The throng edges right down to the waterside and Jesus begins to teach them using **'parables'** (4:2). 'Parable' (from the Greek *para*, meaning 'beside') is a very general word. It can mean anything where some sort of comparison is made; often a word picture is drawn and a particular point is made. Some parables contain more detail; others less. In general, we should not expect that everything in a parable has to 'mean' something. Most parables intend to make one single point and they usually contain some incidental details simply to fill in the picture.[1]

When the Bible gives us images of what people are like, they are most commonly depicted as plants. People are described in terms of plants. Sometimes it may be trees; sometimes grass and sometimes, as in several of the stories in Mark 4, the picture is of a crop in a field. A plant doesn't do much. It's not in control of its own destiny, or of anything else. We like to think that we make our own way through life, shaping our world, making our own decisions. A plant can do none of those things, yet the Bible repeatedly compares us to plants! In these parables, not only are we like plants, we are *plants waiting to be harvested*. There is an end in view: we are planted here for a purpose, and the world does not meander on for ever; it is heading for a conclusion.

The parable of parables

Of all the parables of Jesus, this parable of the sower (4:3-9, with the explanation that follows) is the best known. Here is a farmer; it's the time of year for sowing, and out he goes into his field, scattering the seed by hand of course — and we shall see where it lands. It seems that this farmer is either particularly inaccurate with his aim, or else extremely optimistic. Some of the seeds land on the *path* (4:4), and that's no use; nothing can grow there, and all he does is feed the birds. Some of them land where the soil is very *thin* (4:5-6); there is rock just under the surface and, as soon as the hot Mediterranean sun gets to work, the little shoots which spring up from these seeds wilt, then wither and die. Some of the seeds land on a patch that looks more promising until you see that there are already suspicious little spiky growths emerging from the earth (4:7). As soon as the crop starts to grow, these *thorns* are going to squeeze them out. Even if the plants survive, they won't produce anything useful.

Only in one area of the field is there any chance of success. There is some *good ground*; some of the seed falls there, and that produces a crop (4:8). It's a bumper crop — up to a hundred times what was sown, enough to make up for all the rest. Jesus starts and finishes his story with a command that adds a note of urgency: **'Listen!'** (4:3); **'... let him hear'** (4:9).

This is a parable. Clearly, the point is not to analyse the sowing techniques of Galilean farmers, however indiscriminate they may be. This is not a lecture at an agricultural college! But what *is* this all about? You may have read and heard this story hundreds of times — but would you have understood what this picture is really about if someone hadn't told you? I don't think I would. And, although some of the same ideas are hinted at in the Old Testament, the plain fact is that no one who was present when these words were spoken seems to have got the point. Jesus isn't giving much away. It seems that most of the crowd are content to think, 'That was a nice story. I don't know what it meant, but that reminds me, I must go and see how my runner beans are doing!' But look at verse 10. At some later point, when they can get him on his own, Jesus' disciples and a group of others gather round and ask for an explanation. He says to them, gently I think, 'Come on, if you don't understand *this* one, how are you going to understand any of the others? This is the key to all the parables, because this one is not explaining my message, it's actually about how you *hear* the message' (4:13).

Here it goes. The seed that is sown represents the **'word'** — the message of Jesus (4:14). It is sown all over the place, into the lives of all kinds of people. There are people like the path; the message never gets into them at all. Satan, the Evil One, makes sure it is removed before there is any response (4:15). There are people like the thin, rocky soil. You see a response for a while, like a little seedling growing up, but as soon as the going gets tough, it's burned off (4:16-17). Then there are others who hear about Jesus and think, 'This is great!' But there is so much else they want in life — so much to buy, so much to worry about — just like a mass of weeds growing up from the ground and squeezing the life out of them (4:18-19). But then there are people who hear about Jesus, take the message into their hearts and start to live the life that Jesus gives them (4:20). They do far more than barely survive; they grow up and flourish, and then *they* have the chance to sow more seeds themselves and spread the word to new places.

'So,' Jesus says, 'this is what my parable means. There is the *same* message — and right now I'm the one spreading it — and there are these four different responses.' This is why the parable of the sower comes at this point, as a header, because it explains how the message itself will be received. It explains why people respond to Jesus in so many different ways. We have just come from the story of the religious leaders, who hear the message and say Jesus is possessed by the devil (3:22-30), and his family, who think he is mad (3:20-21,31-35). But exactly the same message has per-suaded and brought together this core group of twelve, plus some others, to be his disciples. Jesus tells them, 'This is how it will be. Not everyone will accept me. Some it will bounce off; some will seem to respond well, but then die away, and you will never see them again. And then there will be the others, who will believe in me, who will do well and ultimately reproduce the message in others too. That is how it will always be.'

The purpose of the parables

But why does Jesus use parables at all? Why doesn't he just say, here, for instance, 'Look, when I preach, people will react in these four different ways?' Why doesn't he say what he means? Clearly, in spite of what we may have thought, the parable is *not* to make the message easy to understand. Our instinct, supported perhaps by what we were taught at Sunday school, is to think that the parables are intended as helpful illustrations, just as a preacher today will use illustrations to get his point across. The disciples come to our assistance here because they ask Jesus specifically what the parables are all about (4:10-12).

Some theologians, such as C. H. Dodd, have argued that Jesus himself never could have said this. Either, they say, this is Mark's own interpretation, in conflict with Jesus' intention, or else someone like Paul must have inserted it later on. Some have said that Jesus could not possibly have intended the parables to be deliberately obscure. One of the most influential books on the subject, Jeremias' *The Parables of Jesus*, claims that although Jesus *did* say these words, he was not describing the purpose of the parables. They claim that Mark has confused things. All these people, in fact, support the traditional Sunday school view that Jesus told parables to make things clearer.

The fact is, as verse 13 proves, that not even the disciples understood the parable of the sower, so if Jesus intended it as a helpful illustration we would have to conclude that he wasn't very good at teaching in this way. Verse 12 is a quotation from Isaiah 6:9-10. The prophet has just had an overwhelming vision of the Lord in the temple and he is being given his commission to bring God's Word to the people. But the shock in that passage, and the shock here in Mark, is that, however faithful the prophet, however clear his message, the people are simply never going to respond. That has an application for anyone who is involved in gospel ministry. You can't guarantee a response just by having the message right, or by being superbly gifted, or by working yourself to death; none of that creates an authentic response to the gospel.

But back to the parables — we see from these verses that many people will not respond because *that is God's purpose*. The parables are told, not to make it *easier* to understand, but actually to make it *harder*. The parables draw a line between

those who will hear and understand and those who never
will. We may not like that interpretation, but it is what
Scripture says. It is what Jesus says. How do we respond to
it? On one level, we can say that people who heard the
parables and didn't understand them would still be able to
come and ask for more — which, in fact, is what the disciples do here (notice that in verse 10 it is not only the
Twelve who pursue the meaning). In that case, the parables
will serve the purpose of arousing people's interest and they
will be drawn in. But, on the other level — and this is the
main emphasis here — this is about God's sovereignty. Over
the whole question of who responds and who does not, who
accepts and who refuses, stands God's majestic decision: he
calls some people to follow him, and others he does not call.

The disciples, Jesus says, are on the *inside*. The 'mystery'
(NIV **'secret'**, v.11) of the kingdom has been made clear to
them. In Scripture, a *mystery* is not something you solve for
yourself; it's a secret that God has to reveal to you. But those
on the outside will never grasp it. The parables create an
opportunity to come and find out more, but for most people
they are a barrier. They are deliberately obscure, like an
instruction book that is written in a foreign language. So, as
we often find in Scripture, God's sovereignty and human
responsibility are placed side by side. God's choice takes
nothing away from our responsibility. Jesus tells the parable
to everyone. The opportunity is there for anyone to come and
ask him for more. In fact this is what verses 24-25 are about.
You are *responsible* for what you get, but at the same time it
is God who *decides* what you will receive. In our limited
human minds we will always find it hard to hold these two
together — they are like parallel lines that never seem to
meet. But they are both true.

Now what does this story have to say to us today? First,
the parable explains why so many people rejected Jesus'
message then and still do today. As the radio comic of

bygone years[2] used to say, 'The answer lies in the soil.' To die or to grow, reject or accept? Even when Jesus himself, the Son of God, walked the earth in person, the great majority of his hearers rejected his message, because most of them were not 'good soil'. So it is not surprising that people today reject Jesus Christ in just the same way. It happened to Jesus; it happened to his first followers; and it will happen to *us*, when we tell people the same story.

But, on the other hand — and this is the second point — for those of us who know Jesus, this story should encourage us to keep sowing. We never know what kind of soil we shall find when we go out to sow. Sometimes we shall be very surprised; sometimes the response will be a wonderful surprise, and sometimes it may be a very nasty surprise. In fact we have no choice but to sow as widely and as indiscriminately as the farmer in the story. But success is in *God's* hands, not ours. There is a fifth kind of soil which doesn't feature in the parable — the soil that gets no seed at all. Whose fault is it if the soil never meets the seed? We need to sow the message widely and, just like any farmer, we long for a successful outcome.

Lastly, this passage holds a very serious warning for anyone who is rejecting Christ's message. Tacked on to the end of Jesus' explanation of the parable of the sower is the cryptic little saying about the lamp (4:21-23). This miniparable has been interpreted in various ways, but in this context the lamp which 'comes' (the literal meaning of **'bring in'** or 'brought in' in 4:21) surely represents Jesus himself and his mission. The message may be hidden to begin with — hidden away in parables, hard to understand. But in the end, truth will out. One day, everyone on earth will be confronted with the truth shining out.[3] As Jesus spoke these words, very few people — a few dozen perhaps — had any real idea of who he was, and even they didn't have the full picture. But, as the years have passed, the truth of Jesus

Christ has spread throughout the world, and now hundreds of millions have seen his light. One day there will be no concealment, as everyone on earth will be forced to see it. But when that day comes, it will be too late for those who have spent their lives rejecting Christ. God will hold each of us accountable for the response we give to his Son. Jesus says, **'If anyone has ears to hear, let him hear'** (4:23). He tells us, **'Consider carefully what you hear'** (4:24).

The kingdom keeps on growing

In the remainder of this section (4:26-34), Jesus tells two more parables on the 'people are plants' theme (4:26-32), and then Mark neatly closes the section on the parables by telling us that Jesus told many others. Mark has given only a small selection. The translation **'understand'** (4:33, NIV) is perhaps a bit misleading — the next sentence implies that the crowds still don't really understand what Jesus is saying. It's probably better to say that he tells them as much as they can cope with (literally, 'as they were able to hear'): he continues to speak in parables, holding out the opportunity for people to come and find out more, until they will listen no longer. The parables continue to divide the people Jesus is calling to himself from those whose minds are closed to his message. So he tells these parables about God's kingdom, and then he gives the full explanation to the disciples, his own inner group.

At this point we might wonder, 'If only the *disciples* got the explanation, how can *we* know the true meaning of the parables except in the rare cases where the explanation is actually recorded?' 'How can you be sure,' you might ask me, 'that you aren't just reading in whatever you like into the story Jesus told?' This is a good question. The answer is that, from where we stand now, we can see the big picture much more clearly than those crowds by Lake Galilee. We have the full record of Jesus' life and death; we have the whole New Testament to give us the big picture of what Jesus came to do, and the themes we see in these parables are part of the story that runs through the whole Bible. These little stories are not the only place where the message is given. So we understand *these* stories just as we read *any* small part of the Bible — in the light of the whole book. That is why it is so important to read the whole Bible and not just cherry-pick our favourite passages!

Now let's look at these final parables. Notice one difference from the parable of the sower. Whereas that first parable was about the *message* of the kingdom and how it is received, Jesus opens each of these parables by saying explicitly that this is what God's kingdom is *like*.

First there is *the parable of the growing seed* (4:26-29). This parable, instead of describing different responses to the seed, zeroes in on the crop growing in the good ground and focuses on what goes on there. Once again, someone is out sowing seed and the seed begins to grow (4:26-27). In a parable we need not worry about every minor detail. The mention of night and day, sleeping and getting up, is just for local colour. The point is that time is passing. All through that time, this mysterious process of growth is going on. Of course, there are actions the farmer can take that help the seed to grow. He can water it; he can make sure it is fed with all the nutrients it needs to grow successfully. But he can't *make* it grow. The basic miracle of growth is just that — it's a miracle. A living seed has all that potential within it — it grows **'all by itself'** (4:28), to the point of producing a crop — the full head of grain. Finally it is ready for harvest (4:29). All this sowing and planting and rooting and growing has been for a purpose, because the harvest is coming.

What is the point of this parable? Actually Jesus has already given us a clue to that when he explained the parable of the sower. In verse 14 we read, 'The farmer sows the word.' This parable is simply about that word — the message of Jesus — taking root and growing in someone's heart. As someone like you or me receives the message, a new life begins and grows. There is a new start, a new birth, when someone knows Jesus. Then the person grows. The growth happens mysteriously; you can't control it. If you have watched a new Christian grow and develop, you recognize the picture. We can encourage it. We can surround a young Christian with all the help and support we can, just as a gardener will feed and water a growing plant, and perhaps support it with a stick — but we can't make the growth happen. That is a miracle, and miracles are God's department. Then, maybe long afterwards, comes the harvest. Grain plants are there for a reason. They are in a farmer's field, and the farmer is coming back. The parable is about us, and the Lord, like the farmer, is coming back. The only question is, what will he find when he does?

Let's move on to the second of these parables about the kingdom — *the mustard seed* (4:30-32). Jesus muses to himself: 'How can I show these people what my Father's kingdom is really like?' (4:30). He chooses a somewhat different picture this time; instead of a field of grain, where each plant stands for a single individual, in this case the one mustard plant stands for the whole kingdom. A single tiny seed is sown in the ground (4:31). The point here is not about scientific accuracy, so don't let's trip over it; seeds do exist which are smaller than mustard seed, but Jewish tradition regarded the mustard seed as proverbially tiny. But see what happens as it grows! In this area, mustard plants can grow up to ten feet (over three metres) high, **'the largest of all garden plants'**, as Jesus says — big enough for birds to perch and hide away in and shelter from the heat of the sun (4:32).

It's a very short, simple parable. The basic point is the contrast between the tiny seed and the fully-grown shrub. Each of those birds that come to perch in the branches weighs thousands of times more than the original seed. This kingdom, whatever else it may be, is something that starts out tiny and ends up enormous — but *it all takes time.* That is the aspect that Jesus' original hearers would not have appreciated.

The Jews of Israel in those days had very clear ideas about the kingdom of God, but their ideas were quite different from what Jesus is teaching here. If they had expected their Messiah to tell parables at all (which is unlikely), they would have expected him to compare the kingdom to a hurricane which sweeps in suddenly and flattens everything in its path, or else to an invading army that sweeps through the land in no time at all, destroying all resistance and ending with the king enthroned. That is what they expected God to do! Holy war would be unleashed, the Day of the Lord would come at once, and God's enemies would immediately be subjugated. The story would end with God's chosen king reigning over the world from Jerusalem and the Jews in their proper place as top nation. So they certainly were not comfortable with this picture of slow, almost invisible growth. The idea that when God's kingdom arrived it would grow within an evil world, that the harvest would be long delayed, that God's people would still need a lot of patience — that was totally unexpected. This, I am convinced, is why Jesus spends so much time teaching them through the parables about the kingdom, using these images of peaceful, quiet, steady growth. As all these parables show, the kingdom *does* end up in triumph, in a successful harvest, but it doesn't all happen in a matter of minutes.

The beginning of the kingdom was indeed like a single seed — tiny, apparently insignificant. It begins with Jesus appearing by Lake Galilee, preaching to the crowds and beginning to gather around him a nucleus of followers. It continues as he sets his face to go up to the capital in Jerusalem, where he faces his death. At that point it seems even to his followers that this tiny plant, this new kingdom, has been finished off before it has even begun. But a couple of days later Jesus has risen from death. A few weeks after that, he returns to his Father God's side in heaven, but the plant continues to grow. Now at last his followers realize that Jesus' death is actually the key to it all. Only after Jesus himself has left the earthly scene, and the Holy Spirit has been given, does the kingdom really start to grow. Within days it is sending out shoots in all directions. In a few years it has branched out beyond Israel into the whole region and then far beyond. It's the kingdom that goes on growing, even today.

Jesus speaks of the birds coming to perch in the branches. It's possible that they are no more than one of those incidental details, included simply to illustrate the size of the mustard bush. But I think there is more to it than that. This parable alludes to Daniel 4, where the great king Nebuchadnezzar is compared to a huge tree that provides shelter for all the birds of the air (Dan. 4:20-22). In that story the birds seem to represent the nations that were incorporated into Nebuchadnezzar's empire. So, here in the parable of Jesus, it's likely that these birds represent people from all the nations of the earth who will be drawn into the kingdom of God.

Even today, God is growing his kingdom — Jesus is growing his church — from among every nation on earth. You can go anywhere in the world and meet people who are part of this kingdom, people who love and follow the Lord Jesus. But the time for growth is limited, because the harvest is coming (4:29). Have you seen what a field of wheat looks like when the harvesters have finished with it? There is nothing left. Everything living has gone. The world we know is coming to an end. It may be sooner or later — we don't know — but it *will* happen. The Bible often uses the picture of a harvest to make this point. It's there in the Old Testament (see Joel 3:12-13, for example). The Bible looks ahead to the day when God will bring an end, and the peoples of the earth will be gathered up as when a farmer takes in the harvest.

This parable gives a positive picture: a field of ripe grain, all safely gathered in. It's a positive picture because it's a picture of the kingdom, of people who are rooted and grounded in Jesus Christ. But the Bible gives us other pictures too, and they don't make such cheerful reading. For people who are outside Christ, people who don't know him, there is a harvest too, but a harvest of judgement and condemnation. Revelation 14:14-20 gives a vision of a double harvest. There is the happy picture of the grain in the field being gathered in, God's people being brought home at last to him. But coupled with that is the haunting picture of people being gathered in for judgement, thrown into the winepress of God's wrath, crushed by God's anger against the evil things they have done. The harvest is coming, and the only way to be ready is to be in Christ, to be part of his great, worldwide kingdom that is growing to fill the whole earth.

6.
Power to restore

Please read Mark 4:35 – 5:43

What does the word 'chaos' convey to you? What picture does it bring to mind? For some, there will spring unbidden a vision of your child's bedroom, that moment when you open the door and you realize that there is not a single inch of floor space visible to the unaided eye. Or maybe it's your *own* bedroom that's like that — or your garage, or your desk at work! But for some, I suspect, the picture is darker. For you, 'chaos' may be the word that best describes your *life*. This kind of chaos means that nothing makes sense; nothing fits together. Life is out of control and there is nothing you can do about it. This kind of chaos brings despair. Real chaos is something we fear. We fear it taking hold of our lives, our streets, our world — our inner world or the world around us.

Chaos, and our fear of chaos, is something the Bible takes very seriously. We now come to a section of Mark's Gospel that contains three stories of miracles which all reveal Jesus' absolute authority over hostile powers. Whether he is facing a violent storm, a violent evil, a violent sickness, or even death, Jesus has the authority to overcome it, to face chaos and bring peace; to take the broken pieces of a man's life, a woman's life, and put them back together. Nothing symbolizes chaos

better than the wild waves of a restless sea — the subject of
the first of these stories.

Power to bring peace

In the previous chapter we looked at the parables of the
kingdom, where Jesus explains that his new kingdom is going
to grow from very small, almost invisible, beginnings ultimately to fill the whole earth. Now he will show that he has
the power to make that happen. Here comes the evidence.

We don't know how much time is covered by the parables
of chapter 4, whether one day or many, but in verse 35
evening is coming, and Jesus makes the decision to move on.
It's possible that he simply stays in the boat he has been
using without stepping ashore at all; that would explain the
odd expression, **'just as he was, in the boat'** (4:36). As we
have noticed before, Jesus does not simply go where the
crowds are. This is the exact opposite of celebrity culture.
Celebrities seek out the crowds; they stay with their public.
Publicity is their life-blood. Jesus is not like that. In fact,
having taught crowds of thousands, he is now setting out for
a rendezvous with one single man, and that man the ultimate
outcast.

Remember that this lake is quite small; the journey can't
be more than ten miles. The disciples are expecting a routine
crossing. There were **'other boats with him'** (4:36); various
ideas have been read into that statement, but most likely the
boats are simply carrying uninvited followers who are keen
to see what Jesus is going to do. Various minor details are
included in this story which sound very like the marks of an
eyewitness account, almost certainly Peter's. In any event,
the people in these other boats are about to benefit from a
miracle, because now, without warning, the storm breaks
(4:37). It seems amazing that such a small lake could be

prone to such wild storms, but that is in fact the case. The
Sea of Galilee is mostly surrounded by mountains and hills,
and when the wind funnels through the gap at the southern
end, where the River Jordan flows out, these violent storms
occur, creating a chaos of short, choppy waves that could
easily swamp a small fishing boat. Even so, from the reaction of the disciples, this storm must be exceptionally bad.
Not all the disciples are experienced boatmen, of course —
at least one (Levi) has come from a desk job — but panic
seems to have been the response of them all (4:38).

So Jesus is asleep, and our eyewitness tells us exactly
where he is. We should note that, in a story that will soon
show us his awesome power and majesty, we are reminded
first that Jesus is completely human as well. This man needs
to sleep. He is asleep because he has been teaching all day
and he is exhausted. This is a man with physical, human
needs just like us. The stern will perhaps be a little drier than
elsewhere, but, even so, this is an open boat, not some luxury
yacht with a soundproofed cabin and stabilizers, and Jesus
sleeps on through the crashing waves, the howling wind, the
pitching of the boat and the yells of the disciples. He sleeps
on, not because he has some magical sleeping pill, but
because he is at peace even while the world around him is in
chaos. When the disciples do rouse him, they say, literally,
'Don't you care that we are *perishing*?' But that is their idea,
not his. *He* knows they are not drowning, however fast the
water is rising and whatever the note of panic in their voices.
It is not clear what the disciples expect him to do — probably just to join in baling out the boat — but they want him
awake.

One of the most striking points of this familiar story is the
sheer casualness of Jesus' response (4:39). He just gets up
and does it. There is no ceremony, no need to gather his
energies: he doesn't even need to pray. He simply calms the
storm. In the space of a moment, everything *is* quiet and still.

And the words he uses are very interesting. In the exorcism story of 1:23-27, Mark tells us that Jesus 'rebukes' the demon; the same word is used here of rebuking the wind. Jesus tells the demon to be silenced, literally to be 'muzzled'; just the same rather unusual word is used here. Jesus speaks to both the demon and the storm as you would speak to a dog. In both cases, the 'dog' obeys instantly. This man has the power to bring peace to a life torn apart by the power of a demon; he has the power to bring peace to nature torn by a raging storm — and all with a word!

In the boat, the disciples' ears are still ringing with the noise, but the noise has already stopped. Their muscles are still tensed against the jolting of the boat, but the boat is not moving. Then through the dusk Jesus looks round at them and speaks (4:40). Clearly, not only the wind and the waves are out of order, but the disciples as well! Surely by now they should know they have nothing to fear when Jesus is with them. Hasn't he told them, just in the last few days, that they are the insiders, the people who have seen what the kingdom is really about? (4:11). It seems they still have a great deal to learn. Verse 41 tells us that the disciples are actually more afraid *after* the storm has been stilled than they were in the middle of it. 'They feared a great fear', the Greek says.

For the answer to the disciples' question in verse 41 we need to go back to the Old Testament, where time after time God is described as the one who brings order out of chaos. Right at the beginning, this is a keynote of the creation story. Out of the primeval chaos of a formless universe, the Almighty God has brought order, design and life (Gen. 1:1-2). Repeatedly, as the Bible's story unfolds, we find this picture of the God who brings order out of chaos — a chaos often represented as a turbulent, storm-ridden sea. Look at Psalm 65:7; Psalm 89:9 and Psalm 46, which celebrates the fact that, even while the mountains are falling into the sea and the waters roar and foam, God's people have no need to fear because he is the one who instructs the chaotic forces in the world: 'Be still, and know that I am God' (Ps. 46:10). Psalm 107 contains the story of seafarers who are caught in a storm and cry out to the Lord in their trouble, and we read, 'He stilled the storm to a whisper; the waves of the sea were hushed' (Ps. 107:29). For the Jews, then, the people to whom Jesus comes, their great Creator God is the one who can still the raging sea — something that as a nation they fear more than almost anything else. He is the God who quells the chaos. Now here is Jesus doing what only God the Creator could possibly do — addressing the elements and literally putting them in their place. He couldn't make his identity much clearer. Here on the lake, as the darkness draws in and with the disciples as the exclusive audience, Jesus reveals himself as the true God — nothing less than God in the form of man. Could it be plainer than that?

This story has something important to say to Christians. Notice that Jesus has actually *suggested* this journey — it is his idea and we can assume he knows exactly what is coming. The storm is violent; it is actually life-threatening. But Jesus brings them through it. Think of Mark's first readers, facing persecution; they might be dragged off to death in the arena at any moment. They need to know that their Lord is with them, where the storm is raging, where it seems their whole world is collapsing and chaos is taking over. The early church drew great comfort from this story. They felt that they were about to be overwhelmed; they felt they were going to sink — but no, because Jesus was there in the storm *with* them. Why should we fear, when our Lord stands here with us? Similarly, this story gives great encouragement for the persecuted church in many corners of the world today. And it is true for every Christian that the Lord Jesus is able to bring us safe through every trial. Jesus is not physically present with us now, of course, but he has given us his Spirit, who is here with us just as surely as Jesus was there in that boat. Whatever furious squalls are frightening us, we can be sure that the Lord who is with us is in charge. He may well lead us into trials; he will certainly lead us through. Jesus says to the disciples that they have no more cause to be agitated and upset than the waves do. Their fear is quite out of place, he says.

This story is not just a message of comfort for Christians who are facing trials in their lives; it's a challenge as well. **'Why are you afraid? Do you still have no faith?'**, Jesus asks. If we are disciples, what is our answer? This Jesus is the same one who can bring peace out of chaos in every place. One day he will do that, in every troubled corner of the world, as he establishes his everlasting kingdom over the whole earth.

Power to liberate

I wonder how you get on with your neighbours. If you are like one in seven of the British public, you don't get on with them at all! That is the proportion who have reported incidents of noisy neighbours, not to mention the many others who have feuds over parking, boundary lines or — a current favourite, this one — overgrown hedges. The whole issue has so gripped the public imagination that the concept of 'neighbours from hell' has inspired several TV series and, most recently, a popular computer game called 'Neighbours from Hell'. It's not much fun living next to a 'neighbour from hell', as you may even have experienced. There are many possible responses: on-line forums to support the victims, going to the police and ultimately the courts. You can form a vigilante group to drive the offenders out. You can move away, or you can simply suffer in silence. And some, though not all, of these remedies were attempted by the inhabitants of the **'region of the Gerasenes'**, just next to the Sea of Galilee. Unfortunately, none of them worked. The offender in this case was the original 'neighbour from hell' — in his case, this is the perfect description. This man — Legion, as he is known — certainly will not listen to reason. The only option for the locals in his case is the vigilante solution — until they meet the man who has the power to liberate.

It is likely that Jesus and the disciples have spent the night in the boat, because the story that follows in 5:1-20 clearly takes place in daylight. There is some confusion about the place name in verse 1 here, as you can see from the footnote included in most Bible versions. There is no doubt that Mark originally wrote **'Gerasenes'**, probably referring to a village by the lakeshore; the main town of the area was Gadara, about six miles away, so to call the area 'the region of the Gadarenes' would be equally accurate. In any case, we are now on the east shore of the lake, the *Gentile* side — that is important.

As Jesus gets out of the boat, without warning a terrifying spectacle appears (5:2-5): a man dressed in rags, at best, scarred and bloody where he has been cutting at himself in his despair. Appropriately, he lives among the tombs, the place of the dead — these would be burial caves, the only place where he can live because the locals have driven him away. They have tried to restrain him with chains and shackles, but to no avail; from somewhere he has found the strength to tear them off. At night and by day they hear his howling cries. This is not a man you would want around. This *is* the neighbour from hell. He is uncontrollable, un-manageable and totally without hope. Even by the standards of demonic activity, this is an extreme case, a man whose life is the very picture of chaos.

As he reaches Jesus he falls down before him (5:6) — the word used usually means 'worship'. The demons who control this man are forced to recognize that they are in the presence of someone totally superior. A shout is wrung out of him (5:7). **'Son of the Most High God'** is a Gentile expression, not a Jewish one, but, as we have seen before, it shows that the demons recognize Jesus far more clearly than any human does. That is why they respond to him with paralysed terror, recognizing a power that is not just infinitely *greater* than their own, but the total *opposite* to theirs as well. In 3:22 the Jewish teachers accused Jesus of working by the power of Satan. These demons would hardly agree! As Jesus commands the spirit to come out, the man is forced to confess that there is not just one spirit there, but a whole army of them (5:8-9). No wonder his life has been so totally devastated. These verses show how his identity has been almost completely submerged: **'"*My* name is Legion … for *we* are many." And *he* begged Jesus … not to send *them*'** away. Once this man had a real name; now he is just 'Legion'. A Roman army legion contained six thousand men. That needn't be taken as a precise count (would you expect accuracy from demons?), but it will soon become clear that it's not far from the truth.

Nearby there is a herd of pigs — this is Gentile country — and soon the demons are pleading to be allowed to transfer to them (5:10-12). Jesus lets them go; they leave the man at once, and moments later there are two thousand pigs hurtling down the steep hillside to drown in the lake (5:13). It's a vivid scene, but a strange one, and many people have wondered why it happens this way. Why does Jesus let the demons destroy the pigs? Why doesn't he simply banish the demons, as he does at other times? Doesn't Jesus care about animals? Is it something to do with pigs being unclean for Jews? These are reasonable questions. The explanation can have nothing to do with pigs being unclean; Jesus has very little interest in the Jewish food laws, as we shall see in chapter 7, and he certainly wouldn't have the destruction of *Gentiles'* pigs on his agenda.

No, there are two reasons why Jesus lets this happen. Firstly, it is not yet time for the powers of evil to be destroyed. Defeated and driven out, yes; but, in God's master plan, Satan and his forces still remain at large for a little longer. So the demons are allowed to continue their destructive work, but this man himself will no longer be their victim. In God's sight, one man is worth far more than two thousand pigs.

Secondly, Jesus wants to give a dramatic visual demonstration of the reality and strength of these demonic powers. 'Legion' has been freed from a whole army of evil spirits. They were intent on destroying the man just as they have now destroyed a whole herd of animals. This is what demons are; they are chaos monsters. Look what happens, Jesus is saying, when they get to work.

The pigs are gone and, not surprisingly, their owners, or the swineherds, are powerfully impressed (5:14-15). Here is the man who has terrorized their district, made their lives a misery, peacefully sitting down. He has been running around naked, or near enough; now, somehow, he is properly dressed. He has been deranged by the demons, maddened, suicidal, but here he is in his right mind. He is liberated. Surely the locals will be delighted. But no, they are *afraid*. This is all too much for them to cope with. When they also hear what has happened to their pigs, there is only one possible outcome: they plead with Jesus to leave (5:16-17). They drive him away, much as they drove their troublesome neighbour away. When it really came down to it, they would rather have their pigs than have Jesus around, like many people we may meet today who will not embrace Jesus because of the disturbance he will inevitably cause to their lives when he takes control — even though he brings the answer to their impossible problem.

Naturally, the man who has been healed feels differently (5:18-20). Today, troublesome neighbours are given a restraining order to keep them away from home, but this man can go home. It's not his first choice. There is a striking point about discipleship in this story. Four times Jesus is begged for something: four times the same Greek word is used. Twice it's the demons who beg (5:10-12): 'Don't send us out of the area'; Jesus agrees. 'Send us into the pigs'; he agrees. The locals beg him to leave (5:17), and he agrees. The healed demoniac begs to go with him (5:18), *and he refuses*. This man is now a disciple; he is part of the new kingdom, and he has to go where the King sends him. He is sent back home as a missionary, and it won't be an easy task. Jesus may never return this way. That is why this man's case is different from that of others whom Jesus heals. Generally he tells them to keep quiet, but this man he tells to speak. This is Gentile country, and now Gentiles will have the chance to hear from one of their own. He does just as he is told — right through the Decapolis region, which stretches down to the east of the Jordan River, telling what wonderful things the Lord Jesus has done for him. It is not surprising that the people are amazed (5:20).

Do you notice how similar Legion's story is to the account of the stilling of the storm? Both stories start with chaos — the howling of the wind, the howling of the demoniac — and end with peace. Both times the Lord Jesus simply speaks a few words, and violent disorder becomes calm; and both times, people respond with fear — greater fear *after* the miracle than *before*, when they were actually in danger! The message is just the same too. This man Jesus holds the power that only God has. The same one who can restore peace to a storm-ridden lake can also restore peace to a demonized life. That's wonderful, but it's frightening too.

Most people who read this book will be much more like the man called Legion as he is at the end of the story, rather than at the beginning. He has experienced the power of God in his life in a wonderful way, and so have we. He is qualified to go out and proclaim the news about Jesus, wherever Jesus tells him to go — *and so are we.* Maybe that thought makes us uncomfortable. First he goes to his own family and tells them. Then he travels, and wherever he goes he tells people what he knows about Jesus. Actually, that isn't much. He has no theology degree. Unlike us, he has never heard a sermon, never attended a Bible study. But he knows who Jesus is. He has experienced God's power in his life and he knows what it means to be set free, to have his life restored. That is enough for this man to have a ministry. That is what people do when they have met Jesus. And what Jesus has done for us is not less than what he did for Legion. He wore his cuts and scars on the outside, but our lives were just as broken and torn on the inside until Jesus restored us.

Power to heal

It's not a comfortable thought, but death is inevitable for all of us. We all have the seeds of death in our system from the day we are conceived. It may work very slowly; we may never give it a thought, especially when we are young; it may even take a hundred years to finish us off, but death is inevitable. Death is the final enemy we have to face. In the double story that forms the remainder of chapter 5, Jesus proves that he has victory over it! We see him here facing first sickness and then the most feared enemy of all, death itself, and proving that he has the power to heal, the power to give life.

Jesus recrosses the lake (5:21), probably back to the area of Capernaum. At once, and in contrast to the loneliness of the other shore, a great crowd gathers, as it does every time Jesus appears in Galilee. But very soon there is a special visitor (5:22). The locals all know him: this is Jairus, the official in charge of the local synagogue, an important dignitary. He has seen Jesus before; there is no doubt about that. He was probably there not long ago when Jesus drove out an evil spirit in his own synagogue, and then there were all those healings that same Saturday night (1:23-34). But today his thoughts are full of his own problems (5:22-23). Whatever suspicions he may have shared with his colleagues about this new teacher, Jairus now has only one thing on his mind. Casting his dignity aside, he falls to the ground in front of Jesus and begs him for help. The situation is desperate. His daughter — twelve years old, as we learn later — is at the point of death. Jesus goes with him (5:24). It's probably only a mile or two to his house in the town, but progress is desperately slow as the great crowd relentlessly presses in. Every moment's delay must be agony for Jairus, and soon there is a much longer one. Will the delay mean that Jesus comes too late?

For in the crowd there is another desperate case. Unlike Jairus, she has no dignity to lose. Unlike him, she approaches Jesus secretly (5:25-28). My guess is that most men who teach or preach on this passage pass over the woman's condition rather quickly. In case it's not clear, this woman has been living with continuous menstruation for twelve years. That kind of problem would be bad enough today; in those times it would be far, far worse. A woman like this is in trouble for no less than five reasons. Firstly, it is *embarrassing* — not so much because people are coy as because it would make them despise her. She lives with constant shame. Secondly, it is physically so *debilitating*. She lives with constant weakness. Thirdly, her desperate attempts to find a cure have driven her into *poverty*. With this condition she would be poor anyway, but, tragically, she has spent her last reserves on hopeless remedies.[1] Fourthly, she will be physically *unable to have children*, with the bitter disappointment

and shame that would bring in a culture where the family line
is all-important. But, perhaps worse than any of these, fifthly,
she will be *ritually unclean* all the time. The Jewish law is
very clear on these matters. It's all to do with the central
importance of blood in the sacrificial system, for blood
represented both life and death. Blood could not be eaten —
hence some of the kosher food laws. Blood was special — it
was reserved for sacrifice. That's why women were unclean
during their periods — not because the law was down on
women, as some people think, but because of the sacredness
of blood. But this woman will be unclean *all* the time. The
Jewish scholars, typically, produced a whole book of rules
about how someone like this had to live — it's there in the
Talmud. No one who wants to worship can touch her. She
herself can never approach the presence of God, can never
enter the temple courts to pray. Just like the man with leprosy
we met in chapter 1, she is a permanent outcast.

Is it any wonder, then, that she simply creeps up through
the dense, jostling crowd to reach out and touch Jesus'
clothes? How could she dare to appear openly? Perhaps there
is an element of superstition in her idea that she need only
touch the healer's robe to be healed, but there is a lot of faith
as well. It has cost her so much even to emerge from her
home and do this! Immediately she does, she is healed
(5:29); somehow she knows it. Perhaps there has been
constant pain, and it has suddenly ceased; more likely it's not
just that the bleeding has stopped, but that all her weakness
has been restored to strength. She feels complete again,
strong again, as she has not felt for twelve long and miser-
able years. But her story is not quite finished. Jesus too
knows that something has happened; the touch may have
been unconscious, but there has been a cost — he **'realized
that power had gone out from him'** (5:30). This does not
mean that he now has less power than he had before, but that
there has been a transaction. She has *touched* him, by faith.

There is a relationship between Jesus and the woman; power has been released.

To the disciples, the question he asks is ridiculous (5:31). Obviously, in a crowd like this, people are touching him all the time. Certainly they are touching him, but not every touch has released his power. We may want to ask, 'Does Jesus *really* not know who has touched him? Is he simply attempting to draw the woman out of the crowd and make her confess?' The short answer to what is quite a difficult question is that Jesus Christ, the incarnate Son of God, was omniscient (all-knowing) in his divine nature, but had limited knowledge in his human nature. We will meet this question again when we reach 13:32. As far as this story is concerned, he certainly does want to draw the woman out, but in his human nature he really doesn't know (5:32). Finally she emerges and, just as Jairus did, falls at his feet and fearfully tells him the whole story (5:33). She knows so little of this man who stands before her. Will he be angry, will he recoil at the thought that an unclean outcast has dared to lay a hand on him? What of these others who can overhear every word as the story pours out of her? Even the miracle of healing she has experienced fills her with fear — just like the disciples in the boat on Galilee, just like the crowd who saw the demoniac restored to his right mind, for the power of God is a fearsome thing.

She need not have worried (5:34). She is healed after twelve years of misery. She has peace after the torment she has known. Once more, Jesus brings in the outsider. Jesus is never bothered about becoming ritually unclean by contact with leprosy, or blood, or even death, because his touch makes everything clean. After her years as an outcast, barred from access to God, he calls her **'daughter'**. Think what that means to her! '*Daughter*, because you have put your faith in me, you are healed, you have peace, you can go.'

Still there is another daughter; and for her it does not look so good. Even as Jairus breathes a sigh of relief that at last they can move on, a delegation from his home appears with the terrible news that his daughter has died (5:35). Bringing Jesus home now would be pointless, they say — perhaps betraying their own suspicions of him. Jesus hears what they say and doesn't bat an eyelid. He turns to Jairus with a word of comfort (5:36). *What* Jairus is to believe, he does not say, but they push on and at last they arrive. Jesus takes with him just his inner circle as he goes on into the house where the girl now lies dead (5:37-38). There is a loud commotion of people crying and wailing — the hired mourners custom demands. To judge by the speed with which they have assembled, the family must have anticipated the girl's death, in which case her last hours of life have been accompanied by funeral preparations.

Jesus now takes charge (5:39-40). The mourners ridicule his statement, of course, because they know perfectly well she is dead. They go round mourning for people every day; it's their job. They know what death looks like. But Jesus knows too, and he has the advantage that he knows what is going to happen next. Sleep is something you wake up from, and so is this. So, with the mourners banished, the six of them enter the room and look down at the dead body (5:41-42). Again, the miracle is so simple. Again, here is the eyewitness record: Mark alone, informed by Peter, records the original Aramaic words which Jesus speaks as he raises the girl to her feet and to life. Mark tells us **'they were ... astonished'** — of course they are! This girl was dead; now she is walking about. Jesus says, 'Give her a meal; she has had a hard day!' (5:43). 'And don't tell anyone.' It's hard to believe *that* instruction is obeyed for long — already far too many people know about it — but maybe Jesus only intends to cover his own withdrawal from the scene.

For twelve years this girl has lived a privileged life in the home of a respected local official. But status and privilege have not protected them from death, the ultimate enemy. At the opposite end of the social scale is the woman in the crowd. If she had not had this affliction, she might have a child now just the age of Jairus' daughter. Twelve years of privileged childhood in one case; twelve years of outcast, childless poverty in the other. Both are far beyond human help, but one Jesus heals and the other he raises from death. By the way, do notice how these two stories demonstrate the high value Jesus places on the lives of women, both adults and children.

The Lord Jesus has power over death. When Jesus died, that too was a sleep. Yes, he was dead — there was no shadow of doubt about that — but two days later, on that triumphant Sunday morning, he burst the bonds of death and rose to life. Death has no more hold on him. For everyone whose faith is in Jesus, that resurrection guarantees that we shall rise to life as well. That's why the early church persisted in calling it 'sleep' when Christians died. It wasn't some silly euphemism. It wasn't that they couldn't cope with thinking about death. No, they knew that, for a Christian, death is something you wake up from. It's *sleep*. That's why Paul could write so triumphantly, 'Where, O death, is your victory? Where, O death, is your sting?' (1 Cor. 15:54-55, filling out the meaning of the words originally used by the prophet in Hosea 13:14), because he knew that the Lord Jesus has the power over death, and his resurrection proves it. Paul knew what death looked like; he had stared it in the eye more than once. But he knew that for a Christian it was a beaten enemy, because of Jesus. There, in the girl's empty bed, that victory was demonstrated clearly. And in the empty tomb of Jesus Christ our own resurrection to eternal life is fully guaranteed.

7.
Prophets without honour

Please read Mark 6:1-30

In 1995, a number of London publishing editors made what was possibly the worst decision of their lives. They had received a manuscript from a new author no one had ever heard of, currently leading a hand-to-mouth existence as a single mother in Edinburgh. It was a children's novel, but this woman had no writing background, no contacts in the industry and, frankly, the whole concept looked distinctly unpromising: a title that would be a complete turn-off for the target audience, a slow-moving opening page and a fat boy who was a horrible villain — how politically incorrect! No, these editors had seen and heard it all before. Struggling author desperate to make a breakthrough — they saw the same thing hundreds of times a year. So publisher after publisher made the same response: put it on the rejection pile and think no more about it. Eventually, of course, J. K. Rowling *did* get her publisher. A new and little-known publisher called Bloomsbury agreed to take the book. In June 1997 *Harry Potter and the Philosopher's Stone* was published in London, and in the next ten years we witnessed a unique publishing sensation, breaking all records and earning that tiny publisher Bloomsbury around ten million pounds every year. What about all the people who rejected the book and its author, those literary experts and publishing editors who made that fateful decision? They are left with the regrets of a dreadful missed opportunity, a decision they will always regret.

In this next section of Mark's Gospel we are looking mainly at two stories of rejection. This brings to a close the second main division of the book, 'Authority and opposition' (1:14 – 6:30). These themes of authority and opposition form part of the wider agenda of the first half of Mark's Gospel (up to 8:21), which is to ask and to answer the question: 'Who is this Jesus?' We have already come across a number of different answers, just as people have different answers to that question today. In this section, we see Jesus going back to his roots in Nazareth and facing opposition there, and we see what happens to his faithful herald, John the Baptist.

Not welcome at home

In verses 1-6, Jesus returns to his home town, in the Galilean hill country where he grew up. Nazareth is not named here by Mark, but there is no doubt that is what he means (compare 6:1 with 1:9,24). In the synagogue the people are amazed; the locals simply don't know how to cope with him (6:2). They have heard what he has been doing in other places — the profound words, the teeming crowds, even the miracles. But where does he get all this power and wisdom? If his family think Jesus is mad (3:21), it's perhaps not surprising that the rest of the village struggle with his identity! They think they know him so well. He is just the local **'carpenter'** (6:3) — the Greek word *tekton* means 'builder' as well. He is **'Mary's son'** — hinting, perhaps, that the real father isn't known — and all his brothers and sisters are here. Listen to them ticking off the names, some of them no doubt still with the family firm. And Jesus — he was just the first of the family. He went away last year and now he is back. He looks just the same as ever; it's not as though he has come back with a degree or a good job, or even a smart suit. Sure, he has gained a bunch of followers, but, frankly, they don't look any more impressive than he does. Any self-respecting rabbi can make a better showing. In fact, they are no more disposed to be impressed with Jesus than the London publishers were with J. K. Rowling.

It is precisely their familiarity with Jesus that breeds their contempt. In verse 4 Jesus uses his own version of that saying. His own people have rejected him. He is not welcome at home. Verse 5 tells us that he can do only a few miracles there — just some healings, not much by his standards. Of course, this means, not that he has lost his power, but that he doesn't find the faith he is looking for, to such an extent that he is **'amazed at their lack of faith'** (6:6). They have seen Jesus himself, in the flesh, walking their own narrow streets, and have decisively rejected him. It's a rejection that will continue and deepen, until he faces his trial and his death. Ultimately the Lord Jesus must face the scorn of his accusers and the contempt of the authorities as he goes to his death. Here at Nazareth he is rejected, and in the next episode, as he sends his disciples out, he warns them at the outset that they will face rejection too. The pattern we should expect is that the world will often reject our message, and therefore they will reject *us*, just as they rejected him. Sharing the gospel is a joyful task, but it's a serious and costly business too. For some Christians, rejection is found even in their own home — and that makes them even more like Jesus, because it's exactly what happened to him.

Multiplying the mission

Jesus' response to the opposition in Nazareth is not to give up or to change his strategy (6:6-7). Nazareth itself is just a small village; its only significance is that Jesus has grown up there. Now, in order to multiply his mission, Jesus sends the disciples out in pairs to do exactly what he has been doing himself. He has been leading up to this for some time. When he first selected the Twelve (3:13-15), this was one of the objectives.

Verses 8-11 give us the pre-mission briefing. This story, by the way, does not teach us exactly what our own ministry should look like. This passage doesn't teach us how much we should emphasize exorcism, healing, or even preaching. If we treat this particular mission of the disciples as a model, we shall also have to stop sending money to our missionaries and, for that matter, ban our ministers from taking a packed lunch to work — which some of us would certainly struggle with! No, this mission is intended for one specific purpose: to do exactly what Jesus is doing in the villages of Galilee and expand it. They must travel light, just as he does, to show that they are depending on God to provide for them. Their confidence must be entirely in him. The message they take is the same as Christ's (6:12): 'Repent, turn away from your evil past; a decisive change is demanded, because now Jesus is here, God's kingdom has arrived and it's time for you to join it.' And to prove that the kingdom is breaking in, to prove that Jesus is taking on and beating the powers of darkness, they too are to heal and drive out demons (6:13). He gives them the authority to do just that. They must find a base where they are welcome and stay there until it's time to move on (6:10-11). If a place refuses to welcome them and rejects their message, they are to leave with the clear message that rejection is mutual.

So the disciples go out in their pairs. We don't know how the pairs are chosen, though it's interesting to wonder whether Jesus takes delight in putting opposites together, like Matthew the former collaborator with Simon the political extremist, or Thomas the hesitant with Peter the impetuous! They go and preach the message of repentance; they drive out demons and they heal the sick — far more than Jesus could do in Nazareth — and in verse 30 they return. They gather round and tell Jesus how their mission has gone. Jesus knows it will be good for them to share their bubbling excitement before they move on. Their first taste of mission has been an exciting success, but, as we shall soon see again, this is in sharp contrast to the potential cost of following their Master.

For us, the story of the apostles' mission — like the account of Jesus' rejection in Nazareth — contains a warning: 'Follow Jesus, and he could send you anywhere!' The disciples have obeyed Jesus' call and they are following him. Already they have seen some amazing sights; these last few months have been full of the most memorable experiences, but all the time they have had Jesus there with them. It hasn't always been easy; it hasn't always felt very safe — it certainly didn't in that storm — but at least he has been there. In all their experiences, he has been teaching them, training them; this could turn into a bit of a comfort zone. Now comes the moment when they are to move out on their own. No longer will there be someone looking over their shoulder, holding their hand, telling them what to do all the time. This is the day when they will sink or swim. When we follow Jesus, this is what happens. You and I, when we followed Christ, placed ourselves at his disposal. Are we ready to move out of the safety zone, as these disciples had to do? Many people in our churches today are spectators. But this is no spectator sport.

There is also a warning here for non-Christians: reject Jesus, and you will face the consequences. Jesus gives the disciples careful instructions as they set out on their mission (6:11). This is the picture. When religious Jews returned to their homeland after visiting foreign countries, their practice was to pause at the border and ceremoniously shake or wipe the dust off their feet as they crossed over. They did not want their own country contaminated by even a single grain of Gentile dust. It was the symbol of utter rejection. When hostile villagers see the disciples making that gesture as they leave, they will understand what it means: 'You have rejected our call, so now you too are rejected.' As Jesus says, it is a **'testimony against them'**. Ultimately, everyone will be judged by how they have responded to Jesus, and those villages and towns which rejected his message will have to pay the price. They will be excluded from his kingdom, excluded from his presence for ever. Exactly the same warning comes to everyone who rejects Jesus today.

The price of truth

The noise of the party, muffled by the weight of stonework, has fallen suddenly silent. From the gloomy depths of his dungeon, John can only guess that Herod is holding another of his imperial-style receptions in the banqueting hall. He has been here for months now. Only rarely has he had the chance to see anything beyond these four walls, though when Herod does make one of his regular visits to this palace fortress, he generally sends for his prisoner and intrigues himself with his spiritual speeches. On those occasions he may get a glimpse of the barren surrounding country, the brown hills rolling down to the Dead Sea. But this is odd — Herod's parties usually last longer than this. Then comes the rapid tread of feet down the stairway and the rattling of the bolt.

The cell door swings open and a dim light shines in. A powerful arm seizes him. As he is pressed down onto a stone block, he barely has time to realize what is about to happen. As a suspicion of the reason begins to form in his mind, the sword swings. And so it is that John the Baptizer meets his end as he pays the price of truth.

This tale of sexual obsession, a ruler's weakness, political tension and a woman's passion for revenge is one of the most grisly and frightening stories in the whole Bible. In such a time, and in such a world, the Christian faith was born. Mark 6:14-29 forms the backdrop to those peaceful stories about a lake and fishing boats, and parables about fields and crops. The story of John's death is unique in Mark's Gospel in that it is the only one that doesn't focus on Jesus himself.

Mark deliberately places this story in the middle of the account of the apostles' mission. This is what he often does — bracketing one story within another so that one incident illustrates or explains the other. There go the disciples on the mission Jesus has given them, faithfully carrying out their God-given task. While that is in progress, Mark tells us, 'This is what serving God may cost. This is where it may lead you — to the executioner's block.' That is what makes the story of John's death so chilling.

Now in fact the whole story of John's death is told in flashback. It has happened a while before. The account here begins with the rumours that are running round about Jesus (6:14-15). All the activity in Galilee is causing a stir, not surprisingly, and everyone has their own idea about who Jesus is.

Some think he is John the Baptist restored to life. Now of course *we* know that John and Jesus are around at the same time: John actually baptized Jesus (1:9) and directed his own followers to him. But John disappeared from the scene round about the time that Jesus began his public ministry in Galilee, so it was just possible to think that John 'finished' before Jesus 'started'. And John didn't do any miracles, but if he had been raised from the dead, perhaps other amazing events might cluster around him — like the miracles that Jesus is doing. Then there are those who think that Jesus' arrival on the scene is the return of the prophet Elijah, who the Jews expected would have a special role in the end times (Mal. 4:5). Others prefer to believe he is simply a prophet like the ones who were around centuries before. There are three options, none of which really fits the evidence, but which seem to be good enough for market-place gossip. I don't think these are any weirder than some of the ideas about Jesus that float around today.

But all this talk about Jesus, which will crop up again in chapter 8, is not the focus of attention here. The point is that one of these theories is worrying the man in charge of Galilee (6:16). At the centre of the story is Herod, a son of King Herod the Great, the Herod of the Christmas story. Herod the Great ruled the whole area, but when he died the country was divided into four parts (or tetrarchies). One part is ruled by his son Herod Antipas, who is the Herod who features in this passage. He is in charge of Galilee, but also of an area called Perea, on the other side of the Jordan, which runs right down to the Dead Sea. Herod Antipas has a half-brother called Herod Philip, and he is married (at first) to Herodias. Confusingly, there is also another Herod Philip, again a half-brother, who rules a territory away to the north-east beyond Galilee. He is mentioned in the Bible (Luke 3:1), but he is not the Philip in this story!

Herod Antipas was married to the daughter of the king of the Nabateans, who occupied an area east of the Dead Sea. (Petra, the city carved from the rock and a well-known tourist destination today, was one of their main cities.) But now Antipas has divorced his first wife, taken Herodias from his brother Philip and married her instead (6:17). By doing

that he has made a number of enemies. He has outraged
many of his Jewish subjects, because his actions are in clear
defiance of God's law, and he has infuriated the Nabateans, a
dangerous action because they are a powerful nation and his
next-door neighbours. What seems to worry Herod Antipas
most is this wilderness preacher named John. John has taken
every opportunity to remind him of what he already knows:
'It is not lawful for you to have your brother's wife'
(6:18). The law is very clear on the subject (Lev. 20:21), and
John's forceful preaching on this could be heard as a call to
an uprising. Religion and politics are never far apart in the
New Testament — the strange idea that you can keep them
separate is a very recent one. Herod has alienated both his
subjects and his neighbours; the last thing he needs is John
cranking up the tension with his preaching, so he arrests and
confines him, probably in the fortress of Machaerus, just east
of the Dead Sea — a fortress which is also a palace — very
close to the area where John has been operating. That is good
enough for Herod, but it doesn't satisfy his new wife. Clearly
the happy couple don't see eye to eye here (6:19-20). Herod
knows there is something special about this man, and although in one sense he can't stand him, he is also drawn to
keep listening to him, and this could carry on for years unless
Herodias can find a way of finishing John off for good.

Eventually the opportunity comes. Herod Antipas, interestingly, is never officially a king; it is his persistent demand
for the title that eventually leads the Romans to sack him.
Mark's use of the title is probably ironic. But his bitter
frustration does not stop Herod from running his own show
like a miniature version of the imperial court in Rome. This
is what we see in the next scene (6:21-23). It's his birthday
party, and Herod invites all his top men to Machaerus for a
lavish display of his rather limited power. Herodias' daughter Salome — the name isn't in the Bible, but we know it
from the writer Josephus — is the daughter of her previous

marriage and is probably in her mid-teens. Herod is no doubt delighted that his step-daughter is willing to perform for the assembled company. He doesn't yet know why she should be so willing, but the reason will soon emerge. Her dancing is certainly seductive and quite possibly sexually explicit — this is Herod's household, after all, where more or less anything goes. The fact that she is the princess merely adds extra spice to the show. No wonder all these powerful men are so **'pleased'**. They probably fail to notice the satisfied expression on the face of the figure who lurks in the shadows, waiting to spring her trap. Drunk on a heady mixture of power, wine and sex, Herod makes his ridiculous promise and seals it with an oath. Salome immediately asks her mother and the answer comes straight back (6:24-25). Herod detests the idea, but he is trapped. They have all heard him make his oath; he will simply have to keep it, even if it proves he has been outwitted by his wife. The executioner is sent; then and there the deed is done, and Salome presents her proud mother with her gruesome prize (6:26-28). All that is left is for John's followers to retrieve his body and give it the dignity in death which it was so horribly denied in life (6:29).

It's a vivid story! Let's revisit two of the key players. First, there is *John*, the voice of truth. John's life story is hardly enviable. It was hard from start to finish. Commissioned by God to prepare the way for Jesus to come, he lived out in the wilderness; he lived rough, on the most bizarre of diets (1:6). He attracted a following, but his greatest moment came when he could point to Jesus and tell his followers to leave and follow him (1:7-8). His bold preaching led to a dungeon and a solitary death. But his story reminds us what we Christians are called to. John is clear, uncompromising and authentic. This is what we too are called to be as God's people.

In the twentieth century, the church in the UK lost its nerve and retreated into a safe ghetto. It bought into the idea that politics are too dangerous and are unsafe ground for a real Christian. It forgot that it was the church of John Newton, William Wilberforce, Charles Spurgeon, the seventh Earl of Shaftesbury and Elizabeth Fry. It retreated from the world; it went into the wilderness. But when John went out into the wilderness it was not a retreat. The wilderness became the vantage point for him to speak to his own culture. Will we recover our nerve in time to challenge our own authorities about injustice, immorality and laws that contradict God's Word?

The challenge is for us as individual believers too. No one thanked John for telling the truth. There is no career structure for a prophet! The terrifying truth from this passage is that John, the hero, the man of God, dies a hideous, undignified death as the result of a sordid marital power struggle. He dies in the company of no one but his executioner, with no kind words, no family at the bedside, not a friendly face in sight. That is the price of truth. Are we willing to stand for the truth if our only support, our only vindication, comes from the Lord?

Then there is *Herod*, the voice of doubt. Herod does not come out of this story well. He arrests John because it's the easiest way to deal with his problem, without regard to justice. He makes John into a kind of spiritual mascot whom he can bring out whenever he feels the need. There are plenty of people today who like the idea that they have a spiritual side to their life. They have no intention of committing themselves to anything, but whenever they feel like it they will look for a spiritual boost. Some even go to church for that reason. People can carry on that way for years, never really understanding that Jesus Christ came into the world to change their life, not to make them feel more comfortable. In the end, of course, Herod is manoeuvred into an action he never means to take and then finds himself living with his regrets, believing John has come back to haunt him. That is where superstition gets you.

History passed its judgement on Herod. A few years later, the Nabateans launched an attack against him to avenge their humiliation. They scored a crushing victory over Herod's forces, and he had even greater reason for regrets. The local populace interpreted this defeat as an act of God avenging John the Baptist's murder; maybe they were right. Three years after that the Romans sacked him, and then he died. You could say that after that night at Machaerus, the career of Herod Antipas went into decline.

But far more serious than the judgement of history is the judgement of God. In this story, the clear loser is John, dying that lonely, meaningless death. But in eternity, it is quite the reverse. On the day when Christ is seated on the judgement throne, there will be vindication and reward for all God's children — for John, for all who suffer today, for us who belong to him. But for everyone who has opposed him, there will be eternal punishment — not just a moment of terror in a palace dungeon, but an eternity of painful, bitter regrets.

John was not the last Bible figure to face an unjust execution. There was another who suffered hideous injustice, who met the same Herod, who was condemned by a weak and vacillating ruler and whose broken body was laid in a tomb by a brave disciple. John's death seems meaningless, but the death of the Lord Jesus gives meaning to the lives of all who know him.

Part III.
From Israel to the nations (6:31 – 8:21)

8.
Catering for Israel

Please read Mark 6:31-56

Catering in the desert

The scene looks distinctly unpromising. Spread out across
the hillside, right down to the edge of the lake below, stands
a great, milling crowd: thousands of people shuffling about,
muttering, wondering what is going to happen next. They are
tired; they have rushed to get here; they have now been
standing for several hours, and in their rush to come out
nearly all of them have forgotten to bring their sandwiches.
It's gradually dawning on them, as the sun begins to go
down behind the ridge to the west, that they are extremely
hungry. There are no corner shops here — hardly even a
house in sight. It's a remote spot. In fact, it seems the only
resources available are a single packed lunch and a dozen
frankly rather grouchy young men who have been hoping for
a good break but instead find themselves having to cope with
this unexpected crowd. But out here in these lonely sur-
roundings, Jesus is about to reveal his identity in a new way:
not just as one who can feed a crowd, not just as one who
can fill their stomachs — though he can certainly do that —
but so much more. Jesus is about to show that he is all they
need.

With this story we begin a new section of the book, which runs through to 8:21, beginning and ending with the two great feeding miracles. The reasons for putting the division after 6:30 are explained in the introduction. The disciples have just returned from their mission, found Jesus and cheerfully reported back (6:30). The dark tale of John's martyrdom forms the backdrop — discipleship is a serious business.

Jesus says to them, 'Right, let's go and have a break. I think you need it.' There's certainly no peace here: people are coming and going all the time, so that there isn't even time to eat (6:31) — and that's ironic, considering they are about to be part of the world's biggest picnic! They set off by boat, across to the eastern shore of the lake, to a **'solitary place'** (literally, in both verses 31 and 32, Mark says 'a desert place'). Unfortunately, by the time they get there, it is no longer solitary. Their departure has been spotted (6:33). The boat may be the easiest means of transport, but it's not necessarily very quick. Under most circumstances, you could walk round along the shore and keep the boat under careful observation all the way. It's not hard to imagine how the disciples feel when they see the crowd — we know how *we* feel when we have been longing for a break and suddenly find we are not going to get it. No doubt on board there is an audible groan as the boat moves in to shore only to meet a host of expectant faces.

Jesus' attitude is very different (6:34). Where the disciples see a nuisance, the Lord Jesus sees people with a need, and his heart goes out to them. They are **'like sheep without a shepherd'**: that's a powerful image, because sheep without a shepherd are lost; they are aimless. These people may think they have been very purposeful in coming out here to meet Jesus, but he can see that in fact they are more like a helpless flock of sheep wandering near a cliff edge, and what they most need is direction. That is why he at once begins, not to heal or to perform other miracles, but to *teach* them.

Time passes and it is getting late. The disciples have had enough. This morning they thought they were off on a quiet camping trip; now Jesus has insisted on dealing with the crowd, and he doesn't even seem to have noticed that there is this huge catering problem. They are in the middle of no-where; it's about to get dark; and there is nothing to eat. Finally, they tackle him (6:35-36). It's not at all clear whether the operation they suggest would even be possible, but Jesus' response shocks them (6:37). They clearly have in mind the most basic provisions at that price, but even so the sum of two hundred denarii is far beyond their means. Worse still, Jesus is simply bouncing the problem back to them, as if it's their fault they are in this mess. It's almost as though Jesus has created this difficulty on purpose. The disciples don't realize that this discussion is all part of their training. Should they really be so worried when Jesus is there with them? Haven't they seen him get them out of tight spots before?

Jesus tells them to start with what they have (6:38). Someone at least has brought something, but since these loaves will be about the size of our bread rolls, it will not go far. 'Come on,' says Jesus, 'sit them all down.' So the disciples spread out among the crowd, get the people into groups and persuade them to sit down (6:39-40). Probably it is only their respect for Jesus that makes the crowd so co-operative, and now a sense of expectancy runs through the throng. As they watch, Jesus takes the bread and the fish, and then he looks up to heaven, he gives thanks to God — and then something amazing happens. He breaks the bread, and then does it again, and again — and somehow every time he passes it out, his hands are full again. The same happens with the fish. Basket after basket is filled with food; basketful after basketful, he gives it to his disciples to distribute to the crowd (6:41-42). Probably they don't all see what has happened; certainly they don't understand it; but they do understand that there is good food in their hands, and soon their hunger pangs are gone. As they sit there in their orderly groups, this feels like a proper meal — the word used for the disciples **'[setting] the food before'** them underlines that. This is no hurried snack; Jesus has provided a feast. So the story closes with the disciples each picking up a basket, moving out among the groups of those taking part in the feast, and filling it with leftovers. They finish with more than they started with. Everyone has had plenty to eat; these people are poor — mainly peasant farmers or fishermen who will rarely have plenty to eat — and when they get the chance they will take full advantage of it. It is easy to imagine how they feel. Five thousand men have eaten, plus women and children — a ratio of one bread roll to over a thousand people. What excitement, what delight, as over five thousand poor, hungry people are fed to bursting point!

What springs out of this story is not the disciples and their grumpy attitude, nor the buzz of the happy crowd as they relax on the grass. It is the person of Jesus himself whose presence fills the stage. There is more to this story than five or ten thousand stomachs being filled, amazing as that is. Let's dig a little deeper.

A great crowd has followed their leader out to a remote spot — a *desert* place. There they have been fed and satisfied with miraculously provided food. If you know your Bible, that should remind you of someone. Fifteen hundred years before, *Moses* was the great leader, the man of God, the great heroic figure who took his people out of slavery in Egypt, into the desert and eventually to the edge of the promised land. On the way, God provided for them in a miraculous way. Every day he sent them manna, which was so unexpected that the name 'manna' itself means 'What's this?' The crowds ate it and were satisfied. At the end of his life, with the desert safely negotiated, Moses told the people that the Lord had promised to send them 'a prophet like you from among their brothers' (Deut. 18:18). Now, here, Jesus appears. Out in the wilds, he stands before the crowd and feeds them. In this story Jesus reveals himself as the new Moses — but better than Moses, because all Moses did was tell the people the manna was coming, by the power of God, and give them instructions what to do with it. But Jesus in the power of God *provides* the food himself. The message is clear: Jesus is the new and greater Moses who has come to rescue his people.

When Moses was about to die, there was one thing that worried him. After he was gone, who would lead the people of Israel into the promised land? Who would take care of them then and lead them home? So he prayed that the Lord would provide a faithful leader to replace him — 'so that the LORD's people will not be like sheep without a shepherd' (Num. 27:15-17). The Lord did give his people other leaders. Some turned out to be good; some of them were dreadful. But when Jesus sees the crowds of his own time, he sees that they are just like **'sheep without a shepherd'** (6:34). They don't have the leadership or the care that they desperately need. All those other leaders, all those other shepherds, at best came and went. In the end, even the best of them would fail. Every human leader ultimately lets us down, but the Lord Jesus never will. He is the true and final shepherd, the *Good* Shepherd.

Mark gives us some other significant pointers in his telling of this story. Look again at verse 39. Why should Mark tell us the colour of the grass? The Bible doesn't waste words. It is a factual detail; it suggests the story takes place in spring, when the rains have fallen and the grass is fresh. But I think there is another reason for saying that the grass is **'green'**. Moreover, Jesus' actual words to the disciples in this verse were: 'Make them *lie down*.' Does that remind you of anything? Look at

Psalm 23:1-2! This shepherd takes the sheep to a place of peace and rest and there provides them with all they need. Jesus has seen the people as sheep without a shepherd, and then reveals himself as the shepherd they need — the shepherd who is in fact 'the LORD', God himself in human form.

We have looked at Moses and at David's psalm. Move on a few centuries more for one last Old Testament reference. God used the prophet Ezekiel to condemn the failed leaders of his people, men who had proved to be corrupt and brutal instead of caring for the flock as he wanted them to. In the same passage, God says, 'I myself will search for my sheep and look after them. As a shepherd looks after his scattered flock when he is with them, so will I look after my sheep' (Ezek. 34:11-12). When Jesus appears, he fulfils that prophecy in full.

All those hopes and promises from Old Testament days, spread over a thousand years — the shepherd who would succeed Moses and lead his people home; the shepherd of Psalm 23 who brings his people into green pastures and beside quiet waters; the shepherd Ezekiel spoke of, who will stay with the sheep and look after them — come together in Jesus Christ, the Good Shepherd who ultimately will lay down his life for the sheep.

Mark has deliberately pointed this story to highlight the way in which Jesus fulfils these Old Testament pictures. The emphasis falls on Jesus' fulfilling the needs and aspirations of Israel. Jesus is literally catering for Israel. That is appropriate because the people who have streamed out to meet him in the 'desert' are from the towns and villages of Galilee; they are Jews. In chapter 8 there is a second feeding miracle, and we shall see that, in sharp contrast to the feeding of the five thousand, none of the special features relating to Israel and its history is present.

The story reminds us all, however, that without Jesus, we are simply sheep without a shepherd, wandering and lost. He is the shepherd who will care for us, who will stay with us, rather than let us down — as every human friend eventually will — the shepherd who will give us rest. Just as in this story the milling crowd becomes a scene of rest and peace when Jesus takes control, so when Jesus is in charge of our lives there will be a place of peace that nothing can destroy, no matter what turmoil is going on outside.

Treading on the sea

'We could never quite remember who saw it first. There we were, out in the middle of the lake, in the middle of the night, struggling on in the moonlight. We had been rowing for hours, into the teeth of the wind, and we were still only halfway across. We were all too tired to talk, too flat even to think about what had happened earlier that day. Even James and John had stopped arguing, and all we could hear was the wind keening and the choppy little waves splashing against our bows. Then someone saw it. Rowing, we were facing back the way we had come, of course. There it was: a misty figure, moving towards us over the water, still several hundred yards away. I wanted to rub my eyes, but I didn't think I should let go of my oar! Tired as we were, this was no hallucination — we knew we could all see it. It came nearer, and now we could see it striding across the waves. It wasn't heading straight for us — it seemed to be going past — but I can tell you the hairs on the back of my head were standing on end. That was when we gave up rowing. We couldn't do anything but stare. You know what they say about spirits of the night. Someone cried out and then we were all yelling, "Help!" — pointless, really, in the middle of a lake. But we were terrified; we didn't know what we were saying. And that's when he turned and came straight towards us. That's when we finally realized who it was. He spoke to us — and it was all right.'

Thus Peter might have described the story in verses 45-51 to Mark, thirty years later as they sat down together in Rome. It's hard to be sure how much the crowd has grasped about the miracle Jesus has performed, but as we move on to verses 45-46 Mark gives us some clues. Clearly, Jesus does not want either the crowd or the disciples hanging around. The Galilean mob is notoriously excitable and there is a real danger that they will get carried away with what has just happened. If they have recognized Jesus as some kind of new Moses figure — and they would be right to do so — they will want to adopt him as their leader, and quite possibly to start an uprising. Remember this is an occupied territory. In fact one of the other Gospel accounts confirms that that is exactly what the crowd want to do (John 6:14-15). But Jesus will have none of it. It's a temptation he has to resist, because he is not going to be that kind of leader.

In fact, it is even possible that Jesus sends the disciples away so quickly to stop them stirring up the crowds by explaining how they saw him multiplying the bread and fish. They are quite excited enough already. So he sends the twelve away in the boat that they arrived in a few hours ago and tells them to go back to the northern end of the Sea of Galilee, to Bethsaida. He will follow later, on foot. As indeed he does!

Meanwhile, once the crowd has finally dispersed peacefully, Jesus climbs up into the hills to pray (6:46). As elsewhere, we see him praying at night, an interval of peace to share time with his Father, no doubt to gather his strength after the demands of the last few hours and to recommit himself to follow the hard road that is laid out ahead of him — not to political uprising, but to the cross.

Out on the lake, the going is also very tough (6:47-48). Jesus looks up and can see them. They are in the middle of the lake, which would mean three or four miles away. From a high hillside, and assuming there is a full moon, it doesn't take supernatural sight to see the boat fighting its way against a strong headwind and the white caps on the waves. This isn't like the sudden, violent squall we read about in chapter 4; this is the steady, hard grind of rowing into the wind. And so, **'about the fourth watch of the night'** — that is, around three in the morning — Jesus comes to them, the account tells us quite simply, **'walking on the lake'**. What a shock for the disciples! They think they are seeing a ghost, not because they are superstitious, but just because there seems to be no other explanation. But Jesus speaks (6:50). He gets in, the wind drops and the disciples are amazed (6:51). Soon they are on their way again. They arrive, not at Bethsaida in the very northern corner of the lake, but at Gennesaret in the north-west (6:53) — probably the wind has blown them off course. And, having arrived, still without having had their much-needed break, what do they see looming up in the grey dawn light but another crowd, people already going about their business in these shoreline fishing villages? They recognized him when he left (6:33), and now they recognize him when he returns (6:54).

The response to his return is immediate (6:55-56). Very soon, people are flocking from far and near, collecting every sick person who can move, or whom they are able to carry, to bring them near to Jesus and have him heal them. They have all heard the stories about how he healed the paralysed man, just a mile or two along the coast in Capernaum (2:1-12) and that woman who just touched him and was instantly cured (5:25-29). So they come from miles around to do the same thing. Wherever Jesus goes, the eager crowds are there, and they know exactly what they want. They want to be well again, and he gives them the healing they are looking for.

This is another vivid, eyewitness account, and we can learn a lot by studying the characters we find here. The first character is *Jesus*, and once again in this incident he has revealed himself in a new and powerful way. Just as the feeding of the five thousand is about much more than filling people's stomachs, so this miracle of walking on the water is far more than Jesus proving that he has an alternative to the boat!

Once again, this story has deep roots in the Old Testament. This time we look back to the book of Job, and to a speech where Job is praising God for his wisdom and power in creating the world: 'He alone' — that is, God alone — 'treads on the waves of the sea' (Job 9:8). Now here is Jesus, treading on the waves of the sea. What does that make Jesus? Here is the first clue to something in the story that was quite puzzling. In verse 48 we read, **'He was about to pass by them.'** If Jesus wants to come and help them, why would he be heading straight past? The passage in Job gives us a hint. In the Old Testament, when people get a glimpse of the glory of God, it's often said that he 'passes by'. When God appears to Moses at Sinai, we read that 'he passed in front of Moses' (Exod. 34:6). 1 Kings 19:11 says something similar. Out on the lake, Jesus is doing what God does: *passing by* in his power and glory. In this story we see him as the majestic Creator, the Lord Jesus who is God himself, who can tread on the waters of the sea because he has *made* them, they belong to him and they obey his command. If walking on the water breaks the laws of physics, which of course it does, that is not a problem for the one who devised those laws before the universe was made. We can call them 'laws' only because they reflect the faithful character of the God who sustains them. If he wills to 'break' them, he can do so!

Yet even that is not the most amazing thing we see about Jesus here. Although he is God, all-powerful, far above and beyond us, who can bestride the waves, he is also the man who gets into the boat. When the frightened disciples cry out, he comes to them, and he says, 'Don't worry, it's me.' Their friend is back, and he gets into the boat. We don't know whether he takes an oar, but he certainly could have done. In chapter 4, where Jesus stills the storm, he stands up in the boat and tells the wind and waves to shut up. Here it's a little different (6:51), as if Jesus brings peace with him, so that once he arrives and joins his followers, it's simply impossible for the wind to keep blowing. When Jesus arrives, calm descends, and all is peace. Jesus is the God-man — God who was there before and right through creation, but also the man who brings peace to his people.

Now look at *the disciples*. They have been struggling to row across the lake; Jesus arrives, walking on the water, and they are terrified. Look again at verses 51-52. Now of course the disciples know that a miracle happened when Jesus fed the crowds. But, for all that, they don't understand. They don't get the point about who Jesus really is. Mark tells us, **'their hearts were hardened'** — they don't have that spiritual openness to grasp the real Jesus and trust him. In fact at this point they don't understand Jesus much better than his enemies do. They have spent so much time with him, seen him do so much, but they still don't get the message. They should realize that if Jesus can make one bread roll feed a thousand people, there is no limit to what he can do; that if he cares enough to feed a whole crowd of strangers, he is hardly likely to abandon his best friends. But this kind of hardness is not about your intelligence; it's about faith, about believing in Jesus.

The disciples should also understand what living with Jesus is like. If you want a good picture of the Christian life, look at this story. You get into trouble; you struggle; you cry for help; and Jesus comes to your rescue. Then before long it all happens again. It's a constant pattern of trial and deliverance, trial and deliverance. Trials and difficulties are

perfectly normal in the Christian life. These disciples are in
difficulty not because they have done anything wrong: they
have done exactly what Jesus has told them to do. They are
not in trouble because they have gone wrong; they are in
trouble because that is what happens. The path of obeying
Christ lies through trials and difficulties. As Jesus says to his
disciples later, 'In this world you will have trouble. But take
heart! I have overcome the world' (John 16:33). That is one
of the simplest but most important lessons a Christian has to
learn. We should never expect the Christian life to be plain
sailing. All too often it's more like rowing into a strong
headwind. It's through these struggles that our faith is built
up. This is how we learn to trust in the Lord for everything
— you don't learn that when everything is going swim-
mingly; you learn it when it's tough.

Finally, what about *the crowd* — this frantic, desperate
crowd? (6:55-56). They want healing. We should try to
understand how desperate people must have felt in days
when there were no hospitals and only the most rudimentary
medicine. There were no benefits if you were disabled; if
you couldn't work you had to beg, or simply hope that your
family would do the right thing and take care of you. Of
course, if you heard that there was someone around who
could heal you, you would do everything in your power to
get near. We can sense their desperation in verse 56. We
don't hear anything about Jesus resuming his teaching
ministry; these people are not ready for that. They see him as
a kind of wandering healer possessed by some divine power
that is communicated by touch. They understand even less
than the disciples do. Yet, wonderfully, Jesus accepts them
with their limited understanding: he doesn't turn them away,
and **'all who touched him were healed'**. Of course, they
need to know more; of course, they too need to recognize
Jesus' true identity — the time will come for that. We don't

need to know everything before we come to him. But he wants us to come.

This story paints a picture of what the Lord Jesus has done for us. It tells the story of his love. At the beginning of the passage there he is, on high, enjoying the unity and fellowship he has with God the Father. He looks down and sees humanity in trouble, unable to help ourselves. So he does not remain 'up there'; instead he comes 'down here'; he crosses over into our space and time and becomes a man, sharing our humanity, our flesh and blood, and he gets into the boat with us. The Creator of the universe enters into our very lives, and where Jesus comes, there is peace.

9.
Tradition!

Please read Mark 7:1-23

Fiddler on the Roof is one of the best-loved musicals of all time, and it features some of the best-loved songs. It tells the story of life in a Jewish community in rural Russia a century ago. The hero is Tevye, the village milkman, and the story revolves round his struggle to defend his family life and his own identity at a time when the Russian authorities are persecuting the Jews, revolution is in the air and everything seems to be changing. Everything Tevye knows so well, everything that always seemed to be so firmly fixed, is shifting before his eyes. Appearing at intervals through the film is the mysterious character of the fiddler, standing on the roof and playing a sad tune on his violin. The fiddler represents all that is constant, all that keeps the family going; he stands for tradition. The opening song of the musical is called 'Tradition', and the family members one by one sing out the role they play in the traditional Jewish family. But on every side tradition is being threatened — and the question is, how will Tevye respond to the challenge? In the story, Tevye's three eldest daughters all want to get married — each, in turn, to a more unsuitable man than the one before — and we follow the painful struggle which he faces in each case.

Fiddler on the Roof is fiction, but the power of tradition is not. When Jesus walked on the earth he lived among a people who clung to their traditions with a tenacity that would have put Tevye to shame. These people too feel that all they hold dear is under threat. Their treasured Jewish culture is being swamped by the rising tide of Greek influence; their national independence has been stolen from them by the Roman Empire; and now some wandering preacher and his bedraggled band of followers are stirring up even more trouble away in the north by saying that their cherished tradition doesn't even matter! The first half of Mark 7 is all about Jesus' response to tradition.

As we begin chapter 7, we find Jesus in fierce dispute with his opponents once more. Whatever they may have heard about his amazing miracles, what bothers them is that Jesus and his disciples seem to have no regard for the tradition that lies at the heart of their own religious system. Already they have been infuriated by the way he hangs around with outcasts, people no respectable Jew would be seen dead with (2:15-16). They have been thoroughly offended by the fact that his followers don't observe the ritual fasts as they should (2:18). And as for the way Jesus plays fast and loose with the rules about the *Sabbath* ...! In chapter 3 we saw that this was the issue that made his enemies seriously begin to think, 'This man simply has to go.' He has no respect for their **'tradition'** — a word which appears five or six times in this passage.[1]

The problem with tradition

Now the inspection team sent by the religious authorities in Jerusalem is back (7:1). They gather round Jesus, on the lookout for anything unorthodox. They soon spot the fact that Jesus' band of disciples are not washing properly before they eat (7:2). In verses 3-4 Mark gives us a careful explanation of what this is all about. The fact that Mark goes to the trouble of explaining these Jewish practices supports the view that he is writing for Gentiles. Matthew, who is writing for Jews, omits this explanation entirely (the equivalent passage is in Matthew 15).

The key point is that this washing is not part of the law which God gave. So how has it come about that the Pharisees insist on it? The law of Moses stipulated that the priests had to wash their hands and feet before they approached the tabernacle and the presence of God; it was one of the signs of ritual purity. But then people thought, 'Well, the whole nation ought to behave like priests, because God has called us all to show the world what he is like.' So, bit by bit, committed Jews began to adopt ritual washing before their daily prayers. The next step was to say, 'We don't want one rule for our worship and one rule for the rest of life, so we should wash before all our meals as well. That way our whole life will be holy and pleasing to God.' Mark also explains that there are many other 'washing' traditions as well, no doubt following on from the ritual cleaning of vessels used in the temple — the idea being that you should wash your own pots and pans in just the same way.

In fact, when you think of it like that, you can understand the sense of it. There is always a logic to tradition, if you go back far enough! Mark describes two kinds of washing here. One is in verse 3; they did this before meals. Literally the expression is: 'they wash with the fist'. It probably means that they would hold an open fist under a stream of water and quickly rub over the front and back of the hand. But then if you had been buying meat in the market (7:4), you would *submerge* your hands in water to purify yourself from anything unclean you had encountered there. It is all perfectly reasonable. In such ways, little by little, a huge body of tradition grew up around the original teachings of the law

— traditions handed down by the elders of the community, passed down by word of mouth until eventually, some time after this, it was all written down in the Talmud. These are traditions which the Pharisees not only follow obsessively themselves but also impose on others, because they believe that only through these traditions will God smile on them and the nation survive and prosper. So it is no wonder that they feel threatened by Jesus when they find out that he doesn't ask his disciples to follow these precious **'trad-ition[s] of the elders'**. They demand to know why (7:5). The whole point of these rules is to make completely sure that God's law is properly obeyed — and surely that is what religion is all about, isn't it? — scrupulously obeying the rules, both what is written down in the book and what all the wise experts have added to it.

But Jesus' answer is devastating (7:6-8). Jesus is picking up what was said centuries before by one of their greatest prophets, who condemned his people for the utter emptiness of the religion they pursued (Isa. 29:13). Jesus says, 'Isaiah was talking about *you*. Yes, you can get all the words right; you know how to perform the right ceremonies, the right rituals — but where are your hearts? The truth is that you are not really following God at all. You long ago gave up caring about the true commands of God — these traditions have taken their place.' By the way, see how Jesus doesn't use their respectful expression 'tradition of the elders'. He simply calls these things **'the traditions of men'** (7:8) or **'your own traditions'** (7:9).

Having answered their accusation, Jesus now goes onto the attack. 'It isn't just that you hide God's true priorities under a great mound of invented tradition,' he says. 'You actually play one command off against another so that people can't follow the law even when they want to.' This is what verses 9-13 are about. In the Ten Commandments, the heart of the law, it says, 'Honour your father and your mother'

(Exod. 20:12). Of course, in these times there are no pensions or benefit systems, so 'honouring your parents' involves the full responsibility of looking after them in old age — housing, feeding, clothing, medical care and generally paying all the bills. But clever legal minds have spotted a potential loophole for escaping that responsibility. It involves a technical term called *Corban* — an Aramaic word meaning a gift irrevocably devoted to God. If you have some property, or some savings, which rightfully you should use to support your ageing parents, you can declare that property *Corban*, removing it from the sphere of everyday use, and devote it to God — which in practice probably means to the temple. The really clever part is that you don't actually have to hand it over at once. It has the label *Corban* on it, and so it's no longer available for normal use, such as keeping a roof over your parents' heads. You can hold on to it.

Now suppose you have second thoughts. You realize that you have been hasty and you want to do what is right by your parents after all. 'No,' say the Pharisees, 'you can't do that. You have made a *vow*, and the law says, a vow is a vow. That property is *Corban*; you can't "honour your father or mother" with *that*!' Now this legal argument has become yet another tradition, which just makes people's lives harder. Worse than that, this time the Pharisees have not just buried the original command; they have made it impossible to keep. Jesus' closing verdict is that this isn't even an isolated case; he says, **'You do many things like that'** (7:13).

We might wonder what all this has to do with us in the twenty-first century — this remote world of religious experts, of tradition passed down by word of mouth from one generation to the next. The answer is that it has a great deal to do with us. Many religions are still like this now. Orthodox Jews still operate this way today — through the Talmud and other traditions which expand, interpret and ultimately bury the law of God. But, on a larger scale, this is also the way that Islam works. Islam is based on the Qur'an, believed to consist of the precise words given by God to Mohammed. After the Qur'an came the Hadiths — the traditions built up and collected by successive generations of Muslim scholars. Islam has thus become a highly complex system of regulations, practices and traditions which are all designed to ensure that, if you follow them, you will truly be pleasing God. If you trace the traditions all the way back, there is probably an explanation for every one of them. Muslims too have ritual washings before prayer — in fact they are much more tightly defined than what the Pharisees taught in Jesus' time. The detailed rules for fasting during Ramadan are phenomenally complex — who is exempt from the fast, what exactly invalidates the fast, and so on.

The fact is that traditions give us a comfort zone. If you ask someone who has converted to Islam why they have done that, they will often tell you that Islam offers a *system*. It tells you exactly what to do in every situation: a structure to fit into; an exact time and place to pray; an exact calculation of how much money to give — in short, precise measurements of godliness. You can always tell exactly how well you are doing. Isn't that appealing? Isn't that attractive? Doesn't that feel *safe*? As it was for the Pharisees in Jesus' day, tradition becomes a security blanket. All that matters is that you keep to the tradition, keep to the rules, and all will be well.

Even closer to home, this is the way that many so-called Christians live their lives. Perhaps their parents brought them up to be religious, to try their best and keep the rules. For them, going to church is about looking right, going through the right motions. Then, whatever happens the rest of the week, at least they have been in church, ticked the box one more time, kept the tradition. But what does Jesus say? **'These people honour me with their lips, but their hearts are far from me. They worship me in vain'** (7:6-7). In other words, their lives are nothing more than outward show. If we have no genuine, live engagement with God, then we have completely missed the point — just as the Pharisees did in the time of Jesus. We are truly following God *only* if he has our hearts.

Inside or outside?

Jesus still hasn't fully answered his opponents' question (7:5). *Why* doesn't Jesus enforce any of these rules? Has he anything better to put in their place — any better fix for the human problem? In verses 14-23, Jesus answers that question at a deeper level. It would seem that the delegation of Pharisees has managed to tackle Jesus more or less alone so far. But now he has had enough of arguing with them and calls the crowd together (7:14). At this stage in his ministry the crowds are never far away.

He picks up the theme by telling them something that comes over as a riddle (7:14-15). When Jesus says, **'Listen ... and understand,'** it's a signal that something really important is coming. But it's a difficult saying. The first part they can possibly understand. But what does Jesus mean by **'what comes out of a man ... makes him "unclean"'**? They are left to wonder, because he will say no more to the crowd for today.[2] He leaves them to chew on what he has said and disappears indoors. The explanation is coming, but it will be for the disciples alone (7:17-18). Going into a house is often a signal in Mark for a private explanation denied to the crowds (9:28,33; 10:10) and, as so often, Jesus is going to explain only to his inner circle, though he seems exasperated that they are not catching on more quickly (7:18).

He begins by explaining the first part of the riddle (7:18-19). By **'his heart'**, of course, Jesus doesn't mean the organ that pumps the blood round your system. The 'heart' was thought of as the centre of your personality — what today we would probably talk about as the mind. Jesus is saying, 'It's not what you eat that causes the problem. After all, food doesn't affect your mind; it only affects your stomach and then it ends up in the toilet or latrine' — that's what he actually says! In the final analysis, what you eat has got nothing whatsoever to do with the state of your heart and mind. So, says Jesus, what you eat can neither destroy nor preserve your relationship with God. If your heart is far away, eating from the approved list is not going to help.

Having said that, Jesus then goes on to explain the second half of his riddle (7:20-23). The list covers most of the Ten Commandments. What makes you unclean in God's sight is not anything you might consume; the problem that needs fixing is what is already inside you, the sin that comes from your heart. So Jesus is saying, '*That*, my friends, is why I don't insist that we go through the Pharisees' washing routine.'

What does this mean for us? There are three important points to get hold of. The first is, *you can eat what you like*! Mark has added a note at the end of verse 19, and from a Jewish point of view this is absolutely explosive: '**Jesus declared all foods "clean".**' This is not what Jesus says at the time; it is what the church concludes later on. Mark is saying, 'When we thought through the implications of what Jesus said that day, we realized this meant that all foods are acceptable.' Remember that Mark is almost certainly getting his information from Peter, who is there with Jesus in the house. If you know your New Testament, you will remember that it takes Peter a very long time to learn this lesson. In Acts 10:9-20, the Lord sends him a vision of all kinds of unclean animals lowered down from heaven in a sheet and he hears a voice telling him to eat them. Peter protests that he never touches anything unclean. It takes three times before

Peter gets the point: it is fine to eat the unclean food; it is fine
to invite the unclean Gentiles into the house. But a few years
later, up the coast at Antioch, Peter gets it wrong again, as
we read in Galatians 2:11-21. This time the problem is that
he lets the strict Jews intimidate him to the point where he
withdraws from the unclean Gentiles. It's Paul who has to
put him right.

Later, perhaps another fifteen years on, Peter sits with
Mark in Rome, talking about the past, remembering all that
the Lord Jesus said and did when he was on earth. I imagine
him at this point with a broad smile on his face, looking back
and saying, 'Yes, that's what Jesus really meant. Write it
down, Mark, so that others will catch on quicker than I did.
Jesus declared all foods clean, that's it! And have another of
these excellent ham sandwiches!'

Yes, there are times for avoiding some foods, if it would
cause too much offence to someone with a sensitive con-
science. And, yes, for the sake of your health, or the health of
the planet, you might want to go easy on the steak — but,
basically, as a follower of Jesus, you are free to eat and drink
what you want. Pork, alcohol, shellfish, snake, black pud-
ding, sheep's eyeballs — whatever — enjoy!

The second point is that *the rules about uncleanness are
finished*. The Jews were clearly told in the law of Moses that
there were many animals they must not eat because they
were unclean; and with the animals they could eat, they must
drain the blood out first. That was the beginning of the
kosher rules. So if Jesus has declared that all foods are clean,
it must mean that this part of the law has done its job and no
longer applies. You may never have worried about the Old
Testament ban on eating shellfish, but people do want to ask,
'How do we know that those parts of the law don't apply to
us?' This is the answer. The laws about what was clean and
unclean were there to teach God's people a vital lesson, a
symbol of the fundamental truth that to come into God's

presence you have to be pure, because he himself is holy and pure. So God set up this system to teach them about holiness, purity and cleanness. The Pharisees hijacked that system and made it into a heavy weight to hang round people's necks, but the basic idea was there in the law, and for good reason. Now, with Jesus' arrival on the scene, none of that is needed any more. Just as all the animal sacrifices point forward to the death of the *real* sacrifice, the Lord Jesus himself, so all the teaching about 'clean and unclean' points to the cleanness on the *inside* that only Jesus can give us. So, when Jesus arrives, no more sacrifices are needed and no more kosher laws either. The rules about uncleanness are *finished.*

The third point is the most important: *what matters is the inside.* Look again at this list in verses 21-23. Notice how Jesus makes no distinction between thoughts and actions. Whatever flows from the heart, from your mind, is what matters. Can any of us say we are not guilty of *any* of these things? Don't we recognize all too clearly that Jesus' picture of the corrupted heart is horribly accurate, horribly true to our own personal experience? The Pharisees thought being unclean is about trivial things that you do or don't do. But the point that leaps out here is that *everyone* is unclean. Jesus hasn't reduced the demand for purity; he has *raised* it. He has raised the bar so high that *everyone* misses it. Nothing that we can do to this old, hardened, rebellious heart does any real good. Washing obviously didn't, but nor do any of the hopeless attempts that people make today. They are all useless fixes, attacking the wrong problem, as pointless as trying to repair a broken-down car by giving it a respray.

Confronted with this truth, we have very few options. We can ignore the problem and hope it will go away — and that is what many people do, whether their drug is the kind you inject, drink or smoke, or the kind you look at on a screen. All these are ways of escape from the grim reality of the sin-ridden, screwed-up human heart. Or we can admit that we are hopelessly broken and the only solution is a complete replacement. The only way to deal with what is on the inside is a new heart. That is our desperate need, and that is what Jesus came to give.

10.
Reaching foreign parts

Please read Mark 7:24-37

My life as a dog

On 3 November 1957, the Soviet Union launched the world's second artificial satellite, Sputnik 2. Strapped into a tiny capsule on board was Laika, the world's first space traveller. She had trained with two companions for the demands of the mission: to bear high acceleration, to endure confinement in small spaces for many days and to cope with the special food which would be needed in the weightless conditions of the spacecraft. Life support was rudimentary. There was a fan which was supposed to operate when it got too hot and a basic system for producing oxygen and absorbing carbon dioxide. Instruments measured the passenger's heartbeat, breathing, blood pressure and movement. As the rocket blasted off, the effects of noise and the harsh acceleration were found to quadruple her breathing rate and sent her heartbeat (literally) sky high, before returning to normal once the craft began its orbit. Unfortunately, as the satellite reached its final altitude, part of its heat shield was torn away and, about six hours into the mission, Laika breathed her last, killed probably by a combination of heat stress and exhaustion. It was over forty years later, long after the demise of the

Soviet Union, that this unfortunate mission failure was
finally admitted. Now that sounds pretty callous. How could
people show such gross disregard for Laika's life and wel-
fare? Even if everything had run perfectly, she would not
have lasted more than a week. There was never any plan for
Sputnik 2 to be recovered so that Laika could return safely to
the earth. How could they be so callous? The answer, as you
probably realize, is that Laika was not a woman; she was a
dog. The world's first space traveller was a dog who started
life as a stray on the streets of Moscow.

The fact is that outside the sentimental Anglo-Saxon
world — countries like Britain and the USA — that is mostly
how dogs are regarded. They are working animals; they are
there to do a job for us. They are at the disposal of their
masters; they are obviously not our equals and they are
unlikely to be our friends, let alone 'man's *best* friend'. To
call someone a dog would be among the harshest of insults,
because dogs are largely dirty, disease-ridden scavengers.
Yet in Mark 7:27 Jesus looks at a woman who has approached him in a state of utter desperation and calls her a
dog — Jesus, the gentlest and kindest man who ever walked
the earth. How can Jesus insult someone like this? 'Dog' was
a traditional Jewish insult for a Gentile, so perhaps Jesus is
simply displaying the standard racial prejudice of his time,
showing that he is just as much bound by his own culture as
any of us are? Or is something else going on?

We follow Jesus as he now travels north, out of Galilee,
where he has been operating for some time, to the region of
Tyre. This is Phoenician territory, a Gentile area, about
twenty miles north-west of Capernaum. This is a place where
almost everyone will be, in Jewish terms, unclean — Gentiles, dogs. Jesus probably comes here to get some rest and to
give his disciples a break as well. The last time they tried this
it was not exactly a success (6:31-44): they go out to the
wilds and are quickly surrounded by a crowd of thousands

who want to hear Jesus speak and then need to be fed. When they return to civilized territory (6:53-56), the demands are just as remorseless as before! So now Jesus goes off in a different direction (7:24). It's likely that this house belongs to some Jewish follower of his. But even here, it seems it is impossible to escape people's notice (7:25-26). On one level, this is nothing new. Mark records several such incidents, and often the plea is made in absolute desperation. Demonic activity is quite capable of ruining someone's life, and if the victim is your son, as in 9:14-29, or your daughter, as in this story, of course you feel desperate — any parent would. So this woman, as soon as she gets wind of Jesus' presence in the area, tracks him down and begs him for help. Even here they have heard some of the amazing stories of miracles and transformed lives that surround his person.

But there is a problem — not a problem about dealing with demons, but a problem with this woman who has burst into the house and now lies at Jesus' feet pleading for help. She is a Gentile. Mark emphasizes this, explaining in detail that she is a Greek-speaker, culturally alien to Israel. She is from Phoenicia, the coastal strip of what is now Lebanon; administratively it is part of Syria, but what counts is who she is: she has nothing to do with the Jews. To understand what this means we must remember how the Jews thought of the Gentiles. One of the daily prayers used by Jewish men of the time went like this: 'Blessed are you, Lord our God, ruler of the universe, who has not created me a *woman*; who has not created me a *Gentile*; who has not created me a slave, or an ignoramus.' But here is a Gentile woman, the lowest of the low for a devout Jewish man. So how will Jesus, a devout Jewish man, respond to her?

Perhaps given that background, his response is not quite so unexpected, but it still shocks us (7:27). His meaning is plain enough: he is here to feed the children, not the dogs. The children, safe inside the family home, are the Jews, who think of themselves collectively as the children of God, his adopted race. The dogs, running around in the yard, are the Gentiles, outsiders, unclean, with no claim whatsoever on God's care or protection.

So is Jesus no different from other Jewish men of his time — grateful that God has spared them from the appalling fate of being born a Gentile or a woman or (perish the thought!) both? More than one explanation has been offered for this very blunt reply. Jesus must be speaking with a smile on his face, or he is joking. Well, we can't say whether he is smiling or not, and Mark doesn't tell us. There is certainly no suggestion that he is joking. There are two reasons why he speaks as he does.

One is that he is simply telling the truth. Jesus' mission at this point is focused on the Jews. Two thousand years of history, beginning with Abraham and running down through the centuries since, have not quite finished yet. Everything about Jesus is Jewish. His royal ancestry through the line of David, his birth in Bethlehem, 'royal David's city', his religious upbringing, his visits to the temple, the language he speaks — all are Jewish, and all reflect the fact that for two thousand years God has been dealing with the world through the nation of Israel and the Jewish race. If people from the rest of the world want to encounter the one, true living God, they need to go up to Jerusalem and become Jews. Up to this point, they are the children and we Gentiles are the dogs. Jesus' mission continues that story. His ministry of teaching, healing and driving out demons is for the Jews. The children must be fed; he cannot take their bread and fling it to the dogs. The Jews come first in the purposes of God.

But there is a second reason for Jesus' response. We know that from the way the story concludes. In the end, Jesus will not reject this woman. This verdict about the children and the dogs is not the final word. Jesus is testing her to see how she herself will respond to such a blunt judgement. If Jesus' response shocks us, the woman's reply to him is breathtaking (7:28). She makes just a small change to the picture he has painted. In the scene she describes, the dogs are under the table, where they can pick up the crumbs that fall from the master's table — but they are still dogs! She is willing to take the lowly position he has assigned her. In effect she is saying, 'I understand that the Jews are your first love and they demand all your attention. But surely there are some small leftovers for me? Surely you can drop me a few crumbs? That is all I am asking!' Almost uniquely in the Gospel story, this Gentile woman, this outsider, holds her own in a conversation with the Lord Jesus. She puts his own dull, male disciples to shame! She does so, not by being proud and laying down the law, as the Pharisees have done; not by trying to outwit him with smart arguments, as the Sadducees would do; but, wonderfully, by listening to his words, looking into his face and asking him for mercy.

Wonderfully too, in response she receives what she is pleading for (7:29-30). Jesus recognizes her faith and her confidence, not only in his power but also in his loving willingness to heal. He sends her home, and always in this Gospel that command is associated with faith that the healing work is done: the paralysed man who was healed (2:11); the woman who was bleeding (5:34); blind Bartimaeus by the Jericho road (10:52) — three Jews and, here, one Gentile woman. Jesus has simply told her, 'Don't worry. The demon has gone.' He hasn't been near her house. He has intoned no incantations such as their pagan priests might have done. There has been no noise, no fuss, just, 'The demon has left.' That is enough; she goes home and finds her daughter is well (7:30). Literally, the girl is found 'thrown' or 'flung' on the bed, no doubt exhausted after the final convulsion of the departing spirit. Jesus' words were true. He has given her dignity, and he has given her what she asked.

Most of us reading this story now are Gentiles. Can we see ourselves here? Can we view ourselves as Gentile dogs? The truth is that for all those thousands of years, we Gentiles truly were the outsiders. Paul describes the situation of the Gentiles in Ephesians 2:11-12. He might just as well have used the word 'dog' to add to his list, describing how outcast we were, how far from hope of ever knowing God. We were Gentile dogs, consigned to running around in the yard while the children were fed in the family home. At the time of this story that is still the case. The story of salvation is moving on, and the time is coming when the barriers are going to come down, but at this point we haven't quite reached that part of the film. This picture gives us a freeze-frame shot of the movie, and it shows us just where we have come from.

This woman has only the sketchiest notion of who Jesus is. What can she understand, as a Gentile of Syro-Phoenicia, of the prophecies and hopes of the Jewish people? Even his own race don't recognize his true identity — what chance does she have? She has heard the stories and a name; that is all. But in her desperation she comes to Jesus. She is prepared to take the humblest position; she is content to receive the insulting name the Jews give to Gentiles. Astonishingly, from her utterly outcast position she is better off than the insiders, better off than the Jewish religious experts with their centuries of tradition, their calm sense of superiority and their certainty that they alone know best. Her encounter with Jesus is even more striking because it anticipates what he is about to do. It's as though she can somehow glimpse the fact that Jesus is here on earth to do something for the dogs as well as for the children, as though she can see a tiny chink of light appearing in the towering wall that has separated the peoples for so long. If so, she is absolutely right. Very soon Jesus will head back south, eventually to Jerusalem to face judgement and a death that will change everything. Paul describes the transformation in Ephesians

2:13-18: in the cross of Christ, the world's greatest dividing wall is broken down as free salvation is offered equally to Gentiles as well as Jews. People who were far away — people like us — are brought near to God through the blood of Christ that was poured out on that day. People who were outsiders are brought inside, into the warmth and the light of the family. So there are no more children and dogs; instead there is a single new humanity born anew in Christ. We who were 'dogs' are given a new status, because the wall of hostility has been broken down and the love of Jesus has crossed every barrier. As we grasp that astounding grace poured into our lives through Jesus' death, we must resolve never to re-erect the barriers which he has demolished — those which divide one race from another, one true Christian from another. We are dogs no longer; we are children, sons and daughters — one family.

From 'can't talk' to 'won't shut up'

Our politicians frequently tell us that global warming is the most important issue facing our planet, but they are wrong. Far more vital than the healing of the planet is the healing of *humanity*. Restoring the creation around us and healing its wounds is important, but re-creating broken men and women is the supreme task. That is the subject of the final story in Mark 7 (vv. 31-37).

At first sight, as we read it, we might think, 'This is just another healing story'. Though that would be amazing enough in itself, perhaps there does not seem much to mark this incident out from a score of other stories in the New Testament. But as we look at it more closely, we find that there is more to it. All the accounts of Jesus' miracles point us to something deeper than the restoration of a single human body. This one in particular takes us to the very heart of Jesus' mission. Mark selects and arranges the material in his Gospel with great care and deliberate skill; the four major episodes in chapter 7 are no exception.

In verses 31-37 we come to the case of a man who is deaf and can barely speak. This is not just a healing story tacked on the end of the chapter; if such a thing is possible, the message of this narrative is even more radical than those which precede it. In verse 31 Jesus leaves the Gentile area of Tyre, moves up through Sidon and then travels south-east to the eastern side of the Sea of Galilee and into the area called Decapolis, which is simply the Greek for 'the Ten Cities'. He may well be taking this roundabout route to avoid the crowds which would meet him instantly in the territory of places like Capernaum and Bethsaida around the western shore of the lake. Not too far from here, as we saw in chapter 5, is where Jesus healed the man called Legion.

Verse 32 tells us what happens next. Whereas the previous story was about a Gentile, a 'dog', this one probably involves Jews. The Decapolis is a mixed area, mostly Gentile but with large Jewish colonies, and if these people were Gentiles Mark would probably tell us. Here is a man who can't hear at all and who has a serious speech impediment. Most likely, from the way Jesus deals with him, some disease has robbed him of hearing and speech; he knows what he is missing. But he is blessed with friends who care about him enough to bring him to Jesus. Here, too, they have heard of him — possibly even from 'Legion'. We don't know if they expect him to heal the man, but they are certainly amazed when he does!

We note first in verses 33-35 the way that Jesus treats the man as an individual. He takes him away privately — Mark stresses that point in verse 33. He gives the man his dignity and he wants his full attention for what he is about to do. Next Jesus performs a thoroughly bizarre series of actions. Of course, he does not need to do all this. We know by now that the Lord Jesus can heal with just a quiet word, or even at a distance, without setting eyes on the patient, and his power is such that even death or a whole horde of demons cannot thwart him. This elaborate drama is solely for the benefit of the man he is about to heal. Picture it: the man cannot hear; he relies on what he can see and feel to connect with the world. So Jesus holds up his own fingers and places them firmly in the man's ears to show that he is going to deal with his deafness. Then he spits, to mime expelling something from his mouth, and to reinforce the point he touches his tongue. Very deliberately he looks up to heaven (7:34), not because he needs to, but in order to show the man where his power originates: it comes from above. He gives an exaggerated sigh to convey that healing power is about to flow from himself to the man. Then he speaks the word: *Ephphatha.* It's one of those words that Mark has preserved in its original language — this may in fact be a Hebrew word, rather than the usual Aramaic. Perhaps Mark records this to make the story more vivid, but it occurs to me also that *ephphatha* would be a very easy word for the man to lip-read; Mark may well be underlining that the point of this little drama is for the man's understanding. He explains to us that the word means, 'Be opened'; what our own, limited English language cannot convey is that Jesus is not addressing this command to the man's ears. The command is in the singular; it is addressed to the man himself. His whole person is to open up to Jesus' healing power.

So, of course, it happens (7:35). The word is spoken and the healing is done. A man's life is restored — a man who must have struggled to support himself, who could not connect with the outside world, and now suddenly he can. Restoration! Suddenly he has a great deal to say for himself. It's a case of from 'can't talk' to 'won't shut up'! (7:36). As 1:38 and 4:35 have already shown us, Jesus' mission is not simply to boost his name-recognition index; anyway, he knows they will simply tell people there is an amazing healer at work in the Decapolis — and all that news will generate is more crowds of excited spectators. But, in spite of Jesus' strict instructions, once again the news goes out. Not just the man who has been so wonderfully healed, but the friends who brought him and everyone in the vicinity all want to spread the news far and wide. A man has been healed, a hopeless case restored. But in fact there is more to it than that. Mark is the only one of the Gospel writers to include this story. Matthew, whose account runs closely parallel to Mark's throughout this section, talks generally about healings at this point (Matt. 15:29-31) but he doesn't mention this man.

The reason Mark decides to use this story is that he is writing with a specific purpose in mind. The first half of the Gospel — up to the end of chapter 8 — is all about answering the question: 'Who is Jesus?' We have already seen that Mark deliberately echoes Old Testament language as he talks about Jesus. We find this again here. In verse 32 Mark uses a very rare word to describe this man's condition. You wouldn't expect a word meaning 'almost unable to speak' to be very common, but in fact this is the only time it comes up in the whole of the New Testament. It is almost as rare in the Septuagint, the Greek translation of the Old Testament. Almost the only place it appears is in the prophecy of Isaiah, in a passage where he looks forward to the day when God will intervene in human history and bring about a restored humanity in a restored creation (Isa. 35:3-10). What a vision! God coming to judge his enemies and to save his people; the ones he has redeemed, ransomed, saved, coming home to the renewed city of God; and, all around them, the world of nature being restored to perfection and beauty! This is God's climate-change programme! And one of the signs of that happening is given in Isaiah 35:5-6, where we read that 'the

ears of the deaf' will be 'unstopped' and 'the mute tongue'—
there is that same unusual word — will 'shout for joy'.

Mark is telling us, 'This is what is happening in the
ministry of Jesus.' The ministry of Jesus is the beginning of
the new age breaking in — the new age that will ultimately
involve the re-creation of the whole earth. It doesn't happen
all at once. That is what the prophets of old couldn't see. But
with Jesus the new creation is beginning. God's great project
is a new humanity who live to enjoy a new heavens and a
new earth, creation perfected once again. It is a place where
there is no disease or disability of movement or speech, no
blindness or deafness, where deserts flow with clean water
— a place perfectly fit for God's clean and renewed people.
What a vision of the future — no dream, but reality! Jesus
came to begin the new creation, and it starts with creating
new people. The Bible makes it clear that the work of new
creation is now well under way — not in the physical world,
for our bodies are still growing old and dying and, for that
matter, the ice caps are still melting. But the new creation is
under way inside us (2 Cor. 5:17).

Finally, did you notice how Mark summarizes the people's
response to Jesus in verse 37? **'He has done everything
well.'** This seems a strange way to describe a healing miracle,
but it echoes another verdict that was given right at the start
of the Bible (Gen. 1:31). When he sees what he is doing in
you and me now, the new creation beginning in us, he says
just the same. It's good!

11.
Catering for the nations

Please read Mark 8:1-21

The catering project, part two

Are you any good at barn dancing? From my experience, there is always someone who doesn't get the hang of it, even if the band is outstanding and the caller is perfect. They have heard it talked through, seen it demonstrated, even walked through it themselves, but when it comes to the actual dancing, they are still going the wrong way round the circle, or swinging by the wrong hand, or simply counting wrong! Of course, it doesn't really matter. Who cares if it takes you a long time to grasp the finer details of barn dancing? But there are more serious aspects of life where being slow on the uptake is far more important, when what is at stake is not whether you might bump into someone on a dance floor, but whether you will miss something of life-or-death importance. Far too many people are desperately slow to grasp the point when it comes to the *spiritual* world — the truth about God and how it is possible for us to know him. Mark 8 is about just that, as we watch the disciples putting on a demonstration of being incredibly slow on the uptake. Here is something they should really have understood very well, but apparently they don't have a clue.

Remember that the first half of Mark's Gospel is about answering the crucial question: 'Who *is* Jesus?' What is his identity? That is one of those vital questions where people are often very slow to grasp the truth. By the end of chapter 8, this question will have finally been answered; we are not quite there yet, but Mark's story has been full of clues, many of them tied up with the miracles that Jesus has done. So surely the disciples, of all people, the disciples who have literally been walked through the miracles, won't be so slow that they will miss the point? Apparently, unfortunately, they do. In Mark 8 we come to another miracle of feeding a huge crowd, which the disciples should already know by heart. This story brings to an end the major section of Mark which began in 6:31 with that first feeding miracle, and which I have called 'From Israel to the nations'. As we conclude it, the last clues which are needed to establish Jesus' identity are given; at the start of the next section, all will be revealed.

There are sceptics who think that these two accounts of feeding miracles really represent a single event. This incident has been remembered in two different ways, they say, or somehow the story has been changed in one tradition, or both, and by the time Mark comes to write all this down he has the idea that there were two separate feeding miracles. But quite apart from the fact that we believe the Bible tells a true and accurate story, this idea does not really make sense. Too many of the details are very different. The crowd, obviously, is a different size. In fact, all the numbers involved are different, as is the location. Jesus' motivation for feeding them is different, and so is the aftermath. Even the recycling bins for the leftovers are different! In a culture where stories are passed on by word of mouth, you don't get away with tampering with such details. Someone will always be there to correct you if you try it; that is how oral culture works. There are two stories because there are two crowds and two miracles. This is the catering project, part two!

   Mark knows exactly what he is doing as he writes his
Gospel. Study the layout of these chapters and you can see
that he is doing something very deliberate. Compare these
two sections of Mark's Gospel, one from 6:31 to 7:37 and
the other from 8:1 to 8:30, and you will see that, in each
case, the section begins with Jesus feeding a crowd, then
there is a journey in a boat, an argument with some Pharisees, a conversation involving bread, a healing and, finally, a
confession of faith.[1] The details of all these incidents are
quite different, but it is clear enough that Mark has deliberately structured his story in this way. There were any number
of episodes about Jesus that he could have chosen to recount,
and he has selected exactly these to make this point. Mark is
telling us that the people closest to Jesus, the disciples, still
haven't understood! Going through the 'dance' once was not
enough. They have to be walked through another cycle of
miracles, of teaching, of close encounters with Jesus, before
they finally grasp his true identity at the end of chapter 8.
The point for us is just as simple — we need to understand
about Jesus too!

   As this story begins, Jesus and his group are in the area
known as the Decapolis. He has been there for a little while,
it seems. People have gathered from near and far to come
and meet Jesus and, just as before, there is a catering problem. Whatever food the people have brought with them has
now gone. This time it is Jesus himself who points out the
problem (8:2-3). He doesn't blame the people for failing to
bring picnic hampers; after all, they have come for the right
reasons, to hear him teaching. He has presented the problem
to the disciples with the implication that they should respond
with proper confidence that Jesus can deal with it. Instead
comes the helpless answer we find in verse 4. They are out in
the wilds; the shops are too far away; so, as far as they are
concerned, the situation is hopeless. Here is the main reason
why the sceptics think this cannot possibly be a separate

incident. Only two chapters back, Jesus has managed exactly the same problem, and they were all there to see it done. It's inconceivable that they would be so dumb! In response, we must remember that those two chapters probably cover a few months of real time. Remember, too, that Jesus often drew huge crowds, and he must often have sent them away at the end of the day *without* feeding them. So perhaps the disciples have a little more excuse than we might imagine. It's even possible that they don't expect or want Jesus to feed this crowd because in this place, east of Galilee, most of them are Gentiles, not Jews.

But, for all that, and even making every allowance we can, the disciples are remarkably slow on the uptake! Their reply is depressingly similar to the one they gave the time before (6:37). So Jesus asks again, 'What do we have to work with?' (8:5). This time the answer is, not five, but seven small loaves, and it turns out that there are a few small fish as well (8:7). Perhaps these are the remnants of the disciples' own supplies but, wherever it comes from, it's not much to feed the crowd that covers the hillside, yet once more that is what Jesus does. He tells the crowd to sit, or lie, down on the ground — and this time, there are none of those distinctive Jewish or Old Testament echoes to the story which we observed in the feeding of the five thousand, because this is not a mainly Jewish crowd. Jesus takes the bread and gives thanks for it in the usual way, and he breaks it and he goes on breaking it, again and again, and before their eyes the disciples see it grow and increase until they are carrying great armfuls of bread to the waiting throng (8:6). Then comes the fish course; it would be unusual for a Jew to give thanks a second time, but Jesus does that — again an indication that this is not a Jewish crowd and he wants to teach them to thank God for the food he provides every day.

In verse 8 we see that exactly what the disciples said could not happen has happened — the word translated

'satisfied' is the same word that is used in verse 4. We who
live in the West probably don't know much about what it is
to be hungry. We are used to having food available when and
how we want it. But this crowd of peasant farmers and
fishermen live from day to day; they know what hunger
means. Some of them may not have eaten for days. I can
guarantee that no one in this crowd is complaining that they
don't like this kind of fish, or that it hasn't been filleted, or
that they will only eat haddock! When there is enough to
satisfy a crowd like that — and to fill baskets with the
leftovers that are strewn across the ground (8:8) — that is
some miracle! By the way, these baskets are different from
the ones the disciples used after the feeding of the five
thousand. On that occasion the word that is used means
something like a small shoulder bag. They filled twelve of
those with leftovers, so probably each of the disciples had his
own personal supply to eat over the next couple of days. But
this time the basket is a much larger one, probably made of
rope, and the fact that they fill seven of them actually means
that there are far more leftovers than the first time. It's as
though Jesus is saying, 'If you didn't get the point the first
time, I will make it even more obvious for you by giving you
a much bigger clearing-up operation today. Now perhaps you
will remember! If not the well-fed crowd, then at least the
clear-up operation will fix it in your minds.'

Show us a sign

Now Jesus moves on (8:10). The crowd he sends away (8:9),
no longer at risk of collapse from starvation. He gets into a
boat and crosses the lake again to Dalmanutha — exact
location unknown, but somewhere back on the western side
in the Jewish area — and there to greet him are his old
friends, the Pharisees again (8:11-12). All through Mark's

narrative, there has been this ongoing conflict in the background. For the most part, the religious establishment has turned strongly against him, even pronouncing that he is inspired by the devil. That opposition lies behind their strange request. At first it sounds stupid: 'Show us a sign.' They know perfectly well that Jesus has been doing miracles; they may even know that he has just got off the boat from doing one of the greatest. Yes, they may be stupid, but they are not that stupid. What they are asking for is not just another miracle, but **'a sign from heaven'** that will authenticate the miracles, something that will prove that they originate with God — which is exactly what they don't believe.

Jesus gives them no encouragement. Their attitude exasperates him. 'No,' he says, 'I will not produce signs and wonders to order. I will not submit myself to your examination, and I will not place myself under your control. If you are so wilfully blind that you cannot see the evidence that is in front of your eyes, I am not going to give you any more help.' And so, we read, he leaves them. He turns his back on these people who will not recognize him; he walks away and he gets back into the boat.

Spiritual halfwits

Piece by piece, the identity of Jesus is emerging from Mark's account. In verse 13 Jesus is once more in the boat with his disciples, setting off across Lake Galilee. As soon as they have pushed off from land, the sail has been set and they are on their way across the water, the conversation begins (8:14-15). It is quite likely that as he speaks Jesus is looking back at the group of Pharisees he has just left standing on the shore. Now what would the disciples have made of this saying? It sounds odd to us, but yeast was regularly used to mean something or someone with a pervasive, undercover influence

— just as the yeast in bread-making spreads its unseen influence throughout the dough. Yeast could be used as a picture of sin, of evil which spreads its sinister effects every-where. So when Jesus talks about the **'yeast of the Phari-sees'**, he means, 'Watch out for the evil influence of their teaching. Watch out for the effects they could have on *you*.' It's a warning against the kind of hypocrisy which they have just seen in the Pharisees, who claim to be open to the truth, but in reality are deliberately blind. In fact, in the Aramaic language which Jesus is originally speaking, there is probably a play on words — between the word for 'yeast', *chamira*, and the word for 'teaching', *amira*. In any case, it should be obvious to the disciples what Jesus is talking about: 'Watch out for the hypocrites, and don't ever be like them. Keep your integrity.'

But the disciples are simply not on the ball. Instead of picking up what Jesus is really saying, they stop at the word 'yeast' and jump to the conclusion that he must be talking about bread. They are already feeling guilty because they have forgotten to bring any — the leftovers from the last miraculous meal are all finished and the disciples have failed to stock up again. In fact, they have a grand total of one bread roll (the probable size of the **'loaf'** in verse 14). Now here is Jesus going on about yeast. Obviously he is getting at them! (8:16). You can just imagine it: 'Oh, John — head in the clouds again — you know it was your turn to go to the supermarket! What on earth are we going to do with pre-cisely one bun?' While Jesus is trying to communicate spiritual realities, all they are concerned about is the absence of a packed lunch.

Is it surprising, then, that Jesus rebukes them? (8:17-18). In Jesus' words here the disciples, at least if they are listen-ing, will hear the echoes of the Old Testament prophets — Isaiah, Jeremiah, Ezekiel — the prophets who rebuked God's people for failing to understand, failing to listen to him, when they should have known so much better.[2] Jesus too is a prophet. Once again, like Israel of old, God's people are proving to be blind and deaf. 'You have got perfectly good eyes,' he says, 'but you don't see! You have got perfectly good ears, but apparently you can't hear.' In all the time they have been together, these twelve men still have not drawn the right conclusions about Jesus, and they still don't understand what he tells them. By the way, this is one of those many places in Mark's Gospel where we are obviously dealing with a vivid eyewitness account. No one would ever make up a story like this one, so clearly true to life!

In verses 19-21, Jesus takes them back to those great miracles, the feeding of the five thousand and then of the four thousand, and he checks their memory. Now this is not some complex mathematical riddle. He is simply saying, 'Do you remember how it turned out that day? … You do? And that other day, last week? … Seven baskets of leftovers, right. Good. But what did it all mean? You remember it so clearly, you remember the clear-up operation down to the last scrap — but you don't get the point. All those miracles, all that food, all that teaching — and still you don't realize who you are with! You are spiritual halfwits.'

Are we there yet?

What is the message of this story for us? I suggest two things — one statement and one question. Here is the statement: *Jesus will satisfy your greatest need.* When Jesus sees the starving crowd, he has compassion and feeds them. He meets their need. Jesus does not come to give you whatever you want, as some people think. He comes to give us what we most need. And that is himself — the bread of life. He came to distribute that life of his to a great crowd of people, a great number of us, so that we would be truly fed. It is wonderful

that Jesus performs *two* special feeding miracles, one for
Jews and one for Gentiles, showing us that he has come to
give the bread of life to people of every nation. Wherever
you may be reading this and whichever earthly nation you
belong to, this living bread is for you. But before he can feed
you, you first need to know that you are hungry. You need to
know that there is no food anywhere else; there is no satis-
faction in anyone else. Your own resources have run out, and
you need the life that only Jesus Christ can give you. Once
you have seen that, he will satisfy your greatest need. He will
feed you with life.

Now here is the question: *are you as dull as the disciples?*
Are you a spiritual halfwit, as they were? I believe that we
Christians often are. How often do we have to walk through
the dance before we learn how it's done? How many times
do we have to hear his reassurance, his promises, before we
learn to trust him — his promises that he will always be with
us, that he will always provide, that he really is working out
his purposes for good in our lives, that he wants to give us
rest? If you are not a Christian, how many times do *you* need
to hear the message? How long before you can see Jesus for
who he really is — God's promised Saviour, come to give
himself for you, to lay down his life at the cross so that you
may have life? When the Pharisees made their demand of
Jesus, he refused to comply. He gave a deep sigh, turned his
back and walked away. Watch out, or Jesus may leave you
too. When God stops speaking to you, that is when you
really have to worry. Have you heard the call? Are you there
yet?

Part IV.
Jesus shows that he must suffer
(8:22 – 10:52)

12.
The turning point

Please read Mark 8:22 – 9:1

On 28 January 1986, the space shuttle *Challenger* exploded in mid-air with the loss of all seven crew. It was one of those unforgettable events when many of us can recall exactly where and how we heard the news. President Reagan had planned to speak live to the crew that evening during the annual State of the Union address to the American people. Instead he found himself leading the nation in their grief.

There was, of course, an inquiry. Who was to blame? The inquiry panel did their work thoroughly. There were dramatic moments during their hearings as one key fact after another came to light. But when all was said and done, the conclusion was simple. The *Challenger* disaster was caused by a single, disastrous decision. The shuttle was launched with the aid of two powerful booster rockets. Each of these rockets was built up of sections which were joined together, and in each of the joins there was a rubber O-ring seal. If that seal failed, gas at a temperature of thousands of degrees would come spurting out, with potentially catastrophic consequences. When the air outside was very cold, this rubber would become brittle and wouldn't seal the gap. That day the shuttle was launched in a temperature of 2° C — much colder than any previous launch. Less than one minute into the flight, gas began escaping from one of the joints on the right-hand booster rocket. A small flame appeared. Within another ten seconds, that flame had burned a hole in the shuttle's fuel tank, causing the escape of a huge mass of liquid hydrogen and liquid oxygen. Another ten seconds later, as all the world saw, the shuttle exploded in a giant fireball.

The bitterest aspect of the tragedy was that the NASA authorities had been warned that exactly this could happen. Engineers were aware that there was a problem with the O-ring seals. For the past year, an engineer named Roger Boisjoly had been writing memos warning his superiors that if this cold-weather problem was not attended to, there could be serious consequences, up to and including the loss of a mission. On the night of 27 January, a meeting was held to discuss whether the launch should go ahead. As the experts sat late into the night arguing about what to do, the shuttle was standing on the launch pad in temperatures well below freezing. This was not just a theoretical exercise; it could mean life or death. The engineers urged a delay until the weather was warmer. The managers overruled them. The launch went ahead; the rest is history. They had the warnings — serious, sober warnings from people who knew what they were talking about, warnings based on the evidence in front of them, but warnings they chose to ignore.

In this story in Mark, the question that is raised is even more serious. Is it possible that a decision could be more important than life or death? Yes it is, if the consequences go beyond this life on earth. **'Who do people say I am?'**, Jesus asks (8:27). For some people today, this is a question for academic discussion — something to give their opinion on around a dinner table, or late at night over coffee in a univer-sity hall of residence, or a subject for glossy TV pro-grammes. Does it matter more than any other question for idle discussion? Yes it does, because, to put it bluntly, our answer will determine whether we live or die in the world to come — whether we go to heaven or to hell. The question being discussed by Jesus' disciples as they sit by the roadside is even bigger than the one the experts had to answer at the Kennedy Space Centre that night.

The prelude: a unique healing

We are now entering a new section of Mark's Gospel which I have called 'Jesus shows that he must suffer'. Like the previous section, it begins and ends with a pair of similar stories — in this case, Mark's only two accounts of healing the blind. The incident in verses 22-26, as we shall soon see, prepares for the crucial account of Peter's confession which immediately follows. The previous section ended with the disciples still baffled (8:21). So if, after all this time, after all the evidence they have seen, they don't understand who Jesus is, what will give them the breakthrough? Mark answers that question in a very distinctive way, by telling us about a most unusual miracle. It is a story that only Mark includes in his Gospel — and that is always significant, especially given that Mark's account is the shortest of the four.

The disciples' boat lands this time at Bethsaida at the northern end of Lake Galilee. Almost at once, as happens so often, a man is brought to Jesus for him to heal (8:22). The blind man is led along by his friends, who beg Jesus to **'touch him'**, to make that physical contact which they believe will bring healing. Maybe this will be another 'routine' miracle — if healing a man could ever be routine! Not so. First, Jesus takes his hand and leads him away from the village. Bethsaida, in fact, is not one of those tiny fishing villages — it has a population of over ten thousand; it will be bustling and noisy. Jesus wants to get this blind man away

from the crowds — partly because he wants the man to hear
what he says, and partly because he has a special audience in
mind: not the crowd in general, but his slow disciples.

Usually when Jesus has healed someone, it happens
instantly and completely. In fact this has been a mark of his
miracles up to this point — they appear effortless: he heals
with a word, calms the storm with a word, multiplies bread
simply by dividing it and watching it increase. But this time
it's different (8:23). In a quiet spot outside the town, in full
view of the disciples, Jesus goes to work. Spitting on the
man's eyes sounds rather distasteful. But, just as he did
before with the deaf-mute man at the end of chapter 7, Jesus
is conducting a mime for the man to understand. This man
can't see, but he can hear and speak, so Jesus does something
that he can hear and feel, and then he talks to him. So far this
is much like what we have seen before. But it seems all is not
well (8:24). Hasn't Jesus just laid on hands and healed him?
Apparently not — apparently he *can* now see, but only in the
vaguest outlines. Presumably he knows what a tree looks
like: either he has been able to see at some point in his life,
or else he can imagine a tree from what others have told him.
But when he looks at the people in front of him, they don't
look like people! The picture he sees makes no sense.

Once more, then, Jesus places his hands on the man's
eyes (8:25). Now, at once, the man is healed and he can see.
He looks around, sight fully restored; everything is clear and
sharp; all is well. So what has happened here? Did Jesus run
out of power to do miracles at the first attempt? Did he
somehow forget how to do it? Of course not! So why go
through this strange two-step process of tackling blindness?
He does it for one simple reason: to point to the blindness of
his audience — the disciples. For all that he has done for
them so far, for all that they have been involved in his
ministry, as yet all they can see is like trees walking. The
picture they see makes no sense. On the boat, Jesus issued a

threefold rebuke of his disciples for their half-wittedness, their inability to see clearly. '*Don't* you understand? *Don't* you comprehend? *Are* your hearts hardened?' (8:17-18). Now in Bethsaida there is a threefold description of this man's restoration: his eyes are **'opened'**; his sight is **'restored'**; he sees everything **'clearly'**. Thus the connection is made explicit: the only way that they will be able to see properly is if Jesus heals their sight. Only God can open the eyes of the spiritually blind.

The right answer

We have seen that Mark's concern in this part of his Gospel is to show us how slowly Jesus' own disciples arrive at the right answer. Mark has just shown us that only a miracle from Jesus can properly open someone's eyes to the truth of who he is. And it is only now, at last, that one of the disciples finally arrives at something like the right answer.

In the next stage of the story, we follow Jesus and the disciples as they move further north from Bethsaida, twenty-five miles up to the region of Caesarea Philippi (8:27). As far as we can tell, they have never been here before. The Gospel writers don't record Jesus doing much public ministry in this region. It's an interlude of peace where Jesus takes his disciples away on a kind of retreat, and it's an interesting place that they go to. It's a great place for a break, away from the crowds, a beautiful green oasis on the slopes of Mount Hermon around the headwaters of the River Jordan. At one time there was a temple here dedicated to the pagan god Pan; more recently the Romans have moved in, rebuilt the town, now renamed in honour of Caesar Augustus, who originally added this area to the territory of Herod the Great. The tetrarch Herod Philip, son of Herod the Great, has his palace here. It is here, in an area devoted to the pagan gods and in a town whose name devotes it to lord Caesar, that the true identity of Jesus will finally become clear: here — perhaps as they pause for food sitting on the grass by the roadside — and it is Jesus who opens up the conversation: **'Who do people say [that] I am?'** (8:27). This is the crucial question.

Immediately it becomes clear that there are plenty of answers on offer (8:28). Jesus' identity is a hot topic — it could hardly be otherwise, given all that he has been doing. Even excluding the miracles that only the disciples have seen, there have been a host of amazing events, some of them right under the noses of the authorities. Of course everyone is talking about Jesus, and not just because of what he has done, but equally because of what he has said. There is no doubt whatever — this man speaks with authority. He is not just passing on other people's ideas, which is all that an ordinary teacher does. The only doubt is whose authority he carries — a question that will follow Jesus all the way to Jerusalem (11:28).

First, the disciples say, some people think he is **'John the Baptist'**. They would be in good company if they think that, because that is what Herod himself thinks (6:16). That would be especially worrying in his case, since he is the one who had John beheaded! Everyone knows that John was killed — he was a popular figure — so this answer has to assume that he has somehow risen from the dead. Jesus and John had certain things in common. As cousins through their mothers, they may have looked alike. They were both popular preachers with a band of disciples and a radical message of repentance; they both appeared and disappeared rather mysteriously; and they both infuriated the authorities. But, on the other hand, John never did any miracles. And if people actually listened, they would know that his main ministry was to prepare the way for someone greater who was to come, whereas Jesus never pointed to any other man. His ministry — both his teaching and the miracles — pointed people to himself.

What about option number two — **'Elijah'**? Now Elijah is a really interesting possibility. He was one of the most dynamic of Old Testament prophets, living during the reigns of some really terrible kings in Israel around 800 years earlier. But the key point is that the very last Old Testament prophet, Malachi, foretold that Elijah would be sent by God to prepare for the Day of the Lord, when he would intervene in human history and bring in his judgement and eternal reign (Mal. 4:5). Faithful Jews are watching for the appearance of this great prophet who will herald the dawning of the new age. Maybe this Jesus is the promised Elijah!

What people don't seem to realize is that these two options are actually one and the same. Consider option one: John — a radical prophet who wears a hair cloak and a leather belt, has an eccentric diet, spends a lot of time in the desert and says he is preparing for a greater one who will follow him. Now look at option two: Elijah — a radical prophet who wears a hair cloak and a leather belt, has an eccentric diet, spends a lot of time in the desert and about whom it was prophesied that he would return and prepare for *God* who would follow him. Doesn't that suggest anything? Yes, John the Baptist *is* the Elijah who was to come — and that is exactly what Jesus says about him in 9:13. Perhaps we need to point out that this is not about reincarnation! It is Elijah's promised *ministry* that is seen in John the Baptist. John is the Elijah who was to return to prepare the way for God's coming — and what does that make Jesus? Here is one more jigsaw piece of evidence about Jesus' identity.

Option three on the disciples' list is a prophet, just **'one of the prophets'**. All these options place Jesus in the category of 'prophet'. It's a supporting role. The prophets were men and women through whom God spoke, but that is all. So, say the disciples, these are the options people are coming up with. They might well have added, 'There are other people who think you are demon-possessed, notably the Pharisees, and don't forget your family, who simply think you are insane.' Perhaps they are too polite to throw that in, but they could have done. 'All sorts of people with all kinds of ideas: some basically friendly, some frankly unfriendly; some thinking they are doing you a great honour, Jesus, by saying you are a prophet.'

Finally, Jesus comes to the real point of the conversation: 'Have *you* reached a decision yet, yourselves? After all, you have seen more of me, heard more of me, than anyone else. Let's turn the spotlight on you: what do *you* say?' Peter comes out with it: **'You are the Christ'** (8:29). In a flash of God-given inspiration he recognizes that here in front of him, this friend sitting there on that rock, is the unique messenger of God: not '*a* prophet', but '*the* Christ'. The word Peter uses is *mashiach*, 'Messiah'. Like the Greek word *christos*, it means 'anointed one'. In Old Testament times, a variety of special people were anointed with oil to represent their appointment to a special, God-given task. Prophets, priests and kings were all anointed. But later on, when people spoke of *the* Messiah, *the* Christ who was to come, they had in mind the promises God made about a future kingly ruler, descended in direct line from King David, who would answer the hopes of the nation and bring in a rule of perfect justice and perfect peace (e.g. Isa. 9:6-7). Finally, after so long, after so much blundering around in the dark, the disciples have arrived at this point — or at least their leader has. It's the right answer at last.

Even so, after all that we have read in the last few chapters of Mark, remembering how slow the disciples have been to get this far, we are not surprised to find that they still have some way to go! That is what Jesus clearly has in mind when he gives them the warning in verse 30. This is exactly what he has said to people he has healed: 'Don't tell anyone.' He

knows that even Peter's moment of inspiration is still far
short of the full truth. Peter and the others have little idea
what Jesus' messiahship will actually mean. In fact with this
verse we are at the very hinge point of Mark's Gospel. So
far, the story has been all about identifying *who Jesus is*.
Ever since Mark announced his message in 1:1, we have
been waiting for someone to recognize Jesus. But now at
last, Peter has done so. This is the turning point and, from
here on, the story will be all about *why Jesus came*. What
does it mean to say that he is the Christ, the Messiah? Jesus'
ideas on that score are very different from Peter's. More
about that shortly — for now, just look at verse 31. Here is
why Jesus doesn't want the disciples spreading the news that
the Messiah is here: this is a Messiah they neither expect nor
want. Literally the Greek reads, 'It is *necessary* for him to
suffer.' It cannot be avoided. If you don't have a Christ who
dies for our sins and rises again in triumph and glory, then
you have no Christ at all.

Today, many people will follow Peter and the others up to
verse 29. Yes, Jesus is a prophet. That's absolutely true — a
prophet is someone who brings messages from God, and
Jesus most emphatically does that. No one ever spoke like
this man, before or since. And, yes, Jesus is the Messiah.
Even Muslims go this far. They agree wholeheartedly with
the idea of *nabi Isa*, the prophet Jesus — one prophet among
many. They call Jesus *Isa al-Masih* — Jesus the Messiah.
But the Messiah they believe in is not the one the Bible tells
us about. He is merely a *human* Messiah who does not
suffer, certainly does not die and cannot rise from the dead.
'Messiah' then becomes just a word for someone special,
and it can mean whatever you want it to mean. Plenty of
people are described as a 'messiah' in that sense even now
— a statesman like Nelson Mandela, or your favourite
sporting hero, for that matter. Today we are constantly told
of the similarities between Christians and Muslims — how

we both believe in one all-powerful God, and how we both honour the name of Jesus the Messiah. But if you cut Jesus down to the size of a prophet, you do him no honour at all. If you say he is no God, but merely a man, you are insulting him and denying the truth that God has revealed.

Who do *you* say Jesus is? This is not some academic discussion-starter. As with that group gathered on the night before the *Challenger* launch, this is a life-or-death decision, a decision with deadly consequences. You can choose to call Jesus whatever you like. You can join those who said he was mad, if you like. You can join those who made him a great teacher, or call him another in a long line of prophets. You can call him a special messenger, or your own kind of Messiah. But in the end, the time will come when you have to face the consequences of your choice. We can't pretend that this doesn't matter, that one opinion is just as good as another, that your sincerity will save you. This decision makes all the difference.

And if you *do* know the real Christ, then don't be taken in. Don't be deluded into thinking that there is any other Jesus than this one. Don't be fooled by people who say they honour Jesus as a teacher, as a guru, as a prophet, as an inspired teacher. No one honours Jesus like that, because that isn't the real Jesus.

The turning point

When Winston Churchill became Prime Minister of Great Britain in May 1940, we were eight months into the Second World War. It wasn't going well and it was about to get worse. When Churchill stood up in the House of Commons to make his first speech as prime minister, he didn't mince his words. Perhaps he could have said that everything was under control and the war was going to be won without much difficulty. Perhaps, to make people feel better, he could have suggested that Hitler was about to give up. Churchill, of course, was not like that. His words on that day are still remembered: 'I have nothing to offer but blood, toil, tears and sweat.' That doesn't sound too encouraging. Did he say the war would be over by Christmas? Hardly. 'We have before us an ordeal of the most grievous kind. We have before us many, many long months of struggle and of suffering.' One of the reasons Churchill was respected and admired so much was simply that he told it like it was. He never claimed that the war was going to be easy. No, the road to victory would be long and painful. To pretend otherwise would have been completely futile.

When the Bible describes the Christian life, it pulls no punches. The Bible says it is going to be tough — more like war than peace. Living as a Christian is going to involve toil, tears, sweat, and maybe blood as well. It's a struggle; it will involve suffering. If we are Christians — or if you are not a Christian, but are wondering what it is like to *be* a Christian — then we need to understand what we are in for. The fact is that all sorts of people have misunderstood or misrepresented the Christian life. For some, being a Christian is like a crutch that you need only if you are weak — if you are too feeble to face life alone, you can believe all this stuff about God and heaven and going to church. For others, to be a Christian is just about having better morals — it's a way of life, based on the Golden Rule and whatever else Jesus taught. You try your best; you live a respectable life; and in the end if it all works out you will get your reward. Sadly, even some church leaders and preachers have presented a very false and distorted notion of the Christian life. They tell us that being a Christian is about finding self-fulfilment, unleashing your full potential — or that if only your faith is strong enough, then God will keep you healthy and God will make you rich.

Can that be right? Is the Christian life a pathway to health and prosperity? Here is Jesus to tell us the plain, unvarnished truth. Here in 8:31 – 9:1, he gives us the straight story. Although the disciples are finally thinking along the right lines as far as Jesus' identity is concerned, they still have no idea what 'Messiah' will really mean. So the last thing Jesus wants is for them to rush off and start a misleading advertising campaign — like saying the war will be over by Christmas! This passage sets out the programme for the rest of Mark's book, as Jesus answers two key questions about himself.

What does it mean that Jesus is the Christ?

Here is the first question: 'What does it mean that he is Christ?' Look at verse 31. He **'began'** to teach them — this is a new start; Jesus hasn't spoken like this before. This is the first of three occasions when Jesus explains to his followers what his mission is to be — the three 'passion predictions'. He describes himself as **'Son of Man'**, and at this point that name won't have sounded like anything special to his disciples. On the face of it, 'Son of Man' means little more than 'human being'. It turns out later that it does have a special significance, as we shall see in full when we reach 13:26 and 14:62, but that is not yet apparent.

The mission of this Messiah is about *suffering*. Far from accepting him as their rightful Saviour, the Jewish authorities will reject him — the word used in verse 31 has the sense of testing something and deciding that it is no good.[1] The **'elders, chief priests and teachers of the law'** are the three groups who make up the official Jewish council, the Sanhedrin (14:53,55). They will reject the one who has come to save them, and as a result he will be killed. Christ's death is not an accident, or a miscalculation, but the focal point of God's plan for him. He must suffer and die, and then he must be raised to life again, for death will not hold him.

This is a dying Messiah, a Christ who *embraces* death. Verse 32 tells us Jesus explains this very clearly; previously so much has been veiled in parable, spoken obliquely, but not now. Peter does not like what he hears. We can easily imagine the scene: he takes Jesus by the arm and leads him away from the others. 'Jesus, what are you talking about? You're upsetting them, talking like this. I know those Pharisees have given you a hard time, and the temple authorities sent those inspectors to check you out, but what do you mean? You can't let them *kill* you!'

Jesus' response to Peter is absolutely uncompromising (8:33). They have walked away from the group — Peter has tried to keep their discussion private — but now Jesus turns back to face them all. Peter is not just mistaken; what he has said is dangerous and has to be put right. Again the strong word 'rebuke' is used. Once before in his ministry, someone has tried to entice Jesus off course, tried to subvert his mission. Jesus beat Satan off that time (1:13), but now he hears Satan's voice again, speaking through the chief disciple, and so he says, **'Get behind me.'** That doesn't mean, 'Get out of my sight.' It means, 'Your place is not to tell me what to do, Peter; your place is to *follow* me. So get in line, get *behind* me. What you are saying is just human ideas, man's ideas. You must understand that I am following *God's* programme.' Jesus the Christ has come to lay down his life, in unimaginable love, at unimaginable cost; that is how he will save his people. The path this Messiah follows is a desperately hard one — a pathway of opposition, of hostility, of rejection and ultimately of death.

What does it mean to follow him?

This leads us on to question two. If this is what Jesus'
mission was like, what does it mean to *follow* him? This is
what we need to know if we call ourselves his followers. Is
this Christian life an easy option, as some tell us — a crutch?
Is it about living a good life? Is it about being healthy and
rich? Look at verse 34. This scene probably takes place a
little later while Jesus is teaching in public. Mark emphasizes
the presence of the crowd because what Jesus is saying here
is not just for an elite group of twelve — it is for everyone
who sets out to follow the Lord Jesus. Step by step now,
Jesus explains what it means to follow him. It's laid out for
us in four steps.

Step 1. The cold headlines (8:34)

Jesus uses the same expression he used to Peter when he
said, 'Get *behind me*'. Now it's 'If anyone wants to come
behind me…' What is involved?

'Deny himself' does not mean what many think it means
today: to 'deny yourself' chocolate, or to 'deny yourself' an
extra holiday. This isn't about giving up something you
enjoy. It's about giving *yourself* up. It means writing yourself off. The way we are all born and love to operate is to
place ourselves at the centre of the universe. Instinctively, we
all think we are the most important being in the world and
everything else revolves around us. Instinctively, we actually
worship ourselves and our achievements. Jesus says, 'No,
my followers don't do that. If you follow me, you are no
longer at the centre. *I* am at the centre.' The last thing that
any follower of Jesus will be found doing is boasting about
himself and whatever he or she has done.

Following Jesus means *taking up the cross*. Now, however people use this expression today, in the time of Jesus it

could only mean one thing. The disciples know exactly what this is referring to. The cross is the Romans' chosen method of execution. When they sentence someone to be killed on a cross, they force him to *take up* that cross and carry it to his own execution. That is what Jesus himself will have to do literally, and it is the way that all his followers must be prepared to take. It means that we are prepared to follow our Master on the path of suffering. It means that if we are called on, we too will literally be willing to die — blood, toil, tears and sweat. There are no detached observers here, no spectators. If you are a Christian, this is what you have already committed yourself to, for Christian discipleship is shaped and determined by the cross.

Step 2. The commercial reality (8:35-37)

In language drawn from the commercial world, Jesus now explains that following him is actually a good deal. Certainly, when you look at the alternative, it is an extremely good deal. In verse 35 the Greek word used can mean either **'life'** or 'soul', so what Jesus is saying is this: 'If you live for yourself, cling on to your own life, you will lose your soul. You may win here and now, in this life, but in eternity you are the loser. But if you give up your life for me and this message of mine, the gospel, then you will save your soul. You will gain eternal life.' You may know the words of Jim Elliot, the missionary to the Auca Indians of Ecuador who was speared to death along with his four friends: 'He is no fool who gives what he cannot keep to gain what he cannot lose.' We cannot keep this earthly life — it is fleeting; it is passing by so fast. But, the Lord Jesus says, if you lay down your life here and now, you will gain what you cannot lose — *eternal* life. The world may say you are a fool to follow Christ — your friends or family may say the same — but the truth is that he is *no* fool who gives what he cannot keep to gain what he cannot lose. By the way, Jim Elliot was only just out of college when he wrote those words in his journal in 1949. He devoted what was left of his life on earth to proving that he believed it literally.

In verses 36-37, Jesus reinforces the message. Even if you could gain the whole world, even if everyone loved you and thought you were great, it would do you no good at all if you lost your soul. There is nothing you can give, nothing you can earn or own that will compensate even a tiny bit for losing your chance of eternal life. That is the commercial reality. That is why following Jesus Christ is the best bargain we can ever find.

Step 3. The clear warning (8:38)

There is that name again — the **'Son of Man'**. Now the title begins to be invested with a fuller meaning. This Son of Man is returning one day, not now to be humiliated and shamed, rejected and killed, but in the glory of his Father God and with the angel armies. In this reference we begin to see the Son of Man figure that the prophet Daniel saw in his vision (Dan. 7:13-14) — the one to whom God gives authority, glory and sovereign power, so that people from all nations and every language bow down and worship him. This Son of Man is returning to the earth in glory as the Judge, and he will judge everyone according to whether they have followed him or opposed him. When Jesus Christ comes back to the earth, there will be just one question: 'Were you with him or against him?' That is what he means by being ashamed of him and his words; it's asking the question: 'Are you glad to associate with Jesus, or do you push his message away and say, "He's not for me"?' If we say that, then he in turn will push us away when he returns. From that rejection there will be no appeal and no reply.

Step 4. The comforting promise (9:1)

Mark has his readers in Rome, where he is writing, and they know about the suffering; they know about the blood and sweat and tears. Mark is telling them here, 'Look, this is normal. This is what the Master told us about. He told us, also, that he is coming back in power and glory as the judge of all the earth — and then, all your suffering will be rewarded.' But their question would be: 'How do we know this? How do we know that this glorious return of Jesus will actually happen?' Maybe we have the same question. Perhaps as a Christian you have your doubts that Jesus will ever return in glory. Here is the answer that proves it will happen.

Now what is Jesus referring to here? What does he mean when he says that some of his listeners that day will live to see the kingdom of God come with power? Commentators have reached different conclusions about that. But I believe Jesus is speaking of what is just going to happen. A week after this, Jesus takes three of his disciples up a mountain and there they see him revealed in heavenly glory (9:2-8). For Mark, the **'kingdom of God'** (9:1) is always closely bound up with the person of Jesus himself. So Jesus might as well be saying, 'You're going to see *me* revealed in power.'

The second pointer is the way that Peter writes about this episode later, in one of his letters. Remember that Peter is probably the source of Mark's information. In 2 Peter 1:16-18, Peter talks about the future coming of the Lord Jesus in terms of the glory that they saw on the mountain that day. That event — what we call the transfiguration — looks a bit like how it will be when the Lord Jesus returns. So Peter links the two events closely together.

The third pointer is simply the way Mark writes it: straight after Jesus makes this promise, he says, 'And six days later, *this* happens.' All this suggests that the transfiguration is exactly what Jesus is promising. Three of the people he is speaking to will see his power and glory re-vealed — the power and glory which we will all see, in full, on the day when he comes to judge his enemies, save his people and welcome us into the home which he has long been preparing for us. It proves it; it is going to happen.

One day Jesus will return, and we shall be asked the question: 'What did you do with Jesus?' Were you ashamed of him? Did you reject him? Or do you belong to him? Have you loved him? Have you followed him? That is the decisive question for all of us, for all eternity. Do we know what it means to follow him? Look back at verse 34. Discipleship means Jesus Christ is at the centre, not me — not me at all, not even a little bit. We set ourselves to follow the Master on a path of suffering and sacrifice and even death; we follow our leader through suffering to glory — and it's worth it!

13.
Glory revealed

Please read Mark 9:2-29

Imagine that you have a distant friend whom you met years ago at a party. You found yourselves talking; he seemed to know a lot of people and you have kept in touch. Every now and again, when he is in town, you meet up and bit by bit you get to know him better. He comes from some European country and apparently he is quite into sport — which, unfortunately, you don't follow very much. Then a couple of weeks ago, he was in town again and gave you a call. 'I've put something in the post for you,' he said. 'I'll see you in a fortnight' — and the phone went dead. Through your letter box the next day dropped an envelope — and inside there was a ticket to the men's final of the Wimbledon tennis tournament. You know nothing about tennis and you have certainly never been to Wimbledon, but you go along anyway; you go in and find your seat and wait for your friend to appear. But this is very strange. There's no sign of him anywhere. It's disappointing that he has let you down, but you are here now, so you may as well soak up the atmosphere. At this point the players walk out onto the court. One of them gives you a wave. And at last, suddenly, you realize that the reason your friend isn't in the seats is that he is out there on court. Shortly after that you realize that your distant friend is in fact the world's greatest tennis player, and this is his day of glory. One thing is for sure — you will never see him in the same light again!

I must admit, this scenario is rather hard to imagine! But you get the idea. You might have had the experience of seeing someone you know, family or friend, performing on stage for the first time, or playing football in a serious team for the first time, or even wearing a suit when you have never seen him in a suit! At that moment you know you will never see that person in the same light again. But my far-fetched story is something like what Jesus' friends experience in 9:2-13. Here is someone they have got to know, bit by bit, over a period of years. Here is a man — a special man, yes, a unique man, they have now realized — but they are about to see him in an entirely new light.

In Christ we see glory revealed

In 9:1 Jesus has told his friends that some of them will see the kingdom of God come with power before they taste death. That promise is fulfilled now, six days later (9:2). Caesarea Philippi (8:27) is in the foothills of the Hermon range; it is reasonable to assume it is Mount Hermon that Jesus climbs, along with the three who are his inner circle, Peter, James and John. The highest summit of Mount Hermon is over 9,000 feet (over 2,700 metres) high and often has snow on it, so even if they don't reach the top this is quite a hike. As they climb, they are no doubt wondering what Jesus wants to share with them. They don't know what it is, but they do know that mountains are places where special things happen. They know that it's on mountains, elevated as it were above and beyond the ordinary life of this world, that God has often met with and spoken to his people.

Hours later, they arrive, worn out from the climb. Jesus has climbed alongside them. Like them, he has been out of breath, sweating, gulping water from their bottles now and again, the drab-coloured clothes they all wear showing the effects of months of travel. But *now*, as he stands there, an astonishing transformation takes place. His clothes become white, dazzlingly bright (9:3); his whole appearance is radically altered into an other-worldly brilliance and purity as if he were clothed in white light. They are witnessing something never seen on earth; it is a glimpse of the Lord Jesus in the glory and majesty he possesses in another realm, a world beyond this one. For these few minutes the splendour of heaven is breaking in on the mountain-top as Jesus stands transfigured before them.

As they blink in amazement at the sight, and as they draw back in fear, they see that Jesus has been joined by two other figures whom they somehow recognize as Elijah and Moses (9:4). Their wonder only increases as they grasp what they are seeing. There is Elijah, the desert prophet of long ago — Elijah, who God promised would return to prepare for the Lord's *own* coming (Mal. 3:1; 4:5). And there is Moses, the great lawgiver from the far-distant past — Moses, who led his people out of captivity on their exodus to freedom. Elijah and Moses — and they are here consulting with Jesus, their *friend*, Jesus, the man they thought they knew. Terror grips the three disciples and inevitably it is the impetuous Peter who fills the silence (9:5-6). If he is thinking anything, it is something like this: 'Moses, Elijah and Jesus — they are all here. The one who gave us the law, the one who was prophesied to return and the Messiah himself — if they are all here, this must be *it*! This is the kingdom. We need to build a base camp. We need somewhere for them to stay!' It's nonsense, but he means well. He is simply as terrified as any of us would be.

In the next moment, his words are forgotten anyway, for suddenly there appears a cloud covering them all and the scene disappears (9:7). They hear a voice, and their awe and terror only deepen as they realize that they are hearing the voice of God. Memories fill their minds: all they were taught as boys about the way God appeared to Moses on Mount Sinai in a cloud; the voice that came out of the cloud; how the people shook with fear at the sound. In this moment, Peter, James and John know exactly how they felt. The voice speaks: **'This is my Son, whom I love. Listen to him!'**

With that, as suddenly as it began, the vision is over (9:8). The voice is silent; the cloud disappears; and there is Jesus, alone and as they know him, the human face they know so well, the old clothes stained with dust. What they have seen they will surely never forget. One day Peter will talk to his friend Mark about this event, so that he knows what to put in his book: 'Mark, I remember how scared we were. I remember that daft line I came out with!' One day, Peter himself will write about it (2 Peter 1:16-18). And one day, sixty years or more on from today, John will see again the same Lord Jesus Christ in his heavenly glory, and write down what he sees (Rev. 1:13-19). But for now, they have to come down again from the mountain. Peter was wrong; this is not yet the arrival of God's final kingdom. It is just a glimpse.

As they descend, as soon as the disciples can summon up the courage to start talking, the discussion begins (9:9-10). One day, Jesus says, all this can be told, but not yet. It's hard enough for these three, the inner circle, to make sense of what has happened. No one else will have a chance of understanding — not yet, not until certain key events have taken place. Again Jesus is talking about **'rising from the dead'**, and again they can't cope with it. Of course, they can understand what the words 'rising from the dead' mean. The problem is not what the saying *means*, but what it *implies*. To *rise* from the dead means Jesus has to be dead, has to *die*.

How in the world can it be possible for God's Messiah to die, especially as they have now seen his glory revealed? What place could *dying* possibly have in God's plans for the king? As they struggle with understanding the big plan, they ask Jesus a very good question: where does Elijah fit in? (9:11). 'Our religious teachers tell us that Elijah is going to appear and prepare the way for the Lord's coming; we saw him up on the mountain, but he disappeared — so what was that about?' The question proves that the disciples do believe Jesus is the Messiah; otherwise there would be no point asking it. But if he is the Messiah, Elijah should already have arrived.

Jesus replies: yes, they are right; Elijah has to come first and prepares the way; in fact his appearance is the first sign that God's plans are moving forward (9:12-13). Jesus says, 'Yes, Elijah *has* already come. And just as the Son of Man, I myself, am going to suffer and be rejected and die, this Elijah too has suffered.' Jesus is making it absolutely clear that the **'Elijah'** he is talking about is John the Baptist. Just like the first Elijah of long ago, John the Baptist was a bold and outspoken prophet of God. Just like the first Elijah, he was persecuted by a combination of a weak king and an evil queen, and in the end they killed him. As they walk on down the mountain, the disciples have plenty to think about — all that they have seen and heard today, all that Jesus has told them afterwards. What will they make of it all?

Here are the conclusions the disciples should be drawing from Jesus' transfiguration. First, that *Jesus fulfils the ancient promises*. Who appeared with Jesus on the mountain? There was Moses, who led his people in the exodus from Egypt — out of slavery and into freedom. At the end of his life, Moses foretold that God would raise up another prophet (Deut. 18:15). Who is that 'prophet like Moses'? The voice on the mountain today echoed those very words: **'Listen to him!'** Jesus is here to lead people on a new exodus, out of sin's slavery into a still greater freedom. What Moses did in a small way, Jesus has come to do in a much greater way. Then there was Elijah, promised to return as the forerunner. Both appearing together, they show beyond doubt that God is moving; he is bringing his plans to fruition, and the ancient promises are being fulfilled in Jesus.

The disciples should also be concluding that *Jesus is the eternal Son of God*. The voice said, **'This is my Son.'** While the transfiguration was only a brief glimpse, and it passed quickly, Jesus has always been, and always remains, the Son of God. From eternity past to eternity future, he has always enjoyed the presence and the approval of God the Father, and that is why the disciples must listen to him. His words must be heard; they demand to be heard — and especially the words he has so recently been speaking, words about his own mission that explain his identity as Messiah.

So, thirdly, the disciples should grasp that *Jesus has to suffer before his glory*. What Peter, James and John have seen today is a glimpse ahead. Yes, this vision of glory is the proof that Jesus will come in power one day. The transfiguration guarantees that the power and glory are there, as it were, waiting to break through so that, as John would later write, 'The kingdom of the world has become the kingdom of our Lord and of his Christ, and he will reign for ever and ever' (Rev. 11:15). But the disciples must understand that it hasn't happened *yet*. Messiah is here, but the battle is still on. Before Jesus' glory, he has to **'suffer much'**. That is the true meaning of the Messiah, and that is how his great battle will be won.

Did the disciples understand all this? They were beginning to. They wouldn't see it all until after the cross, after they at last understood what **'rising from the dead'** really meant. But we need to realize what this experience means for us. This glory that the disciples saw that day is what *we* shall be living with in eternity! We shall see what they saw and, what is more, we shall be transformed ourselves! As Paul writes in Philippians 3:20-21, we shall *ourselves* participate in the glory that the disciples saw that day on Mount Hermon — a glory that won't just break in for a few minutes, but will endure for ever and ever. After the resurrection we shall be living in the new heavens and the new earth that is in every part beautiful, glorious and perfect.

But in the meantime, and certainly until we die, that is not yet. When the Lord gives us mountain-top experiences, those times when we see a fresh vision of him, it is always so that we can live more faithfully for him back at the bottom of the mountain. The Christian life is modelled on the life of Jesus. He has warned us to expect suffering, rejection and difficulty as long as we live here. So we should not be surprised when that happens. The joy that we have comes from knowing and loving the Lord Jesus Christ — whether we are on the mountain-top or in the valley below — and knowing that we have a destiny and a destination with him.

In Christ we see evil banished

For the disciples, that 'valley experience' follows all too quickly as we move on to verses 14-29. Immediately after the wonder of the transfiguration, as they come to the foot of Mount Hermon, they quickly make out a scene of turmoil (9:14). A crowd has gathered; in the middle of the crowd they spot the figures of their fellow-disciples, the other nine, in heated argument with a group they soon recognize as a delegation of religious leaders from Jerusalem. We can almost hear Peter and company groan as they see them: 'Oh no, not those guys again!' We have met these hostile delegations before, although here they are a bit further afield than usual. Almost certainly they are here today to gather more evidence against Jesus; they have tracked him to Mount

Hermon and they will be intensely annoyed that he seems to have given them the slip. Engrossed in the argument, they haven't spotted his approach, but now, as Jesus makes his way down the final slopes, they all see him and come running. They are all excited to see him and, immediately, Jesus becomes the focal point of the story. 'Right,' he says, 'what's the argument about? (9:16).

But instead of either the disciples or the religious leaders, it's a member of the crowd who comes forward, and it soon turns out that this is the cause of the dispute (9:17-18). This boy is in a terrible condition. According to his father, he is possessed by an evil spirit. At once, perhaps, our twenty-first-century eyebrows are raised: 'Evil spirit? Hmm, I don't think so. These symptoms actually sound just like epilepsy.' So at this point, let's stand back and ask some questions about the reality of evil powers.

Not long ago our church office took a call from a woman who wanted to know if we had any holy water. We explained that we didn't! But we did offer to meet her and pray, and we went on to ask, 'What did you want it for?' It turned out that this lady had moved house, and since then her life had taken a turn for the worse. One trouble had followed another, and a helpful neighbour had suggested to her that she ought to get hold of some holy water and sprinkle it round her house, and that would deal with the evil presence that was ruining her life. At least she had recognized that she had problems in her life and needed to find some way of dealing with them. But the story illustrates one of the ways that people respond to the problem of personal evil. She clearly believed that there was some presence in her new house that was upsetting the balance of her life; she simply needed to find the right remedy — even if in reality all she was experiencing was a series of unfortunate events. And so, in the spirit of the film *Ghost Busters* she thought, 'Who do you call?' — and the answer she was given was to call a church and get hold of some holy water.

That is how some people think. There are others who think that the whole idea of personal evil is just a myth, part of the great lie of religion that talks about unseen powers of good and evil, gods and angels and devils, when in fact the reality is only what we can see and feel. This belief is characteristic of the 'new atheism' championed by Richard Dawkins and Christopher Hitchens. Of course, they say, there are no such things as demons and devils. The problem is in our heads; the problem is that we *believe* these fairy stories in the first place, while in fact science has all the answers we need. Then there are others, and they too are on the rise, who find the whole idea of a personal power of evil fascinating, darkly attractive — people who get drawn by the occult, by witchcraft, by the idea of sharing some of that power for themselves. Then there are some Christians who certainly believe in a personal devil and in demons, to the point where they attribute every struggle, every seeming setback, to their ubiquitous influence.

So who is right? Is there really no such thing as a personal power of evil? Or if it does exist, what is it trying to do? How is it trying to attack us? And what do we do about it? Is there anything we *can* do against a power that we cannot see, hear or feel? This passage takes the problem of personal evil very seriously, because here we see Jesus Christ confronting the power of evil head-on. The nine disciples have been incapable of dealing with the family's problem (9:18). They have tried but failed, which is no doubt highly embarrassing. So how will Jesus deal with it? His first response is frustration (9:19) — words addressed to the disciples who have proved powerless to help. It's frankly depressing, heartbreaking, that his own followers have performed so badly. Jesus takes over the case himself. The boy at once goes into convulsions, rolling around on the ground (9:20). As Jesus talks to the father, it becomes clear that this is not a new problem; there is a long history of near-fatal episodes. He appeals to Jesus to do whatever he might be able to do (9:22). But Jesus immediately picks up on his plea (9:23). There is no 'if' about Jesus' ability to help him; the question is whether the father *believes* he can. His confidence shaken by the disciples' failure, the man doesn't feel too sure, but he appeals to Jesus to step in and rescue his son (9:24).

Now the moment has arrived. The crowd have kept their distance for a while, presumably because Jesus has deliberately withdrawn from their noise, but their patience has quickly expired and now they are rapidly approaching once more (9:25). In the seconds that remain before they are surrounded, Jesus speaks. His words make it quite clear that he knows what he is dealing with, and he has the answer. The evil spirit's response is violent (9:26) but, in obedience to Jesus' command, it comes out of the boy and leaves for good, and he lies still. The gathering crowd take a look and immediately conclude that he is dead. But Jesus knows otherwise and raises the boy to his feet alive (9:27), and there he stands, delivered, healthy, released. Then, as he often does, Mark gives us a postscript and once again this takes place when Jesus and his disciples are alone together indoors (9:28). Not surprisingly, the nine want to know the reason for their failure. Jesus simply responds, 'This kind comes out only by prayer' (9:29).

It's a dramatic story, and it's one that Mark clearly wants to highlight. Both Matthew and Luke include this incident in their narrative, but Mark's version, in a much shorter Gospel, is more than twice as long. To find out why, let's review the characters in the story — some of whom don't even appear in the versions recorded in the other Gospels.

First, there is *the demon* itself. We are left with no doubt that this is the boy's problem. The symptoms may be those of epilepsy, but in this particular case they are being produced, not by an ordinary disease, but by a demon — which, unlike epilepsy, is making him deaf and dumb as well. When the demon takes control of the boy, its intention is to destroy him, and if it cannot do that, then utterly to ruin his remaining life. It is real, and it is tormenting this human life in full view of a thousand eyes. It is a power that hates and fears Jesus, as its reaction to his presence here clearly shows.

Then there is *the boy*, the demon's helpless victim. He is living at most a half-life, parasitized by this evil power. In this story, we notice, he is completely passive; he does nothing, except to be taken from A to B, to be thrown around by the demon and then to be delivered and raised to his feet by the Lord Jesus. Although he isn't really dead, Mark deliberately uses the language of death and life to show us that he might as well be dead — he is completely helpless in the stern grip of evil, and only Jesus can give him life.

As for the various figures who surround the demonized boy, there is first *the group of nine disciples*, embarrassed and dejected by their failure to heal him. To make matters worse, they have failed in full view of their sworn enemies, the teachers of the law. They need to understand why they have failed. Remember, they are not new to this: they have dealt with demons quite successfully in the past. In chapter 6 Jesus sent them out on a mission to do exactly that. In verse 29 Jesus explains, **'This kind can come out only by prayer.'** Some have taken these words to mean that this is an especially intractable breed of spirit, a sort of Premier League demon. That would explain why the disciples aren't up to dealing with it: they have only done basic demonology, Exorcism 1A, not the advanced level they need here. That notion is encouraged by the words which some Bibles include here: 'This kind can come out only by prayer *and fasting*' — which just heightens the impression that exceptional preparation is needed to tackle it. But the original Gospel almost certainly did not have those extra words.[1]

Anyway, Jesus clearly expects his disciples to be able to deal with the demon — otherwise why is he so disappointed in them? It makes more sense to understand Jesus as simply meaning: *all* demons, the whole 'race' of demons, can be dealt with only by prayer. In other words, '*You* couldn't deal with it because you didn't pray! When I sent you out before, you could deal with the demons, because you prayed. This time, you didn't. You thought you could do it on your own.' By the way, this should remind us all that if we stop depending on the Lord in our own ministry, we will face the same powerlessness.

As for *the teachers of the law*, they are only here to cause trouble, really. They have probably started by accusing the disciples of not having the proper authority to attempt an exorcism — which raises the question: 'Why can't they sort the poor boy out themselves?' But no, they are happier standing on the sidelines inspecting the paperwork!

Then there is *the boy's father*. He is desperate. He has spent the last few years watching his son suffering, afraid to leave him alone for a moment in case the demon strikes again; he has come in search of hope, yet already today he has been disappointed. But at last, when he meets Jesus, he finds all that he needs. Only Mark gives us this conversation. When the father cries out, 'I believe; help my unbelief,' he is not asking for a bigger faith, a faith that will impress God enough to give him what he wants. He is saying to Jesus, 'Yes, I believe you can do something, but I have nothing else to offer. I'm pleading with you to help, because I have nowhere else to turn and no other resources.' We have a word for that. We call it 'praying'. The man is doing what the disciples did not do. He is *praying*, and Jesus answers his prayer.

Finally, look at *Jesus*, who dominates the story from beginning to end. He ignores the carping scribes; he is exasperated with the nine disciples; and his heart goes out to the desperate father and the helpless boy. He takes on the evil spirit and drives it out, never to return. He gives the boy new life in place of the living death he has experienced until now. So here is the reason why Mark takes such an interest in the story and tells it at such length. This is exactly what he is showing us at this point in his Gospel. The mission of the Christ is to overthrow the power of evil and bring people from death to life. Into the middle of this turbulent crowd of characters comes Jesus the Messiah; he takes control, applies his authority and banishes the evil. This is the message: you need to have faith in him. Don't be like the hostile religious leaders, grumbling and accusing from the sidelines. Don't be like these disciples, who forget that they are nothing without the Lord Jesus. In fact, be like this dad, who doesn't understand much, but knows that Jesus is the answer he needs — the only answer. If you don't belong to Jesus Christ, then nothing stands between you and the untamed power of evil; you have no defence against it either in this life or the next. Until we encounter Christ, that half-dead child is every one of us. Until we have Jesus Christ in our lives, then we are in just as bad shape as the boy in the story. Only Jesus could bring him from death to life; only Jesus can do the same for us. There is no 'if you can' with him.

This passage confronts us with the reality of personal evil. The story makes no sense without that. It's no figment of our imagination. It's real; it's vicious; in fact it's deadly. So what can we do about it?

First, we need to be aware of personal powers of evil in the world. It's not fantasy to talk about Satan's power, or to say that demons are still around. We are not to be obsessed with them, nor to go hunting them down, but they exist. We sophisticated Westerners are about the only people in the world who have trouble believing in evil spirits. From time to time church leaders — and perhaps other Christians too — will have to deal with demonic activity. In answer to prayer, exactly as the Bible tells us here, we will see evil banished in the name of Jesus and by his power. Is that a surprise? Not at all. Why should it be? The key is simply prayer. Prayer is when we say to the Lord, 'I do believe; help my unbelief! Take control, in Jesus' name.'

You have probably seen at least excerpts of some of those famous horror films — *The Exorcist*, *Omen*, *Carrie* and a host of others. Frankly, this is where most people get their idea of the power of the demonic, whether they actually believe in it or not. But if we are Christians, we should have a far better idea of the way Satan works than the people who made those films. When I come across those films (and I am not recommending them!), I remind myself that these things cannot hurt me. I am stronger than any of them. Not because I am clever, or strong in myself — I'm not — but because Jesus has won the victory, and part of that victory is *me*. Satan's powers will yield to us — if we belong to the Lord Jesus.

14.
Priorities overturned

Please read Mark 9:30-50

'Greed, for lack of a better word, is *good*. Greed is *right*. Greed *works*. Greed clarifies, cuts through, and captures the essence of the evolutionary spirit. Greed, in all of its forms, greed for life, for money, for love, knowledge has marked the upward surge of mankind.' Those were the words of Gordon Gekko, the anti-hero of the 1987 film *Wall Street*. The wonderfully named Gekko is a corporate raider who makes his millions by buying and selling shares and by making and breaking companies. In pursuit of his goals, Gekko is prepared to manipulate everything and everybody. His attitude is reflected in the way that he dresses. In fact Gekko's own particular brand of power dressing and coiffure set a trend for corporate culture in the *real* world. One of my favourite quotes of his is 'Lunch is for wimps' — in other words, if you have got time in the day to stop for lunch, you aren't working hard enough. You aren't ruthless enough!

Now we might doubt that anyone in the real world could possibly be as ruthless and unpleasant as that. But Gekko's character and story were based rather closely on a number of famously corrupt Wall Street traders whose cases came to court in the mid-1980s. They might not *say*, 'Greed is good', but they surely believed it. Even on a smaller scale, the corporate world today is full of characters who are constantly struggling to reach the top, invariably by scrambling over the backs of others, people with egos the size of the planet — as you will know if you have ever worked in a large organiz- ation, be it industry, commerce, a city council or even a school. Often in these places, leadership is about doing whatever you need to do to get wherever you want to be, until the day when you have a boardroom to sit in and an army of minions to call you the boss.

That is the model of leadership, and those are the priori- ties, that the world most commonly offers us. Even for those who would laugh at a Gordon Gekko, the objective of leadership is status and security and having those below you do your bidding. But what about the church? What about people like us, who say we follow Jesus Christ? Here is a man who is uniquely qualified for leadership and control. After all, Jesus is God! Yet Jesus' model of leadership is exactly the reverse. When Jesus talks about leadership, he speaks in terms of being a servant, of being at the bottom of the pile, not the top. That's revolutionary. In this section of Mark 9, then, we see how Jesus redefines leadership and revolutionizes our priorities.

In Christ we see leadership redefined

Jesus now heads south from the Mount Hermon area on the first stage of the journey that will eventually bring him to Jerusalem and the cross. Fittingly, as they begin that journey, Jesus again explains to his disciples, and again only to them, what will lie at the end of it (9:30-31). This is the second of the 'passion predictions'. Time and again in these chapters, the narrative is punctuated with warnings about what lies ahead for Jesus and what that will mean for his followers. For the first time now, he speaks of *betrayal*, of being delivered over into human hands. The worst of it is that this betrayal, which now begins to cast its shadow, will be at the hands of one of the very group he is addressing.

The problem is that the disciples still don't understand what he is talking about (9:32). Once again, they hear the words, which are clear enough, but the implications of a Messiah who wins his victory by dying are still completely beyond them. They are afraid to ask for an explanation, maybe because they are worried that they will hear something even more explicit, and even more painful, if they do. So, instead, they get on with something they can understand only too well (9:33-34). It's not hard to imagine how this might start, as they make their way along the narrow tracks winding through the hills, maybe with a division between the privileged three who have been up the mountain with Jesus and the other nine. Maybe it's James and John who set the ball rolling with a typical opening gambit: 'Ah, there's something we saw up there that we can't tell you about just yet — you guys aren't ready for it. Jesus made sure it was just the three of us who went with him, remember, not you!' Or perhaps it's Peter, explaining just how he would have tackled the demon-possessed boy, when the other nine so abjectly failed. Or he could be reminding them just who it was last week who first saw the light, that Jesus is the Messiah. But the basic problem is that these twelve men are aware that they are part of something big. They are not quite sure what that something is, but it's exciting, it's important and they have got wind of what they see as an opportunity to push themselves forward.

So up and down the line the arguments have been raging, and probably by the time they arrive in Capernaum they are all tired of each other. When Jesus asks them what they were discussing so vigorously on the road, they are too ashamed to answer. Of course he knows; in any case it's nigh on impossible to keep an argument secret when you are out for a walk,

and no doubt Jesus has heard snatches of the angry words! It
has been a long day's walk, especially if they have come all
the way from Mount Hermon today, and they are tired.
Probably the house where they come to stay is Peter's family
home. This is the setting for Jesus to show them what true
greatness and true leadership are really all about (9:35). They
are indoors, so it's private. We have seen before that Mark
often highlights going into a house as the setting for significant private teaching, and here he pointedly tells us that
Jesus is **'sitting down'** — the traditional posture for serious
teaching. Deliberately he calls the Twelve around him.
Clearly something important is to be said.

'Look,' says Jesus, 'in *my* kingdom, in order to be the
first, you have to make yourself the last and the least, taking
the lowest priority and the place of the servant, not the big
boss. Yes, you need to be *first* — the first to jump up when
there's a job to be done, while someone else gets the arm-
chair.' Then, to hammer home the point, Jesus does something very unexpected (9:36-37). We are familiar with the
idea of Jesus picking up children and blessing them, so we
don't realize how odd this must have seemed to the disciples.
When they see a child standing in front of them, they won't
be thinking, 'How sweet!' Rather, they will be thinking,
'How insignificant!' In that culture, children simply do not
matter. They have no status. They are absolutely the 'very
last'. So why is Jesus doing this? This is not some sentimental Victorian picture about Jesus cuddling children. In fact,
this story isn't really about children at all. Jesus does love
children, and there *is* a story about Jesus welcoming children, but that is in chapter 10, not here. This is a little parable
using a child as the object lesson, just as we have heard Jesus
using farmers, fields, plants and lamps as the subjects of
previous parables. Jesus is saying, 'If you want to know
about being great in the kingdom of God, look at this child
here in my arms. What sort of people are welcome in the

kingdom? People like this — people with no status, people who know they are nothing, people like an insignificant *child*. Welcome people like that, if they belong to me' — that's what **'in my name'** means. 'If you welcome someone like that, you are actually welcoming *me*. If you welcome *me*, you are welcoming God himself, my Father who sent me here.'

The world of that day is obsessed with greatness. For them it is a question of honour — who deserves the top spot at the dinner table, who is worthy of the most respect, what is the pecking order in the family, whom do you need to greet properly at the town gate, and so on. There are cultures like that in the world today — cultures based on preserving and increasing your honour. So as Jesus tells them that their role model is an insignificant little child, he is cutting right across their notion of what greatness and leadership really mean. In the twenty-first-century West, we are a bit less bothered about issues of honour and dignity, but we are still very concerned about status and power. Whether it is management culture where people are scrambling over each other to reach the top — as if every day at work were an episode of *The Apprentice* — or the celebrity culture which fills the media, our world too is obsessed with success, being admired and being in control. The spirit of Gordon Gekko is alive and well. Even in the church you can find it, from men who reach the heights of church leadership and use their position to control or abuse their congregation — sometimes outright and openly, sometimes horribly behind closed doors, at other times (and much more often) in very subtle ways. But here in this fisherman's cottage in Capernaum, Jesus has just *re-defined* leadership. He can do that because of what he is himself. He is not simply issuing a policy statement or handing down some consultation document on 'The future of leadership in the church of Christ'. He can say this about leadership because *this is what he is about to do himself.* He has only recently explained what leadership will imply for him — probably that very morning (9:31).

For Jesus, 'success' will mean being nailed to a cross and then hung up to die. 'Admiration' will mean public humiliation and abuse — or, to use the biblical expression, he is 'despised and rejected by men, a man of sorrows, and familiar with suffering' (Isa. 53:3). For Jesus, being 'in control' will mean letting himself be betrayed by one of his closest friends, allowing himself to be totally helpless, refusing even to speak in his own defence. It is ironic that on the day when Jesus explains what lies ahead, his disciples pass their time on the road fighting over who is the greatest. Their arguments that day, and their misunderstandings, simply make him a still lonelier figure, all the more isolated, as he sets his face to go on to Jerusalem and strides on ahead. It's often the sheer, persistent nobility of the Lord Jesus that amazes me the most!

If we want to be great, as the disciples did, the only way is to follow his pattern. Jesus has abolished status as the criterion for greatness. In the church, leadership is not about being seen and admired, exerting control, or arguing over who is the greatest. Of course, we would never do that, would we? But we might think it: 'I'm better than him because…' 'I might make mistakes occasionally, but at least I never did *that*…' No, leaders are here to serve the church. A leader is not a doormat. A leader is to lead — but he leads as a servant. A servant doesn't get the comfortable chair very often. He is willing to do the unpopular jobs, the jobs he might think are beneath him, the jobs that no one else sees, that are left when everyone else has gone home. That is leadership, whether you are labelled a leader or not. When we see someone's weakness, it's not an opening for us to exploit; instead we will help to heal it, like Jesus, the great servant: 'A bruised reed he will not break' (Isa. 42:3). Wherever we are serving the Lord — whether in an office, classroom, business, or even our own homes, as well as in our churches — he is our leadership model.

In Christ we see priorities overturned

This chapter ends with one of the most chilling warnings that Jesus ever gave. Mark 9:38-50 is a passage that many have puzzled over. It is not clear at first sight how it all fits together, especially the two final verses. Some have suggested that these teachings may originally have been given at different times, and in different places; Mark has collected them here simply because they have some catchphrases or key words in common, so that they will be easier to remember. That is possible, but in any case this passage does turn out to be coherent, as we shall see. Jesus gives us three stages, three priorities we need to get right, and in the right order.

Priority 1. Knowing where you stand

In verses 38-41 Jesus is still sitting in the home in Capernaum, where he has just been talking very seriously to his argumentative disciples. Now John recalls an incident — where this happened, we don't know — in which some of them encountered a man driving out demons in the name of Jesus and tried to stop him. The Greek suggests that they tried but didn't succeed. John is saying, 'I hear what you say, Lord, but that's not what we have been doing. We have worked on the basis that if we don't know someone, they're not one of us, and we close them down.' Now Jesus could have replied, 'You have got some nerve, talking about stopping someone driving out demons, given that only yesterday you completely failed to do the same thing yourselves!' But he doesn't say that. Jesus says, 'No, this man, whoever he is, is doing miracles *in my name*. That means he is on my side, he is connected with me. **"Whoever is not against us is for us."**' That is the crucial point. According to Jesus, the whole world (**'whoever'**) is divided into two camps, two groups — and only two: 'Either you are part of my "group", part of my kingdom, or you are not. In the case of that unknown man you met, clearly, he is one of us.' God is doing amazing works through him **'in my name'** — which means 'under my authority', 'belonging to me'. 'So accept him, welcome him in my name.'

Jesus immediately illustrates that fact with this little saying about giving someone a cup of water (9:41), a trivial act of kindness. Jesus says, 'Anyone who does that for you *because you belong to me* will get a reward!' The most minor actions assume great significance when they are done for Jesus. Nothing that we do to serve Christ, not even the tiniest little thing, will go unrewarded. It is how the action relates to him that gives everything its value.

Priority 2. Choosing the way to life

In verses 42-48, Jesus gives a stark warning about where people are heading and what they need to do about it. He gives this warning in two different ways, but they are tied together by the key expression **'causes … to sin'**.

Verse 42 is not a pleasant thought. In the recent past, a man named Judas the Galilean, a rebel against the Romans, had been executed in just this way. A **'millstone'** is a heavy, circular stone used for grinding grain into flour. It has a hole in the middle where you feed in the grain, so it would be quite possible literally to hang it round someone's neck. Jesus makes the picture even more graphic by describing it as a 'donkey millstone' (NIV **'large millstone'**), meaning one that is too heavy to turn by hand, requiring an animal to drag it round and round — a stone weighing perhaps a hundred pounds, or fifty kilos. Jesus' saying is a statement of the seriousness of sin. If you are someone who encourages people to sin, who drags other people further away from God, then frankly, in his sight, you are better off dead.

Worse is to follow (9:43-48). Jesus has warned us about causing *others* to sin. Now he warns us about what causes *us* to sin. Yes, Jesus *does* talk about hell, and more than once. The actual word he uses here is 'Gehenna', the name of a location just outside Jerusalem. Centuries before, in the days of the evil kings, it was a place of human sacrifice. King Josiah of Judah put an end to that, and it became instead a great rubbish dump. In Jesus' time, Gehenna is the place where all the refuse ends up, and not just what we would think of as household waste, but the carcasses of animals and even the unburied bodies of criminals. Parts of the dump are on fire; the whole of it is permanently smouldering — so it is not surprising that Gehenna has become for the Jews another word for hell, the place of eternal torment, of rejection, of fire and decay. Just as Jesus has already said, 'Whoever is not against us is for us,' dividing the whole world into two camps, now he says that there are only two *destinations*. There is **'life'**, also described as **'the kingdom of God'** (9:47), because God's kingdom is the place of life; and there is Gehenna, or **'hell'**. They are both real, and your priority is to make sure that you end up in the right place. That may mean some very difficult choices, because sin will keep you out of God's kingdom and send you to hell instead.

Jesus says that it is so important to get rid of sin that if your hand, foot or eye is causing you to sin, you would be better off without it. With your hands you can do violence; with your feet you can walk into places where you really should not go; with your eyes you can see what is not yours, and from that come lust, stealing and envy. Exaggeration? Not at all! Because sin and hell are every bit as serious as that. Jesus overturns our priorities. How different from the

priority scale of this world! Celebrities go to great lengths to
insure various parts of their bodies. The Beatles, Keith
Richards and others insured their fingers. Bruce Spring-
steen's voice was insured for three million dollars. Betty
Grable, Lana Turner and Marlene Dietrich all insured their
legs for around a million dollars — a lot of money in their
day. The food critic Egon Ronay even insured his taste buds!
And probably most of us would regard it as an utter disaster
to lose the use of a hand or an eye. But according to Jesus'
scale of priorities, that loss is nothing compared to losing
your chance of eternal life. Even a top international foot-
baller at the peak of his powers would be far better off
without his right foot and knowing Christ, than fit and well
and on his way to hell. In verse 48 he quotes Isaiah 66:24,
the very last verse of Isaiah in fact; the disciples will know it
well. The prophet declares that everyone, all peoples, all
languages, will see the glory of God on that day. Isaiah
speaks of the new heavens and the new earth which God will
make, and his own people will live there. But for those rebels
who have stayed in their sin there is eternal punishment, and
Jesus does not hesitate to affirm it in the strongest terms. So
choose Christ! Choose the way of life.

Priority 3. Living in the kingdom of Jesus

Jesus continues in verses 49-50, the segment which sometimes people find hard to connect with the rest. But having
warned people who are on the *outside*, he now addresses
the question of what it will be like for those on the *inside*.
Verse 49 is special because only Mark includes it. There are
two clues to the meaning of this unique saying. One is that
salt in those days was an absolute necessity. If you wanted
to keep food edible, you had to have salt. The second clue
is Mark's audience: probably the Christians in Rome in the
time of Nero. It's a time when spectacularly awful things

are happening to faithful Christians. Everyone — all believers, that is, all the people who belong to Jesus — will face the fires of persecution. That is normal; it is necessary. Mark wants to reassure his readers. 'Yes,' he says, 'you too will face the fires. But for you it will be just a brief experience of suffering, here in this world. You have been saved from the eternal fire and your destiny is *life*.' All Christians, all believers, must be prepared to suffer for Christ — including us. It should never be a surprise when this world gives us trouble, because that is exactly what Jesus repeatedly promises will happen. It's more of a surprise, and in a sense much more worrying, when the world leaves us alone because we are no different from the people around us.

That leads on to verse 50 and the second mysterious statement about salt. Jesus is saying, 'You, my people, you all have a quality about you, a saltiness that is special and distinctive. Don't ever lose that. Don't become bland and dull: live a life that is flagrantly different from what this world thinks is important. That's your priority. This morning, on our way here, you people were having a row about who was the greatest. But if you have this wonderful kingdom saltiness about you, you won't fight like that. You will be humble with each other. You won't be scrambling over each other to reach the top of the pile.'

15.
The demands of the kingdom

Please read Mark 10:1-31

It is January 1943, at the height of the Second World War. The outcome of the war is still not certain. Winston Churchill and Franklin Roosevelt are in Casablanca to discuss their strategy to win the war in Europe. Finally they reach a decision which will cause endless controversy. Roosevelt and Churchill decide to demand the unconditional surrender of Nazi Germany. There will be no negotiation, no opportunity to halt the war; the enemy will be permitted no concessions whatsoever. Unconditional surrender is the only way the war will end. In the two years which follow, the Allies finally gain the upper hand in the war, the outcome becomes obvious, and various individuals and groups on the German side try to open negotiations. All their overtures are rejected. There will be *no* negotiation; there will be *no* conditions; the only message the Allies will accept is the very simple one: 'We surrender.' Eventually, of course, it happens. In May 1945 the armies and the government of Nazi Germany finally sign the instruments of unconditional surrender.

The message of this passage in Mark 10 is this: if you want to encounter Jesus, if you want to be his disciple, then you have only one option — *unconditional surrender*. Just as with Nazi Germany in 1945, that is the only way to find peace. You may not feel the comparison does you any favours. But in fact, according to the Bible, the comparison is much closer than we like to think. We prefer to think of ourselves as pretty good; we look at murderers, we look at sex offenders, or we look at Nazi Germany, and we say, 'I am not like that.' The truth is that we are not really any different. Until we come to Christ, we are at war with God, and if we are looking to make our peace with God we need to admit to the fact that we have nothing at all to offer. We bring nothing to the table. Mark 10:1-31 applies this unconditional message of Jesus to three different areas: to marriage and divorce (10:1-12), to children and what they represent (10:13-16), and to the wealthy (10:17-31).

Jesus and divorce

In America, pre-nuptial agreements are recognized and legally enforceable in all fifty states, and if you are foolish enough to go into marriage without one, you have only yourself to blame when divorce leaves you broke as well as heartbroken. In the UK they are not yet recognized in law, but according to a recent poll many believe that they should be. Divorce, not just in the stratosphere inhabited by celebrities but in the world of normal people as well, has become so common now that financial and legal experts routinely advise people to adopt these agreements. Divorce has become something normal, even expected, with estimates showing that 45% of new marriages in the UK will now end in divorce. We might find ourselves asking, 'Should we be advising engaged couples in our churches to be realistic and set up pre-nuptial agreements?' What do we say to couples in struggling marriages? Just 'Call it a day'? Could the Bible possibly have anything useful or relevant to say on such a uniquely contemporary issue?

Interestingly, if the twenty-first-century advocates of pre-nuptial agreements, and the legal minds who draft them, were transported back to the first century, to the time of Jesus, they would find themselves with some very strange bedfellows (if you will forgive the expression!). They would find themselves in the company of our old friends the Phari-sees. Here were people who liked nothing better than a good argument about divorce, the permitted grounds for it and the best way to handle it. Of course, the world was a very different place then. There were no gold-digging wives pursuing their husbands' fortunes through the courts in those days. Women had few rights in marriage. Among the great legal minds of the day, there were two schools of thought about divorce. There was the school of Shammai, who said that a man could divorce his wife only on grounds of adul-tery or some equivalent moral failure. Then there was the school of Hillel, who agreed that those were grounds for divorce, but said that you could also divorce your wife for *anything* you found embarrassing or annoying about her, including the quality of her cooking. But both these groups took the view, like many authorities in our own day, that divorce is something to be anticipated, accepted and legis-lated for. When the Talmud was written some years later, it would contain an entire volume of legal definitions about the proper way to serve a certificate of divorce. It is called Tractate *Gittin*, a *get* being Aramaic for a bill of divorce.

This, then, is the background when the Pharisees come up to Jesus and quiz him about divorce (10:1-2). Jesus has moved south through Judea and now crosses the River Jordan into Perea, the region on its eastern side. That is significant, as we shall soon see — these geographical notes in Mark always are. Again there are crowds and, just as he has done in Galilee, Jesus begins to teach them. But in this story his business will not be with the crowds. Here come the Pharisees, whose representatives have dogged Jesus' foot- steps ever since the start of his ministry. They tackle him with a question, not because they really want to know what he thinks, but in order to *test* him. They probably have two thoughts in mind. One is that they have serious doubts whether Jesus is solid on the Jewish law. After all, he has proved himself unreliable on issues like the Sabbath, and he isn't nearly careful enough about the company he keeps, so now they will try him out on the grey area of divorce.

There is also a more sinister angle to their question. In Perea, Jesus is in the territory ruled by Herod Antipas. Not long ago, this Herod took a wife named Herodias, who had been his brother's wife. It was a very unsavoury business, and John the Baptist had pointed out to Herod that it was completely unlawful for him to take her. Very close to the spot where Jesus is now standing, John was arrested and later executed as a result (6:14-29). What better way to trap Jesus than to force him, in his turn, into making critical statements about Herod and Herodias? Maybe Herod would then take Jesus off their backs, as he had done with John.

In reply, Jesus takes his questioners straight to the law, to their own home ground (10:3). Verse 4 gives their reply. It's true, Deuteronomy 24 provides for the case of divorce. A man who divorced his wife had to give her a certificate to prove that she was released from the marriage contract and was therefore free to marry again. The law therefore gave her some degree of protection, because it prevented a man from simply telling his wife to go and then later claiming that he still had some rights over her. Jesus' comment on this law turns out to be surprising. First, see verse 5. Divorce was never what God intended. Divorce is permitted, but it is never something good. It appeared in the law because it was necessary to regularize it and to prevent even worse abuses. It is there only as a concession to human sin.

Now Jesus makes another move. Instead of arguing from the law, debating the finer points of what does or does not constitute grounds for divorce, he goes right back to the time of creation, before there was any sin in the world at all (10:6-9). In effect, Jesus is saying, 'Don't let's talk about divorce; let's talk about *marriage* and where it comes from.' Marriage comes from the very beginning: a male and a female human joined together in a union so strong that it can be described as **'one flesh'** — a bond so strong that for the sake of it they leave behind the closest relationship they have ever known. So we should focus on that oneness, and not even think about pulling the relationship apart. As he so often does, as he did in chapter 2 when he was challenged about holding a party with the 'sinners', and then about the Sabbath, Jesus responds to these accusing questions by going right back to the will and purposes of God. God's purpose here is for the man and woman to be united and to stay together.

The end of the story sees Jesus in private conference with his disciples — **'in the house'** as Mark puts it, which is his regular signal for private follow-up. The disciples want to know more. From Matthew's account of this story (Matt. 19:1-12), we know they are amazed that Jesus can make such absolute demands. In 10:11-12 Jesus makes it very clear that you can't just divorce without consequences. Marriage is not something you can walk away from when it gets tough. It's possible that the original text of verse 12 read a little differently: it may mean to say, if a woman *abandons* her husband — walks out and leaves — then she commits adultery if she marries another man. That would be very pointed if so, because it would exactly fit what Herodias has done to her first husband — left him for Herod Antipas without even a divorce. But the fundamental meaning remains the same: you can't just walk out on a marriage because you feel like it.

This story remains relevant in three ways. First, *Jesus takes marriage back to creation.* In verse 6 he says that God made us male and female. That very fact indicates that God made us for relationships, not to be alone. In fact the differentness of men and women reflects what God himself is like — he is Father, Son and Holy Spirit, three persons in perfect, eternal relationship with one another. God himself is relational; we are created in his image for relationships. We enjoy being part of a race with two sexes: it makes life much more interesting! Our sexuality is a gift to us, whether we are married or single. That was God's intention, right from the day of creation. As the fullest expression of that relatedness, God gave us marriage — again, that was a gift to mankind before sin entered the world. The verses Jesus quotes here come from *before* the Fall. Marriage was introduced when people were still perfect. It is not some later invention, or some human construct, which we can manipulate or reinterpret if we think we can come up with something better. Marriage as Jesus describes it here is lifelong — **'let man not separate'** — and exclusive — **'one flesh'**; so it is unthinkable that this 'one flesh' sexual union could find its place outside the bond of marriage. Sex is for marriage only. Therefore we have the warning of verse 9. It is not only directed at husbands who might think they could lightly duck out of the demanding commitment of marriage; it is also a warning to everyone not to come between the partners in a marriage and encourage them to separate. Whether that means telling people that divorce is OK, or whether it means enticing one partner away from their unique commitment to their spouse, the warning is clear: don't do it. Very practically, this means we need to be careful as single people in the way we relate to married couples, and as married couples in the way we relate to singles. The marriage relationship is to be guarded, and it has to be exclusive.

What does this passage tell us, in practice, about divorce? Jesus' words here could be taken as an absolute prohibition of divorce; that is how some Christians have understood them. But if we look at the account of the same incident in Matthew, we read something slightly different. There, Jesus says that if anyone divorces his wife, *except for marital unfaithfulness*, he commits adultery (Matt. 19:9). There is an exception. In Matthew, Jesus makes an exception for the case where one partner has betrayed the marriage through adultery. Why hasn't Mark — or Luke either, for that matter — included that vital extra clause? Almost certainly, it's because it was seen as obvious. Jewish custom actually *required* divorce in such a case (which Jesus certainly does not say). It was not necessary to add that divorce was permitted in cases of adultery.

Divorce is never a good thing. Malachi 2:16 expresses it most bluntly. At best, it is the lesser of two evils. If you have been through a divorce, or been close to people when it happened to them, you know that. But we do need to recognize that there are times when divorce is the only option that is left: sometimes in cases of adultery, and sometimes in cases of deliberate desertion. We must respond to those realities with compassion and sensitivity, and help hurting people to find healing through God's grace.[1]

Secondly, *Jesus lifts women to a new level of dignity.* Jesus comes to a culture which believes that a man can divorce his wife simply by scribbling a note and pushing her out of the door, a culture where for many, as Rabbi Akiba will shortly put it, divorce is justifiable if he finds someone prettier. Jesus rejects that. A woman is not property, to be dispensed with if a man tires of her. In today's culture, we should add, neither is a man! In fact, Jesus speaks of men's and women's rights in precisely equivalent terms. The idea in verse 11 that a husband might actually commit adultery *against his wife* — the concept that she might be the injured party — was quite revolutionary. Jesus gives women dignity in a world where they do not possess it. Thus in the early church, you find a Lydia hosting a newly planted church (Acts 16:15,40), a Priscilla teaching in her home (Acts 18:26) and the hard-working Tryphena, Tryphosa and Persis (Rom. 16:12), along with many others, playing key roles. If that dignity and equality were later forgotten, or even buried by some parts of the church, that is not the fault of Jesus.

Thirdly, *Jesus gives us pause for thought before marriage*. Maybe you are thinking about marriage and, like these disciples, you are feeling rather startled about the commitment that seems to be involved. Perhaps you *are* married and thinking exactly the same! If this passage makes you pause for thought, that is a good thing. Marriage is a very serious business. For a Christian it should be out of the question to go into marriage thinking in terms of pre-nuptial agreements, or of what might happen if you get divorced. The only way in is to say, 'Yes, this is for life.' It doesn't matter what everyone else is doing, or what the media tells us; it makes no difference if people tell you that a string of casual relationships will do you no damage, which is a lie. In the sight of God, this is how it is: **'What God has joined together, let man not separate.'** That line is in the marriage service for a very good reason. What Jesus says here is not an impossible aspiration. It is real, and it works — but not if you go in with your fingers crossed because you think you might break up in a few years' time.

Jesus and children

In the Harry Potter stories, 'gobbledegook' is the language spoken by goblins. But in English, 'gobbledegook' refers to any kind of writing or speaking that is needlessly long, complex and difficult to understand — the kind of verbiage

sadly familiar from official documents and books of instructions! Gobbledegook is everywhere, as the Plain English
Campaign constantly reminds us — even in job titles. What,
for instance, is an 'ambient replenishment controller'? It's a
shelf stacker! How about the 'regional head of services,
infrastructure and procurement'? That's the caretaker! And a
'flueologist'? A chimney sweep! The Plain English Campaign provides a kind of translation service in which they
will take a stream of high-sounding nonsense and reduce it to
its basic essentials. For example, here is a 'before and after'.
Before: 'High-quality learning environments are a necessary
precondition for facilitation and enhancement of the ongoing
learning process.' And after: 'Children need good schools if
they are to learn properly'!

Unfortunately, it is very easy for important messages to
get lost in a mass of useless wordiness. Religious leaders —
church leaders — are often as guilty of this as anyone! We
sometimes hide what is really a simple message in a complex
maze of language that normal people will never penetrate.
But, at its heart, the Christian message is a very simple one,
simple enough for anyone to understand. You may have
heard this story about Karl Barth, one of the great theologians of the twentieth century. Towards the end of his life,
Barth was asked for the greatest insight he had ever gained
throughout his long years of study and scholarship. The
audience craned their necks to hear his pearl of wisdom. His
reply was beautifully simple — in the words of that old and
much-loved children's song:

Jesus loves me, this I know,
For the Bible tells me so.

When I checked that story, I discovered that there are at least
three versions of it — but they all end up with Karl Barth

saying those words! Barth did not get everything right, but this time he certainly did. To finish the verse of the song:

Little ones to him belong;
They are weak, but he is strong.

In verses 13-16 we find Jesus embarking on his own version of the Plain English Campaign as he distils his message into the simplest possible form. 'Little ones to him belong; they are weak, but he is strong.' It's very appropriate that this story about the children coming to Jesus immediately follows the one about divorce. It's appropriate not just because marriage and children generally go together, but because it points up the sharp contrast between the sophisticated Pharisees whom Jesus has just brushed off and the ordinary people whom he now welcomes literally with open arms! These ordinary people are rather despised by the very religious groups like the Pharisees. The Pharisees feel that they are the cause of many of the nation's troubles, because they don't observe the law carefully enough (see comments on 2:16). The world of the Pharisees and their teachers was a complex and impenetrable one, far removed from the simple world of every day which was inhabited by the 'people of the land'; fittingly, they don't appear in this beautiful and simple story about ordinary families coming to Jesus to have him bless their children.

At some point — we are not told how or when — people begin to bring their children along, not just to listen, but to have Jesus touch them (10:13). In itself, this is nothing unusual — the respected Jewish rabbis would often place their hands on young children in blessing. However, the disciples don't like the idea. It's not hard to guess why. Jesus' time and energy are too precious to waste on children, they feel; he has a busy schedule — we know there are crowds around him constantly. If there isn't enough time to

deal with all the adults in the crowd, Jesus certainly
shouldn't be wasting it on the kids. The disciples, in fact,
have appointed themselves as his minders, trying to decide
for Jesus whom he should and should not see. But Jesus
doesn't want to be 'minded' like that (10:14). Jesus is
'indignant' — the only time in all the Gospels that this word
is used of him. He is disgusted that his own disciples are
keeping the children away. **'Do not hinder them,'** he says
— referring to the children themselves. Jesus is saying that
it's people like these children who are able to enter this
kingdom (10:14-15). Having said that, Jesus proceeds to
defy his minders by giving these parents more than they have
asked. He doesn't just reach out a hand and touch the children; he opens his arms to them, he places his hands on them
and he blesses them (10:16). We don't know how many
there are, but I think it's safe to assume that there are many
more than one armful of kids. What a beautiful picture!

The big question, of course, is just what does Jesus mean
by **'[receiving] the kingdom of God like a little child'**?
The language is simple enough, but in what way exactly does
he mean that we must be *like children*? This is where people
have come up with some rather strange ideas. Is Jesus
thinking that children are sweet and innocent, and so *we*
must be sweet and innocent in order to enter God's kingdom? I know some sentimental grandparents, but I don't
think anyone who is actually living and grappling with real-
life children truly believes they are innocent of wrong.
Children are sinful; they don't even need to be taught how to
sin, as anyone who has encountered a toddler tantrum knows
full well. Jesus is certainly not naïve about sin. The answer is
found in 9:35-37, where Jesus is talking about something
slightly different — leadership and humility — but the
illustration of the child says much the same. The little child
here is a picture of weakness, the one who is 'the very last'.
A child is someone who does not have status in society, is

more than happy to ask for help and cannot repay you for what you do for them. Jesus says, you have to come to the kingdom like *that*.

The force of this story can be expressed simply in three stages: promise, warning and welcome.

1. The promise (10:14)

The kingdom is for people who will come simply and with open hands. Anyone can do that. The disciples look out and see a crowd of children approaching with their parents. They see them as people with nothing to offer, nothing to add to the kingdom. Jesus looks at them and says, 'That's just the point. The people I will welcome into the kingdom are *precisely* those who come with nothing to offer but are not ashamed to ask me. So don't hinder them; they can come.'

2. The warning (10:15)

Now Jesus inverts the promise: 'Come like a child, come with nothing, and I will let you in. But *refuse* to come like a child and you will absolutely never enter it' — the Greek words are that strong. Many people want to 'come to Jesus' with something in their hands. They believe, like the Pharisees, that they are basically good people. They already have that — they feel good about themselves — but in one way or another they think that Jesus can offer them something extra. They come to Jesus like an adult, to pay, or to bargain, or to negotiate. But Jesus says, 'There is *nothing* you can offer me — except your unconditional surrender. You have to ask for what I can offer *you*. It's a gift.' With his death, Jesus will buy people like us into God's kingdom. It is a very high price for an entry ticket, but it is the price Jesus pays. That is why there is nothing that we can offer. That is why we have to come like children, with no status, with no resources and with no pretence.

3. The welcome (10:14,16)

Here we see plainly that Jesus loves children! Jesus takes the kids in his arms and hugs them to his heart — so different from many in Jesus' own time, who at best saw children as insignificant nobodies, and very different from some people now, who see children as a nuisance — especially if they are disabled, in which case we are advised to get rid of them before they are even born. In the ancient world they disposed of many babies, usually after they were born rather than before; it's not really any different. We have a letter written in Alexandria in the time of Jesus, sent by a man to his wife who he assumes has just given birth. His instructions? 'If it was a male child, let it live; if it was a female, cast it out.' But Jesus *loves* children, old and young. They are important to him. Whatever the disciples think, they are worth his time — and ours.

We see, too, that Jesus affirms the ordinary people. These common-as-muck people who bring their children with them — these people the Pharisees look down their noses at — it's true, they don't know much, but they act on what they know. Jesus honours the faith of these parents. He is not saying that all children are automatically included in the kingdom, but he is saying, 'I will welcome and accept everyone who comes to me like this — not because they understand everything; they don't — but because they come like children.'

Jesus and the wealthy

In verses 17-31 we see the unconditional demands of the kingdom again, though in a slightly different way. This is the story of the rich man who comes to Jesus, who seems to have so much going for him — so much energy, so much vitality, such resources — and yet who, alone among all the Gospel stories, goes away sad, because he will not offer to Jesus his unconditional surrender. Once again Jesus' verdict will come as a shock.

Jesus is just setting off when up runs this man and kneels before him (10:17). Now this is quite a sight. We find out later that this man is very rich; presumably he dresses accordingly. Running and kneeling are undignified actions, especially for someone who has a position in society. Clearly, he has something very serious on his mind.

He calls Jesus **'Good teacher'** (10:17). This is interesting, because the Jews hardly ever called one another 'good'; Jesus must have made a big impression on him. Jesus picks the word up in his answer (10:18-19). This has nothing to do with whether Jesus himself is God. Jesus is focusing on the vital issue of what it means to be good. Only God sets the standards of goodness — and that is what the commandments are about. Jesus quotes several of the Ten Commandments — in fact all the second half of them, the ones about how God wants us to relate to other people, with one glaring exception. He does *not* quote the *tenth* commandment: 'Do not covet.'

In response, the man blithely claims that he has always kept all these (10:20). Isn't that enough? Jesus' response stuns him (10:21). Jesus doesn't condemn this man or send him away. We read that he *loves* him. He sees someone in front of him who is sincere, who all his life has been trying to do what is right and good, someone who has recognized Jesus as an outstanding teacher. Knowing that something is still missing in his life, that he has not yet found that peace he is searching for, that certainty of life with God, he has come to Jesus looking for the answer. He answers the man's question, telling him what the terms are for 'inheriting eternal life': **'One thing you lack.'** The man thinks: 'Here it comes.' 'Sell everything, give it away, and come and follow me. And you will have the eternal treasure you are looking for.' Jesus pointedly omitted the tenth commandment, but now he has put his finger right on the button. This is an absolute demand. **'Sell everything'** — that's not what the law says; in fact the rabbis say you should avoid poverty like the plague. Jesus has pointed to the place where this man will find it hardest to surrender. Yes, he can glibly say he has never murdered or slept around, told a lie, stolen or neglected his parents — and it might even be true, or at least he has had a decent try — but his heart is not set on God. He is not willing to abandon the property he loves so much (10:22), so he walks away, out of the story, away from the greatest chance of his life, because he will not sign that unconditional surrender.

Now Jesus gives his verdict (10:23). It's the disciples' turn to be shocked. They have just seen someone who looked so promising, now retreating with his tail between his legs, and Jesus tells them that it's actually his *wealth* that is the problem! So Jesus repeats and accentuates his words (10:25). It's a ridiculous picture — so ridiculous that people have tried to invent explanations according to which Jesus doesn't really mean a camel, or he doesn't mean a real needle. But Jesus means exactly what he says. Maybe the glum face of the rich man who has just left so disconsolate has reminded him of a sulky camel, or maybe it's simply that a camel is the biggest animal you would ever see in that part of the world. How much of a camel could you actually thread through a needle? A couple of hairs, I suppose. Not surprisingly, faced with such an image, the disciples are more amazed than ever (10:26).

All these expressions, 'being saved', 'entering the king-dom' and 'receiving eternal life', are used interchangeably here, which is interesting in itself. They all mean being rescued by God and brought into the safe place which is his eternal kingdom. That is what the man wanted; it is what the disciples are talking about now; and it's what Jesus has to offer. For the third time in the story, Jesus 'looks' and gives his verdict (10:27). 'You are absolutely right,' he says. 'It's impossible for the rich to be saved. It's impossible for *anyone* to be saved — in human terms; but God can do the impossible.' Being saved is not something you can *do*. It's a gift you receive from the God of the impossible.

At this point, Peter wants his say (10:28). It's true, Peter and the others have done exactly what Jesus asked the rich man to do. Jesus agrees (10:29-31), and he promises that no one who gives up home, family, or property for him and his message will miss out as a result.

There are two clear messages for us in this story. The first is that *only unconditional surrender can bring us peace with God*. We might protest that we have never murdered, stolen or committed adultery. Perhaps not. But even so, we come with a long track record of cheating, lying, lust, anger and greed. Each single, individual action on that list is enough to alienate us from God, because God is good, and we are not. The problem is worse than that. Even if we could somehow clear that long record of sinful behaviour and thoughts, we would still have a sinful inclination at the very core of our being — what the Bible calls the sinful nature. We are born incapable of pleasing God. That is what the rich man in the story has not realized — that when we come to God, we have nothing to offer, no cards to play. The man himself and the onlooking disciples think he has all sorts of cards to play. Look at him. He is young — you can see that from his energy and enthusiasm; Matthew specifically tells us he is young (Matt. 19:20-22). He is extraordinarily rich — far above the peasant farmers, fishermen and small businessmen who make up the usual crowds. He is sincere — he really wants to find the way. He wants to find this peace with God, this assurance of eternal safety. That is why he has made such an effort to track Jesus down; he is not one of the point-scoring time-wasters who have plagued Jesus' ministry. He is law-abiding, the epitome of the upright citizen. We would like him, and we would want to give him the benefit of the doubt, but it is not enough. Not even this elite, successful, well-meaning character can offer anything to God. The only way to eternal life is to come to God in unconditional sur-render and let him do the impossible. In this one human heart, Jesus identifies his wealth as the main problem. It will have to go — otherwise there will be no surrender. But the main focus is on what will happen afterwards. **'Come, follow me'**, Jesus says (10:21). His demands are absolute. The Lord does not ask all of us in literal terms to give it all up. We are not all called to give everything away. Many things the Lord picks up and uses in new ways when we come into the kingdom. But, for all that, we *cannot* enter unless we are willing to let it all go. The demands of the kingdom are absolute and unconditional. If any of us haven't grasped this, then we are probably still outside.

Secondly, *unconditional surrender brings us into a new world.* Look again at verses 29-31. These are the sacrifices which a disciple makes; Peter and friends have made them quite literally. They haven't sold great country estates or stately homes like the rich man would have had to, but the end result is the same. Sometimes if you have very little to begin with, it is even harder to give it up. But when Jesus said, 'Follow me', the Twelve did exactly that. Jesus recog-nizes their sacrifice. 'That's right,' he says, 'that's what a disciple does — for my sake, because you love me, and for the gospel message which brings life to those who accept it.' But just look at the blessings which will follow. Notice how he says this — the NIV doesn't quite bring it out: 'No one who has left home *or* brothers *or* sisters *or* mother *or* father *or* children *or* fields for me and the gospel will fail to receive a hundred times as much in this present age (homes, *and* brothers, *and* sisters, *and* mothers, *and* children, *and* fields...)' — as if to say, 'You may have given up only *one* of these, but you will receive a hundred times *everything* on the list' — except for fathers, you see, because in the kingdom you have a new Father, and he is unique!

Clearly this is not a promise of material wealth and prosperity. These are not things that we will own for ourselves in the kingdom — who wants a hundred literal mothers, anyway! — but, rather, all these will be yours because you will belong to a new family. In chapter 3, Jesus' own human family came to see him; his reply was to look around at the people who were listening to him teach, and to own *them* as his family (3:34-35). Jesus is saying, 'This is what God's kingdom will be like.' It's the family of God, where everyone is related to God and to each other in deeper and sounder relationships than the outside world ever knows. Unlike many merely human families, it will be a family at peace. It's not a place of grasping hold of what we can and defending our own patch. Those days are over when we join the kingdom. So we should make sure that our own little corners of the kingdom, in our own churches, actually look like this. In the kingdom there should not be anyone who is in real need, none who is lonely. There should be hospitality — and not just for those whom we view as our type. That kind of thinking doesn't belong in the kingdom.

Uniquely among the Gospels, Mark includes a pointed little addition at the end of Jesus' list: **'... and with them, persecutions'**. That is also in store for people who come into the kingdom. That is normal. Persecution was normal for Mark's first readers, just as it is in many parts of the world today. Joining the kingdom brings persecution — which we share as members of the family even before it touches us personally.

Jesus sums it all up in verse 31. What he means is quite simple. Jesus is talking about the last day, the Day of Judgement. It will be a day when fortunes are reversed. The rich man, with all his advantages, a man who would be at the front of every queue, who is **'first'** in every sense, will find himself **'last'** — because he would not surrender to Jesus. The disciples, who have left everything behind to join up with Jesus, the one who will shortly be disgraced and executed, and who will later be executed in their turn — this scum of the earth, these rejects of society — they will be 'first' on that great day. Where will you and I be, when we stand before God to give an account of ourselves at the last day? The answer depends on what we have done with Jesus.

16.
Following the real Jesus

Please read Mark 10:32-52

Abraham Lincoln is acknowledged as one of the greatest US presidents. From a young age he began to campaign against the evils of slavery. In 1860 he was elected president, and his well-known stance on the slavery issue precipitated the secession of the southern, slave-owning states and the American Civil War. For four years Lincoln led his country through that war. In January 1863, the Emancipation Proclamation came into effect, declaring all slaves free throughout the United States. Before the civil war was over, Lincoln was seeking reconciliation and the swift rebuilding of the southern states. A great man — and on 14 April 1865, in Ford's Theatre in Washington, a Confederate spy named John Wilkes Booth shot Abraham Lincoln dead.

Mahatma Gandhi is acknowledged as India's greatest founding father. For many years, following his painful formative experiences in South Africa, he gave a moral and political lead in the fight against British rule in India. He refused to use violence. He longed to bring about an independent and united India where people of different religions were able to live in peace. Independence came at last, but to Gandhi's intense sorrow it came with partition into two separate states and bloodshed on a huge scale. Even so, he continued to struggle for reconciliation. A great man — and on 30 January 1948, in New Delhi, a Hindu extremist named Nathuran Godse shot Mahatma Gandhi dead.

Martin Luther King is acknowledged as the noblest and greatest leader of the American civil rights movement. In the face of abuse, intimidation and violence, he provided moral leadership through his stirring speeches and bold campaigns. He too refused the path of violence, even though other civil rights leaders were taking that route. Instead, he refused to condemn the white population and even offered friendship to those who felt threatened by his movement. A great man — and on 4 April 1968, in Memphis, Tennessee, Martin Luther King was shot dead, probably — though no one is really sure — by James Earl Ray.

Jesus Christ is widely acknowledged as the greatest moral teacher in human history. Born in very humble circumstances, like Lincoln, he lived a simple and basic lifestyle, like Gandhi. He taught people to love God and to love their neighbours. He challenged the corruption and hypocrisy of the national leadership. Like Gandhi and King, he refused the pathway of violence. His people were to be peacemakers, he said. A great man — and in the spring of AD 30, just outside Jerusalem, Jesus Christ was executed by the Roman authorities.

The question is, what did any of these deaths *achieve*? Clearly, for Lincoln, Gandhi and King, violent death was hardly in their plan. Death was a tragic and widely mourned ending to their heroic careers; that was all. The most their deaths could achieve was to inspire their followers to carry on the cause of their fallen leader. But was the death of *Jesus* like that? Many people think so. Some people think that Jesus' death was simply the result of the risks he took. He pushed the authorities one step too far, provoked them one time too often, until their patience finally ran out. Then, after he was gone, his followers — refusing to give up his cause

— carried on his work, expanded on his teachings, followed his shining example and built up his movement, until it became the worldwide church we know today. His death was an inspiration, and Jesus is placed in the pantheon of the great, along with men like Gandhi or, for the more religious, in a great line of prophets, or avatars of the gods. But, either way, his death was the end of the story, and it has no more power to achieve anything than the death of those other great leaders. That is what so many think of Jesus Christ, but the facts say otherwise. In Mark 10:32-52, Jesus speaks about his *own* leadership. He speaks of what it will really mean for him to be a great leader, and it's startling. In the cases of Lincoln, Gandhi or King, you could never say that their death was an expression of their leadership. The most you could say is that they knew the risks they were taking and they bravely accepted those risks. But the idea that their leadership was supremely focused in their deaths would be ridiculous. Yet that is exactly what Jesus says about himself here. For Jesus, his leadership is supremely expressed in his own, deliberate, violent death.

Jesus the servant leader

Jesus is on his way, his face fixed on Jerusalem, leading the way — and about to show us what his leadership really is. Look at verses 32-34. It's an energetic picture of Jesus, determinedly striding ahead while his disciples straggle along behind, worrying about what lies ahead of them. There is something uncanny, something daunting, about the look on his face, and clearly they don't know quite what to make of it. It seems that it's in response to this fear and bewilderment that Jesus explains, in not very comforting terms, just what is going to happen. For the third time Jesus tells them very directly what awaits him: he is going to Jerusalem to die. The first of these passion predictions came in 8:31, the second in 9:31, and this is all part of Mark's big theme of setting out what it means for Jesus to be the Christ, the promised Jewish Messiah, which the disciples now know him to be. This third prediction is the clearest and most detailed of all.

There are two new elements in what Jesus says. In verse 34 he explains the detail of the hideous treatment he will receive. This death will not simply be a clinical, judicial execution. It will be accompanied by vicious verbal and physical abuse. Jesus will suffer agonizing pain and humiliation even before he is led out to die. The second new element is really more shocking still. His condemnation will begin with the Jewish religious leaders, but they will then hand him over to **'the Gentiles'** — in other words, the Roman authorities — and it is they who will both abuse and execute him. The Jewish Messiah — the hoped-for, longed-for, prayed-for national saviour — is to be handed over to their oppressors, the very people who are crushing them, the very people who surely they need to be saved from! What a bitter ending this will be! And all this will take place in Jerusalem, their ancient and beloved capital city, the place where kings are enthroned — but the place where their Messiah declares he is now going to die horribly, and at enemy hands! True, Jesus does say he will rise again. Three days later that amazing reversal will come. Jesus gives that as a word of assurance that all will finally be well, that beyond the darkness of his passion there lies the glorious light of his new life. But at this stage he does not dwell on his resurrection. The prediction is given.

Was Jesus' death an unfortunate accident? The result of one risk too many? It doesn't look like it. Whatever else it may mean, Jesus' death is something he goes to face quite deliberately, by his own choosing. This is no mere premonition. He knows, and he goes knowing full well the horror which it will involve.

It seems incredible that James and John can now react in the way that they do (10:35-37). It must be the thought of going up to Jerusalem that sparks off their train of thought, some sense that Jesus' mission is reaching its conclusion; and he *is* the Messiah after all, so surely there will be some important jobs up for grabs. So here they come to make a pre-emptive request for the two places of highest honour at the top table. Surely they have a phenomenal nerve to make this request at this highly inappropriate moment. But, on the other hand, for all its clumsy awkwardness, their request also shows that they have some kind of faith in Jesus; they do believe there will be a top table to sit at! Perhaps that is why Jesus responds rather gently to their approach (10:38). But also, sadly, their request proves that James and John have completely missed the point of what Jesus has told them all. He is going to suffer and die, and this is no time to be making a grab for glory. When it happens, when Jesus comes to his moment of greatest triumph, the places on his right and left will be occupied by a pair of crucified robbers (15:27). That was Jesus' path to glory. 'Can you really face what I am going to go through? Would you dare to face the same yourselves?' Jesus asks. And, so glibly and with such blind self-confidence, they reply, 'Yes, we can!'

What exactly does Jesus mean by these mysterious expressions in verse 38, the **'cup'** he is going to drink and the **'baptism'** he will undergo? 'Drinking a cup' is a common Old Testament expression describing the effects of God's wrath, his anger against evil. For example, in Psalm 75: 8 the 'cup' is the fury of God against the evildoers. The theme recurs in Jeremiah 25:15-16, where the following verses describe the different nations who will have to drink this cup of wrath. This is what Jesus says he is going to do. Not the nations now, but Christ himself, will drink the cup of God's wrath, face the fury of the Father against the sins of the world. The 'baptism' he speaks of is his submission to suffering and death. Just as Jesus submitted to water baptism by John the Baptist, identifying himself with all the sinners who stood in that line in front and behind, so now he will submit himself to the death that rightfully belongs to them all.

Jesus goes on to assure them that they will indeed share in his sufferings (10:39-40). Of course, this doesn't mean the same for them as it does for Jesus. His death is unique. Even so, the suffering will be real. James will be executed in his turn by Herod Agrippa, the grandson of Herod the Great (Acts 12:2). John, on the other hand, James' brother, will live to old age and as far as we know dies peacefully in his bed. But still his life will be hard and full of suffering. In later years he is exiled to the stone quarries of Patmos, and no doubt he reflects on the day long ago when he so lightly told his Master he was ready to face what he faced. A long life, but a disciple's life of suffering — that is what following Jesus the Messiah will mean for him.

Jesus does not commit himself on the question of who gets the top places in the end. He leaves such matters to his Father. Gently but firmly, then, James and John are put in their place. Now how will the other ten disciples react? With greater restraint? With more understanding? Not a bit of it! (10:41). They aren't shocked at what James and John have done — they probably wish they had thought of the idea first! Even his closest friends squabble and grab rather than give him support, and we can only imagine how that must feel. They are **'indignant'** — the last time we heard that word was in verse 14, but the circumstances could hardly be more different. *Jesus* was indignant because the disciples were barring the children who wanted to see him. Now the *disciples* are indignant because James and John have tried to jump the queue!

Just as he has done in previous episodes, Jesus now picks up what has happened and turns it into a teaching session for the disciples (10:42-45). There is an earthly model of leadership readily available as an object lesson — the same authorities who will shortly crucify him. For those pagan Romans, says Jesus, leadership is about grasping whatever power and influence comes within your reach. The Roman emperors of the time are minting coins which describe them as gods, or as the sons of gods. Leadership means lording it over people — that is normal. Now we know that not all human leadership is like that, but much of it is. It was Lord Acton, writing in 1887, who famously said, 'Power tends to corrupt, and absolute power corrupts absolutely.' He added, 'Great men are almost always bad men.' At the very least, *all* human leaders have feet of clay, whether in the political world, in business, or even in the church. Too often, leaders are people on a power trip, relishing the opportunity to make or break the lives of their underlings. Jesus says, 'Not you, my friends.' He said much the same in 9:35, but he says it more fully here, and in a moment he will take it much further. Look at verses 43-44 and see what he is doing here. Verse 43 says that if you want to be **'great'**, you must become a **'servant'**. Then verse 44 reinforces it by making both parts of the saying more extreme: if you want to be **'first'**, you must be a **'slave'**. This is Jesus' picture of leadership: not high and mighty, but humble; not lording it, but longsuffering; not a tiara, but a tea towel! 'If you want a position of leadership in the kingdom,' says Jesus, 'that's fine. It's not a bad thing to want. But understand what comes with the territory. To lead my people means serving them in humility, not standing on your dignity.'

That brings us to the climax of this passage, and in a sense of the whole of Mark's Gospel — hence the title of this book! Verse 45 is the clearest, most magnificent expression anywhere in the Gospels of the meaning of Jesus' death. He has explained very clearly what lies ahead of him; he has made it crystal clear that he is going deliberately to his death;

but now he spells out just what it will mean. Far from being an accident or a mistake, he says that his mission is exactly this, to lay down his life. Without his death — and this is diametrically opposite to all those other heroes — his life makes no sense at all! He lives *in order to* die.

Jesus says his death means *service*. Here is Jesus, the supreme example of leadership, and he has shown it by abandoning his status, which was as high as it could possibly be, and making himself nothing (Phil. 2:5-8). He is just this: the **'first'** who made himself the **'slave of all'**. He says his death means **'a ransom'**. A ransom is what is paid to get a hostage or prisoner set free. In that sense, the ransom is the exact equivalent of the one who is bought out: the ransom takes their place. It is a direct, one-for-one substitution. Jesus' death pays the ransom for[1] **'many'**. It pays what was due — the penalty of death, our death sentence for sin. There are echoes in this verse of that great passage in Isaiah 53 that describes the mission of the one who is known as 'the Servant of the LORD', especially in verses 11-12. Jesus has come to save 'the many'.

Seeing the real Jesus

Although Jesus must have healed hundreds of blind people during his ministry, Mark picks out just two of them — the story of Bartimaeus which follows in verses 46-52 is the second — and, remarkably, both of these stories he uses in this same way, to show us the real Jesus. They form the beginning and end of the section I have called 'Jesus shows that he must suffer'. Giving sight to blind eyes symbolizes the way God opens our eyes to see the real Jesus and what he has come to do; it is thus a highly appropriate commentary on what Jesus has just taught. Mark, like the other Gospel writers, does not throw stories together at random. He has not picked out these episodes just because they are the most appealing stories, or the most dramatic, or even the most memorable, but for what they show us about the Lord Jesus Christ. Jesus' three years of public ministry would have produced hundreds of stories like this — teaching, parables and miracles by the score — and most of them we never hear about. But we hear about this one, because Mark has chosen it to reveal more about the real Jesus as he heads up to Jerusalem.

The scene Mark paints for us in verse 46 is of a noisy, bustling throng leaving the ancient city of Jericho: Jesus himself, the twelve disciples and a large crowd. Jesus has been on this journey for some time now. By this point he has recrossed the River Jordan; Jericho is five miles west of the river and just eighteen miles, one day's walk, short of Jerusalem. Most of this crowd will be pilgrims on their way up to the great city. The Passover festival is probably only a couple of weeks away, and thousands of people are converging on the capital — Jews from all over Israel and beyond. This cavalcade in Jericho is just one component of that great movement of people. But some of them undoubtedly are also keeping a very close eye on Jesus. He has done so many amazing deeds, spoken so many startling words, and the rumours about him have flown far and wide. They know he is heading up to Jerusalem; they have realized there is something special about him; and now they will make sure they are travelling along with him, just to see what he is going to do next.

It's not an unusual sight to come across a beggar at the side of the road — a busy road, this, even if it is known to be dangerous. This man is blind and therefore unable to support himself through work. (Mark's is the only Gospel to tell us that his name is Bartimaeus — or 'the son of Timai'. It's unusual for Mark to name people in the miracle stories; this may mean that Bartimaeus later becomes well known in the

church, but we don't know.) It is obvious to Bartimaeus that
a crowd is approaching. There is a noise down the street, the
pounding of feet on the ground and the smell of dust in the
air. As soon as he discovers the identity of the man in the
middle of it all, Bartimaeus starts to shout (10:47). Clearly,
he has heard of this Jesus of Nazareth. The stories about him
are being swapped up and down every road in the land, and a
blind man learns to be very skilled at tuning in to the latest
news. We can't be sure how much he knows about Jesus, but
he knows this is someone special — someone who can give
him a chance. Normally he calls out for money — it's the
only way he can survive — but not this time. **'Mercy'** is
what you ask from someone who is *greater* than you. Bartimaeus understands this at least: Jesus can give him something better than money. Jesus can give him his sight back.

The crowd around Jesus tell him in no uncertain terms to
be quiet (10:48). It wouldn't be surprising if this was Jesus'
own disciples again, reprising their performance in verse 13.
'Jesus has other matters on his mind,' they think. 'He has a
schedule to keep; he doesn't want to be bothered with *you*.'
But Bartimaeus is still shouting, refusing to be put off. It
soon turns out that Jesus does want to bother with him. He
stops, and no doubt everyone else stops too. Whatever is
Jesus going to do now? As Jesus says, **'Call him'** (10:49),
the crowd suddenly switches sides! Bartimaeus becomes the
focus of everyone's attention as they call him: 'Come on,
over here!' The man has been seated by the roadside, ready
to receive whatever people drop in his begging bowl. But the
moment he hears this call, he springs into action. Not a
second is wasted (10:50). Guided by the sounds, he makes
his way over to where Jesus stands waiting.

Jesus' question in verse 51, **'What do you want me to do
for you?'** is exactly the same question he asked James and
John in verse 36. What *they* wanted was glory, honour,
prestige — pride of place alongside Jesus in the kingdom of

God. Here is a clue to why Mark has included this story! Still blind to the true nature of Jesus' mission, James and John made a grab for glory. Now here stands a man who is literally blind. 'What do you want me to do for you?' The answer is obvious, but Jesus wants him to speak it out, because that makes his need clearer and encourages his faith. **'I want to see'**! In fact he calls Jesus 'Rabboni', the more respectful form of the word **'Rabbi'** — 'my lord', 'my master'.

Jesus needs no dramatic gestures. In a moment, without any fuss, Bartimaeus receives what he asks for. Suddenly, his darkness is ended. The sun shines again. Bartimaeus can see (10:52). And with that he turns, falls in behind Jesus, and sets off with the crowd. He too is now heading for Jerusalem. But Bartimaeus has a special, additional reason for going there. He will be making a sacrifice to thank God for giving him back his sight. No longer a helpless beggar, Bartimaeus now has a life!

In this short passage Mark gives us a great deal of help in seeing the real Jesus. He shows us that *Jesus is a real man*, the one who grew up in Nazareth and was known in that way (10:47). But he also shows us that *Jesus is the coming King*. Bartimaeus calls repeatedly to Jesus as the **'Son of David'** (10:47,48). **'David'** is King David, who reigned over Israel a thousand years ago — the greatest of all their kings. The great longing of the Jewish people at this time is that God would intervene in their nation's sad story again, place a descendant of David on the royal throne once more and bring in a golden age. The prophets have promised it and the people yearn for it, especially now, after a hundred years of Roman occupation have snuffed out the last living memory of national independence. The expression 'Son of David' evokes that picture of the promised, coming King. Quite possibly, Bartimaeus does not know that Jesus of Nazareth is literally a descendant of David. It may simply be a respectful title that indicates someone worthy to be mentioned in the

same breath as the great David — and someone whom God
is using to bring healing and blessing to the land. The fact
that Jerusalem is just up the road — Jerusalem, the city
David himself established as his capital and where he
reigned supreme — is always there in the background too.
But even if Bartimaeus does not have the full picture, Mark
does, and Bartimaeus may well have guessed it. Jesus is
indeed David's literal descendant; Jesus is indeed the coming
King, promised by God through the prophets (Jer. 23:5-6).
That is the dream, and in Jesus it will become reality.

Mark began his story with Jesus' identity a secret. Little
by little, the curtain has been lifted, and more and more has
been revealed. Now, just a day out from Jerusalem, the time
for secrecy is past. Jesus has accepted the title which a blind
man has given him, and very soon now, as the crowds
acclaim his entry into Jerusalem itself, this is just what they
will be crying (11:10). Jesus' true identity must be made
known so that when he dies in Jerusalem, it will be known
that he dies as the Messiah; he dies as the coming King.

Finally, Mark shows us that *Jesus is the splendour of
God*. Here is what Bartimaeus certainly doesn't know — not
yet at least — but Mark does, and he has put the clues in the
story. Read verses 49-52 again and note that the literal
translation of verse 49 is not **'cheer up'**, but 'take courage'.
Now look at Isaiah 35:1-10, where the prophet speaks in
poetic words about what it will be like when God intervenes
to save his people. Remember that 'Zion' is Jerusalem.
When God at last breaks in, we read, the land will be glad,
breaking into new life as God reveals his glory and splendour. We read about specific signs that will be seen as God
begins to move. We read of a highway of pilgrimage, God's
people streaming up to Zion, singing his praises and being
crowned with everlasting joy. And the signs that Isaiah
mentions that will be seen in the land are these: the feeble
and weak will be made strong so that they can stand strongly

on their feet; a message of *courage* to those who fear, because God is coming; the eyes of the *blind* will be opened;
the *deaf* will hear; the lame will leap, and the mute will shout
for joy (Isa. 35:3-6).

Now Mark has already pointed us to this passage, in the
story at the end of chapter 7 about the man who was deaf and
tongue-tied (see comments on 7:31-37). Now we see it again.
In this story the onlookers say to Bartimaeus, 'Take *courage*,
and get on your feet.' On the face of it, these are not the most
obvious words you would say to a blind man! But Mark is
pointing us back to Isaiah 35. Then, of course, the eyes of the
blind are *opened*. And in events like these, Isaiah says, 'They
will see the glory of the LORD, the splendour of our God'
(Isa. 35:2). The appearance of Jesus is the splendour of God
revealed. Not completely, as yet: we are not yet at the place
of everlasting joy; sorrow and sighing have not yet fled
away. Isaiah 35 has not been completely fulfilled, but for
those who are on the pilgrimage highway up to Zion, it
should be dawning that in Jesus the glory and splendour of
God are shining out on the earth. Little by little it becomes
evident that this is nothing less than the coming of God
himself.

Part V.
Jesus declares judgement (11:1 – 13:37)

17.
The judgement of the King

Please read Mark 11:1-25

Carved into a towering cliff in central Afghanistan stand two
gigantic statues. Hewn out of the living sandstone rock, they
are figures of the Buddha, dominating the Bamiyan Valley
which they overlook. The statues stand on the ancient Silk
Road, the old trade route which stretched through Afghanistan and right across Asia, and as a result they have long
been known far and wide. There they have stood for around
fifteen hundred years, a lasting monument to the religious
devotion of their builders, surviving invasions, suffering
mainly from the slow erosion of wind and weather, and a
magnet for tourists and travellers. Or at least, that was the
situation until March 2001, when the Taliban were in power
in Kabul. They decided that these Buddhas were idols and
un-Islamic; they simply had to go. So, against the pleas of
the entire international community, they demolished the two
statues. It proved harder than they expected, taking a month
of intensive effort, but at last the two Buddhas were obliterated. While the rest of the world regards the destruction of
the Bamiyan Buddhas as a supreme act of cultural vandalism, the Taliban simply feel that they have made their point.
Judgement has been given. The old order is finished; the
golden age of hard-line Islamist rule has arrived.

In Mark 11:1-25, Jesus is declaring judgement on the old order. As he arrives in Jerusalem in dramatic procession, he is staking his claim to what belongs to him by right. Then, as he marches into the temple and drives out the stallholders and the money-changers, he is publicly declaring that the temple's days are finished and something new and wonderful has come. This is no empty act of vandalism. Whereas the Taliban were simply striking out at something they disapprove of, making a statement about what they regard as unacceptable, with Jesus Christ it is quite different. When he declares judgement on the old ways, he is actually bringing it about. These are not acts of frustration; they are acts of decision. This is the judgement of the King. This passage begins a new section of Mark's Gospel, running to the end of chapter 13, which I have called 'Jesus declares judgement'. The running theme here is the end of the old religion, the temple and its ways. It forms the prelude to the passion narratives in which Jesus inaugurates the new covenant in his blood.

These days leading up to Passover are a time of excitement, a time of longing, as people remember the days when they were freed at last from slavery, and when they have to face the fact that now, just like last year, just like every year for the past century, they are captive once more under the Roman occupation. That is what the coming Passover means to the crowds who are now flocking to the city: the glory of the past, the bitterness of the present.

The arrival of the King

As we begin this story at the start of chapter 11, the trek up from Jericho is nearly over. The account in John's Gospel suggests that Jesus himself has not made this journey in a single day, but many of the pilgrims certainly will have done.

The only obstacle still ahead is the Mount of Olives, stretching from north to south between them and Jerusalem, and so from here the city itself is still out of sight. Bethphage is on the edge of Jerusalem itself, and Bethany about two miles before it, on the eastern slopes of the Mount of Olives. It's at this point that Jesus picks out two of the disciples and sends them on a mission (11:1-3). It's probably safe to say that Jesus has made some prior arrangement with the owner — so this is not an early account of donkey rustling — which explains why Jesus' delegation are politely permitted to remove the animal when they eventually find it (11:4-6).

The two disciples now return with their prize. With their cloaks they create a makeshift saddle; Jesus gets on board and the little cavalcade moves forward (11:7). It is now that the story takes off. Already the crowd is excited. As they reach the crest of the Mount of Olives, they are just coming to the place where for the first time on this pilgrim journey they sight Jerusalem. And what a sight it is! For every pilgrim on the road today, this is the greatest view they will ever see. The holy city stands before them, there across the Kidron Valley, the city whose name features time after time after time in their poetry and their history and which burns in their hearts — Jerusalem, Zion, the city known by the name of the greatest king of all, the city of David.

Dominating the city, towering over every other building and occupying as much as a quarter of its area, stands the temple. According to the contemporary historian Josephus, who knew this scene well, the temple from a distance, as the pilgrims see it now, appears 'like a mountain of snow', the marble and the gold of its walls brilliantly reflecting the sun. The temple — the heart of their religion and one of the wonders of the world — finally appears before them. And on this occasion, to add to the excitement they feel every time the city comes in sight, there is the figure of Jesus mounted on a donkey riding off down the road. Many of them have seen the miracles he has done, met the people he has healed, heard him speaking, or at least heard the stories. They know he is something special, some messenger of God. They know Jerusalem is where it all happens, and they can see him *riding* in — which ordinary pilgrims never do. You are supposed to arrive on foot. And in this atmosphere of general excitement and longing for God to do something for their nation, his appearing makes them boil over (11:7-10). The cloaks and foliage they spread in the road are the first-century equivalent of the red carpet. The pilgrimage becomes a procession as they march in front and behind calling out words which they always sing as they come this way: **'Blessed is he who comes in the name of the Lord!'** could be said of any pilgrim, but **'Blessed is the coming kingdom of our father David!'** means that they are expecting something more — that Jesus' coming to the capital means that God's longed-for kingdom is one step closer.

So the crowd moves down the Mount of Olives, across the valley and up to the city gates, with Jesus surrounded by the cheering throng. Finally he enters through the massive gateway. Like many others, he makes straight for the temple (11:11). But the story ends in a strangely anti-climactic manner. It seems that, for all their excitement on the way, the crowds around Jesus disperse as soon as he reaches Jerusalem: they go their separate ways and he goes his. The tragic fact, the ironic truth, is that they have failed to recognize that they are witnessing the arrival of the *King*. They know Jesus is someone special; some of them undoubtedly can glimpse something more; but none of them, not even Jesus' own disciples, really understand what this day means. Yet the clues are here. For those with eyes to see, what Jesus has done this day is enough to show them that he himself is the King they long for. We will look at those clues and draw some conclusions now.

1. The King brings the kingdom

'Blessed is the coming kingdom of our father David!' The crowds are looking back to the days of the kings, especially King David, and remembering the prophecies which God has given their people over the years, that one day the descendant of David will come, appearing like a shoot from a dry stump, and a new kingdom will be born. They understand those words to mean that the glory days will return, that the king will reign again from Jerusalem and the nation of Israel will stand strong and tall once more. Right now that has to mean a military leader who will drive their Roman overlords into the sea and set them free again. But Jesus has not come like that — that's why they do not recognize him.

Yet he has come in exactly the way the prophets foretold (Zech. 9:9-10). For anyone looking for a king, what Jesus does this day can hardly make it more obvious. Jesus is coming to bring a kingdom, sure enough, but not as they expect. The King will not come with violence, but with a sign of peace, as he rides in on the most humble and inconsequential of animals, a world away from the military might of the day. Military power has nothing to do with it. He will speak *peace* to the nations. The kingdom of Jesus does not simply go back to square one. Instead, he brings a kingdom for *every* nation. This is the kingdom Jesus spoke of in his parables, one that grows quietly, unseen. It spreads unobtrusively throughout the world, not by might, not by power, but by the Spirit of God (Zech. 4:6).

Although he comes peacefully, Jesus comes to claim what belongs to him. He calls everyone, in every nation, to accept him as their King and Judge. Verse 11 is not really an anticlimax. Jesus has not come to Jerusalem as a tourist. He makes his way directly to these awe-inspiring buildings, which have already taken a generation to construct, because he is here as their *Judge*. Mark says Jesus **'looked around'**;

that is a word Mark uses quite distinctively in his Gospel. In the synagogue in 3:5, Jesus 'looks around' at his enemies in anger and grief. With the rich man who will not abandon his wealth in 10:23, Jesus 'looks around' and passes judgement. Now again, he 'looks around' before he declares judgement on the temple. He comes in peace, but he also comes as Judge. Ultimately, he will condemn anyone who does not submit to his rule.

2. The King brings salvation

Again, the clue is in the words the crowds are chanting. If only they knew, they are themselves using words which acclaim his coming (Ps. 118:25-27) — words they are used to singing, especially at times of pilgrimage like this, but with a meaning far deeper than they realize. **'Hosanna!'** has become by now a cry of praise, but originally it means, 'Please save us', as in Psalm 118. So the crowd are calling out in the presence of Jesus, 'Save us', without realizing that he is the true Saviour. But the salvation he brings is what he has explained three times in the past few months on his way towards Jerusalem. As he has moved nearer and nearer to the city, so the day when salvation will dawn has moved closer and closer; now it lies mere days ahead. The crowd do not understand that this is what he has come to Jerusalem to do — not to lead a rampaging mob against the Roman garrison, but to pick up a wooden cross, be marched outside the walls and hung up to die, at the hands of those same hated over-lords. There is no doubt, because Luke's account tells us explicitly, that as he rides towards the city and hears the clamour around him, this is what fills Jesus' thoughts — this and the tragic fact that the people have failed to recognize him (Luke 19:41-44).

There is one further clue about this salvation: Jesus singles out a colt that has never been ridden. In days gone by,

when an animal was needed for a sacred purpose, they had to
select one that had never done any ordinary work. Especially
was that true in the case of sacrifice (Num. 19:2; Deut. 21:3).
Jesus deliberately chooses such an animal to carry him to the
place where he will be the once-and-for-all sacrifice for our
sins.[1] The psalm the crowds are singing speaks of an altar.
The altar Jesus is going to is his cross.

3. The King brings joy

It's clear from the story that this crowd is full of joy, even if
they don't really understand what they are saying or what
Jesus is coming to do. It's the joy of the pilgrimage, of
arriving at the end of the journey, of singing praises to their
God. They celebrate, but as soon as they get inside the city,
the joy dissipates. The journey is over. Normal life continues
and in a few days they will all go home again, back to the
unrelieved daily grind of their usual existence. This day will
soon be forgotten. But following King Jesus brings joy that
lasts. If we are following Jesus, we too are on a journey. He
is with us on our journey through this life, every step of the
way, in good times and in bad, and he is leading us to our
final destination, which is not an earthly city but a heavenly
one; not the Jerusalem of bricks and mortar, the Jerusalem
which would soon be no more, but the new, the heavenly
Jerusalem, the eternal home of everyone who loves him.

The judgement of the King

After that first triumphal entry into the city, Jesus returns to
Bethany for the night (11:11), a pattern which he will follow
throughout the week. As far as we can tell, he and his disciples are staying with Lazarus, Mary and Martha, who
therefore have to cope with the addition of thirteen men with

healthy appetites for a week's bed and breakfast! This may
explain why, as they leave Bethany to return to Jerusalem the
next morning, verse 12 tells us that Jesus is hungry —
perhaps Martha has provided only a continental breakfast!
He sees a fig tree and goes to see if there are any figs, but all
he finds is leaves — no fruit at all (11:13). Mark points out
that it is not the right time of year for figs, which ripen in the
autumn, not in the spring. Then Jesus does something very
surprising. The fig tree, with leaves but no fruit, is cursed
(11:14). Mark pointedly adds that **'his disciples heard him
say it'**.

Now it's on to Jerusalem, and directly to the temple
(11:15-17). To understand this story, we need to know that
around the actual buildings of the temple there is a wide area
known as the Court of the Gentiles, so called because this is
the only area of the temple where non-Jews are allowed to
go. This is where the action now takes place. We also need to
remember that this temple is not some kind of museum or
tourist attraction. It is busy; it is noisy; it is constantly full of
crowds. In the inner court, a constant stream of animals is
being slaughtered and sacrificed by fire on the great altar,
fifty feet (or fifteen metres) square. At this point, with the
Passover just a few days away, all this activity is reaching a
climax. At Passover, every family in the land is supposed to
come and sacrifice a lamb; the regulations are set out in
Deuteronomy 16:1-8. The number of animals involved is
vast. According to Josephus, at the Passover in AD 66, a
generation after these events, as many as 255,000 lambs will
be needed for sacrifice. They all have to come from somewhere. That's in addition to all the *regular* sacrifices which
the Jewish law prescribes for so many different events. The
poor — the majority of the population — are allowed to
sacrifice doves at some of these occasions, but again the
doves have to come from somewhere.

The Jewish authorities have solved this supply problem in a very sensible way. Over the years, several large animal markets were set up on the Mount of Olives. People can buy their animals there for sacrifice, bring them in to the temple, and all is well. But now, as if this were not enough, additional markets have sprung up in the temple courts themselves, in the Court of the Gentiles. Probably this has been done in deliberate, direct competition with the markets on the Mount of Olives. You can imagine the advertising slogans: 'Don't walk your lambs all the way in from the hills! Buy right here on site!' So the temple *itself* has become a livestock market.

To make matters worse, there is the problem of the temple tax, paid annually by every Jewish man to support the ministry of the temple. The tax is set at half a shekel — and that's the problem. Israel is occupied territory now, and the Hebrew shekel is no more. So everyone who comes to pay his tax has to change his Roman denarii or sestertii into the nearest possible equivalent of the Hebrew shekel, which happens to be the Tyrian shekel. This means that in addition to the livestock markets, there are also lines of money-changing kiosks. There are supposed to be strict rules about what goes on in the temple court. There is even a rule about not using it as a short-cut, but the rules have been conveniently forgotten!

All of this activity is what Jesus takes exception to — we shall see why shortly. Jesus takes direct action. He dives into the crowd and drives out the merchants. He throws over the money tables; of course all the money is in coins, which fly in all directions, no doubt sending people scrabbling on the ground to grab what they can! Briefly, he brings all commercial activity to a halt. Then he explains what he is doing. The authorities, hardly surprisingly, don't like it (11:18). Two different parties unite against Jesus here — the **'chief priests'**, who are Sadducees, and **'the teachers of the law'**, or scribes, who are mostly Pharisees; both see that Jesus is dangerous, and they are afraid. For all kinds of reasons, religious, political and probably commercial as well, they are now absolutely determined that Jesus has to go. But at the end of another remarkable day, Jesus retreats to the safe haven of Bethany once more (11:19).

The next day arrives and the group once again make their way over the Mount of Olives and into Jerusalem. There is the fig tree, now withered and dead — withered **'from the roots'** (11:20), so there can be no mistake. This tree will indeed never bear fruit again. Peter remarks on it (11:21) and Jesus takes the opportunity to give them some teaching on prayer. He starts off by saying, in essence, 'Yes, of course it's withered. What did you expect? That's what happens when you pray with faith' (11:22-24). **'This mountain'** presumably refers to the Mount of Olives, where they are standing, but Jesus is speaking in general terms.

It is easy to take this passage the wrong way; many have done so, as though Jesus is speaking of the power of positive thinking as a guarantee of dramatic answers to prayer. We cannot use these verses in that way. Submitting to God's will is an essential aspect of prayer, yet our knowledge of his will is far from perfect; often we simply do not know what to pray for in a situation. Jesus is saying that if we want our prayers to be answered, we must be people of commitment, not people of doubt. James (Jesus' brother, not one of the Twelve) picks up this theme in his letter, especially in James 1:5-8 and then in 5:15-16. The first of those passages is a particularly helpful commentary on Jesus' words here. Doubting is a state of mind, a condition which makes it impossible for God to work through our prayers.

Mark adds verse 25 here, quite possibly a saying from a different occasion which he has chosen to include at this point because of the common theme — 'barriers to success-ful prayer'. Prayer can be effective only on the basis of a clear and open relationship with the Lord; holding onto resentment or bitterness interrupts that relationship. We need to be people who, like him, forgive easily. We cannot claim to walk in intimate fellowship with the Lord when we are *out* of fellowship with our fellow believers.[2]

The judgement sandwich

Let's now look at the way Mark has put this passage together. Do you see how he has bracketed the account of clearing the temple inside the story of the fig tree? By doing that, Mark makes it crystal clear that the two stories are really saying the same thing. It's a judgement sandwich, where what happens to the fig tree acts as a commentary on the incident in the temple. So now let's try to understand what it all means. We will look at the outside of the sandwich first, and then at the filling.

The judgement of the King comes, first, because his people have produced no fruit. This is the fig-tree story. Some have struggled to make sense of it. Someone described it as 'a tale of miraculous power wasted in the service of ill-temper … and as it stands it is simply incredible'.[3] In other words, Jesus is simply lashing out in anger when he doesn't get his free breakfast, rather like the Taliban taking out their fury on the statues at Bamiyan. How could Jesus not know that figs are out of season? And if he does know, why curse the tree? It has even been suggested that this is simply a legend about Jesus which grew up around a mysteriously withered fig tree that used to stand near Bethany.

People who say this sort of thing have simply not understood the story. It's not difficult to understand: Jesus is acting out a parable of judgement. Of course he knows it isn't the time of year for figs! But he uses the fact of his real hunger — Jesus is a real man, and men do need their breakfast! —

as an opportunity to teach this lesson. The Lord looks for fruit; he sees a tree that looks alive, full of leaves, but he finds no fruit.

What does it mean? The fig tree is a picture of Israel frequently used in the Old Testament; we will confine ourselves to two references in the prophets. First, in Hosea 9:10, Israel is depicted as a fig tree; she shows early promise, but later on, there is nothing but disappointment. The second reference is found in Micah 7:1, a passage which goes on to describe the dreadful spiritual condition into which God's people have fallen. There is no righteousness, no good fruit to be found. And now, when the Lord Jesus looks at Israel, he finds no fruit. In verse 11 we saw Jesus '*looking* round' at the temple; now right after that, in verse 13, he is *looking* for fruit, and there is none. Thus the verdict is pronounced: 'There is no fruit in you; your time is up. No one will eat fruit from you again.' Israel's unique role, her special place in God's plan, is no more. This is devastating.

Now I don't want to be misunderstood. Jesus is *not* saying that the Jewish people are all under a special curse. That would be a foundation for the appalling anti-Semitism of which the church has sometimes been guilty. As we shall see, what Jesus is doing is placing the Jews on the same level as everyone else. He *is* saying, though, that the unique place of ethnic Israel, the Jewish people, is ended. Some Christians try to escape the full force of this by saying that Jesus is judging *only* the corrupt leaders, or *only* the generation that saw him on earth, or by limiting it in some other way, but that will not work. The fig tree does not stand for the national leadership, or for one specific generation. It stands for *Israel*. That means that there is no separate route to salvation for the Jewish people. They have no advantage when it comes to salvation, and they need Christ in exactly the same way as members of every other nation. So is there hope for the Jews? Absolutely! There is the glorious hope of trusting in the Jewish Messiah, the Lord Jesus Christ — exactly the same hope that we all have. Paul in Romans 11:26 declares that a great number of Jews will be saved before Christ returns. They will be saved through the *cross*!

Now for the filling of the sandwich. The judgement of the King comes, secondly, because his people have cut out the Gentiles. Here we are dealing with the story of Jesus clearing the temple, in verses 15-19. If the first cause of judgement was general — no fruit, no righteousness — this one is very specific. The key question is this: why does Jesus take such extreme objection to all the commercial activity in the Court of the Gentiles? It's often said that Jesus is taking exception to the simple fact of buying and selling, and the dodgy dealing that no doubt goes with it. In John's account of a similar incident (John 2:13-16), that does seem to be the emphasis, but not so here. Jesus explains in verse 17 why he is so outraged. He is quoting from two prophecies.

The first is from Isaiah 56:6-8, where the prophet says that even people who would be seen as outcasts in Israel are to be welcomed in — notably, foreigners, *Gentiles*. So the key words in Jesus' quotation are the last three: **'for all nations'**. But how can the Gentiles come and worship in the house of God when the only area open to them is blocked by a cattle and bird market and line after line of money-changers? Israel's God-given mission was to be a light to the nations. Gentiles were supposed to be drawn in to that light like moths to a flame. But what is happening here in the Court of the Gentiles proves beyond doubt that Israel has completely lost the plot.

The second quote is from Jeremiah 7:11. Again, the context is vital. Jeremiah himself was standing at the en-trance of the temple (Solomon's Temple, not Herod's), addressing people who trusted in it as if it were indestruct-ible. The people were in an appalling state of sin: Jeremiah speaks of widespread adultery, theft, murder and perjury as

well as rank idolatry. Yet they believed they were utterly
secure, because they had the temple they were so proud of;
and God would never let anything happen to the temple.
Jeremiah stood there and told them they were utterly wrong.
If they continued to sin, they would fall, and so would their
temple. That is the passage Jesus now refers to. Just as in
Jeremiah's day, he says, this temple has become **'a den of
robbers'**. That word 'robber' is the Greek *lestes*. It doesn't
mean someone who short-changes you when he sells you a
couple of doves for your sacrifice. In fact, 'robber' is the
mildest possible translation. A *lestes* is a bandit, an outlaw,
like Barabbas, whom we shall meet in chapter 15. Jesus is
saying that the temple has once again become a symbol of
nationalistic pride — not a house of prayer but a hotbed of
political plotting. History shows clearly how that worked out.
When the Jews rebel against the Romans a generation later,
the temple is taken over by the Zealots and becomes the
focal point of military resistance. The seeds of that movement are being sown as Jesus speaks. How in the world can
Gentiles feel at home in a place like that?

The outrage Jesus sees is that God's people have cut out
the Gentiles — firstly, by physically denying them the space
to worship and, secondly, by making the temple a focus of
Jewish nationalism. Just as Jesus has acted out a judgement
parable with the fig tree, so now, symbolically, he clears the
temple courts for the Gentiles to come in. It won't last, of
course: in an hour or two, everything will be back to normal.
The sacrifices continue uninterrupted. But in taking these
actions, Jesus is declaring judgement. His own ministry —
his death and resurrection — will make the temple obsolete.
But, more than that, because the people have failed to recognize their King, and because they have failed to carry out the
mission God has given them, their temple and their nation
will be judged and will fall. Forty years later, that finally
happens, as Jesus will explain in chapter 13. For now, God

through Christ is drawing a line under the old regime and will very soon bring in the new. With Jesus, a new day has dawned. To be the people of God now means something decisively different.

The changes that Jesus has brought

This is what it means to be God's people today, after Christ and his ministry.

1. Instead of one temple, we have everywhere!

The temple was the very heart of Jewish worship. So when people went there, they were absolutely right. God lived there among his people (amazing!) *until* the coming of Christ. After Christ, it's better still: we are no longer tied down to a single place for God to meet with us, because he meets with us in *every* place. After Christ, God has poured out his Spirit on all his people, and that's why the New Testament can speak of our bodies as God's temple (1 Cor. 6:19). So for us, buildings are no longer important. We don't need temples any more! We just need a roof to keep us dry when we meet. Some people still call a church 'the house of God', but really it isn't. Not long ago, on a weekday, a man walked past our church building and told us we shouldn't let the local kids sit out there on the front steps, because this is the house of God. (I believe he was a leader of another church.) But that's bad theology! The steps are just steps, and the building is just a building. The Lord doesn't live there! After Christ, there are no more holy places, only holy *people*.

2. Instead of one nation, we are from every nation

For two thousand years, God's plans were focused on a single nation, the people of Israel. But it was always his intention that salvation should be for people of *every* nation (Isa. 56). But even if the temple really had worked like that, its days would still have been finished when Christ came. The temple itself was marked out into zones. Gentiles could only go so far in. A Jewish woman was better off; a Jewish man was better off still. And only priests could go right inside. But in Christ, all these barriers are broken down (Eph. 2:11-14). In Jesus Christ there is no more Jew and Gentile. In Christ, racial distinctions no longer stand, and the gospel of Jesus is advancing day by day, and year by year, in every nation under heaven. Before Christ returns, the good news will come to every people group on the face of the earth. The wonderful truth is that it has come to *us*. Whether you come from Africa or Asia, from the Americas or from Europe, and wherever you heard it, the glorious fact is that the gospel came to *you*.

3. Instead of many sacrifices, we have one cross

As Jesus deals with the money-changers, as he stands there teaching the people, just yards away, from that high altar can be heard the dying cries of the animal sacrifices in endless succession. At the same moment, the priests responsible for those very sacrifices are plotting to put Jesus to death. Did you notice how Mark has carefully dropped that into the middle of the story as well? (11:18). In a few days, they will get their way; at Passover, the Lord Jesus, the Lamb of God, will meet his own death on the cross, as the one, final, perfect sacrifice that puts an end to all the others.

18.
The authority of the King

Please read Mark 11:27 – 12:12

In the Steven Spielberg film, *Catch me if you can*, Leonardo di Caprio plays the part of con man Frank Abagnale, Jr, who has an astonishing ability to pull the wool over people's eyes. It's not just that he has good looks and a way with words; he adds to that the confidence to bluff his way through any situation and an astonishing attention to detail. For years, Abagnale succeeds in keeping one step ahead of the pursuing FBI agent, who is a formidable figure in his own right. Featured in Abagnale's career of con tricks are episodes where he successfully poses as a teacher, a doctor, a lawyer and, most memorably, an airline pilot, complete with resplendent PanAm uniform. He also manages to cash forged cheques to the value of around three million dollars — and this at 1960s prices. At one point, to distract the FBI who have surrounded Miami airport, he puts on his pilot's uniform, drops into a nearby college to 'recruit' some stewardesses, returns to the airport next day with these girls in uniform and successfully makes his escape to Europe. All this at the age of eighteen!

Catch me if you can is great fun. What makes it even more remarkable is that it is based on a true story — hence the film's tag line: 'The true story of a real fake'. The scams

depicted in this film are of many kinds, but they all have one
feature in common. In every case, Abagnale has to persuade
his victim to believe that he is genuine, that his qualifications
are real, that his uniform is what it claims to be, that it really
is PanAm who have given him these pay cheques. The issue
is one of *authority*. The cheques are real only if they come
with the authority of the bank. The uniform is genuine only if
the airline has issued it; otherwise it's just fancy dress.

It is this issue of authority that looms large in Mark
11:27 – 12:12. Jesus is apparently claiming the authority for
some fairly extreme and dramatic actions and, perhaps not
surprisingly, people want to know where he gets that authority *from*. Down through the ages, people have been asking
the same kind of questions about Jesus. Can we accept him
as someone with authority — someone who has the right to
tell us what to do, and whose way we must therefore follow?
Whether we are Christians or not, these are questions we
must get to grips with. Whose authority are we going to
accept in our own lives? We are looking here at two closely
connected stories: in the first Jesus is challenged directly to
explain and defend his authority, while in the second the
parable of the tenants sets out his authority and issues the
sternest of warnings to those who reject it.

Jesus' authority is challenged

Already in verse 18, we have seen the response of the leaders
to what Jesus is doing. Now in verses 27-33 the threat grows
stronger, the storm grows closer, as Jesus is confronted by an
official delegation. This story begins as Jesus arrives in
Jerusalem for the third time in as many days (11:27-28). At
some point in the temple's outer courts, probably under one
of the covered walkways which run round the Court of the
Gentiles, Jesus will now continue his teaching programme.

This is where his opponents finally catch up with him. To say the least, it is an impressive delegation. These three groups, the chief priests, the teachers of the law and the elders, represent the main components of the Jewish ruling council, the Sanhedrin. The **'chief priests'** are very senior figures in national life: they are in charge of the temple, which also gives them a key role in liaising with the Romans. The **'teachers of the law'**, or scribes, are responsible for teaching people how to understand and apply God's law. The **'elders'** are respected community leaders who are expected to bring the wisdom of their years to the council's debates. Many of their faces are known to the crowd, who stand back to let them pass — the stern faces of their nation's leaders, intent on dealing with this wandering Galilean teacher who has created such a stir here in the capital. Already they have had their discussion in private (11:18); now it's time for the confrontation.

It is the authority question that they ask. The day before yesterday, Jesus arrived in this holy city accompanied by a procession who were shouting and chanting all sorts of dangerous things, and he accepted their acclaim. Yesterday, still worse, he arrived on this very spot and started driving out our perfectly legal and licensed stallholders, who were doing no more than providing services for the worshippers, and generally creating mayhem in the house of the Lord! Abusing the words of the holy prophets, causing uproar, disturbing the peace, almost starting a riot, threatening to attract the attention of the Romans...! Jesus, what gives you any right to do this? Whatever their attitude, whatever their motives, it's a good question. What gives Jesus the right to say that the venerable leaders of the established religion have got it all wrong? Who does he think he is to come storming through the temple like this? To put it bluntly — is Jesus just bluffing, or is he for real?

Jesus' response in verses 29-30 is not straightforward. He answers a question with another question — a very pointed one. Twice he demands an answer, which requires some nerve in this company. John the Baptist has been dead for some time by now, grubbily executed by Herod Antipas (6:14-29), but memories of him are still fresh. The crucial point is that John is closely linked with Jesus (1:7-8). The authorities didn't approve of John, just as they don't approve of Jesus. That explains Jesus' question. He is implying that the answers to the two questions are the same. 'Where did John's *baptism* come from? Where does my *authority* come from? There are two options: either John and I get our authority from heaven, from God himself; or else we are just men, making claims that we can't back up — con men, in fact.' Jesus asks this question not as a trick, but as a test to see whether they are really interested in discovering the truth or not.

Their reply in verses 31-33 shows them up. These leaders know about John's popularity. They know the crowds accept him as a genuine prophet from God. But to accept John now would leave them open to a charge of hypocrisy. Worse still, to accept John's authority means accepting the one he points to — the Jesus who is standing in front of them now. But, on the other hand, if they say John was not genuine, as they really believe, they risk the anger of the crowds, and this conversation is happening in a very public place. So they fudge: **'We don't know'**! What an answer! It's like a top tennis player saying he doesn't know which end of the racket to hold. It's their job to know such things, but Jesus' simple question has put them in a fix from which they cannot escape — these great leaders! They know, and so does he, that they have simply dodged the issue. Jesus says, 'If you cannot even commit yourself to an answer about John, I am certainly not going to give you anything else about *me*.'

This vivid little narrative shows us starkly why and how people react as they do to Jesus Christ and the authority he claims. We will look at three issues that arise as people face the authority of the King.

1. The advantages that fail (11:27)

Think what these leaders' lives have been like. From a young age they have been taught the Word of God. They learned to read by poring over a copy of the Torah; they probably learned to write by scribing the Ten Commandments. Every one of them has spent his life in study and memorizing and discussion of the Law, the Prophets and the history of their nation. They have every advantage that a sound religious background can give, but when it comes to recognizing God's King, to acknowledging his authority and his rule, all these advantages get them nowhere. In fact these religious leaders are precisely the people who will be responsible for condemning the King to death. We need to understand that being religious is not the same as knowing God. However good you are at going to church, quoting the Bible, or having any other religious advantage, it does not put you in a re-lationship with God through Christ. Knowing God, being a Christian, is not something you gain by being religious. Nor is it something you can be born into, whoever your parents might be. Someone can say, 'I was born a *Hindu*.' 'I was born a *Buddhist*.' 'I was born a *Muslim*.' But no one can say, 'I was born a Christian.' Until there is that personal encoun-ter, that individual recognition, there is no relationship.

2. The barriers that intrude

Look at the attitude that the delegation adopts. Jesus' un-answered question shows that they are not interested in finding out the truth, but only with playing it safe. At no point does it enter their heads to accept the claims of Jesus. They are trapped by the fear of what they will lose if they accept him: they will lose face, status and control. It is much the same today. People who reject the claims of Jesus Christ don't usually have an intellectual problem — or at least, it's not the *main* problem. Solving people's intellectual problems can only take you so far. Very often, behind every problem you will only find another one.

Yes, it's right that we tackle the problems that people bring up: questions about the Bible and where it comes from, or about evolution, or about the absoluteness of truth, or whatever it may be. Our faith is reasonable; it is rational; it is not full of holes; and God has given us our minds so that we can explore the truth and so that we can think through the important questions. But being more clever is not the answer. Being clever is just another of those 'advantages' that cannot bring you to God. In my lifetime I have encountered many very clever people, including several Nobel prize-winners and the like — some of them rather bizarre; some of them perfectly normal — and while their brains may be up in the stratosphere, I can assure you they are just the same as the rest of us. They have the same kind of problems, the same kind of hang-ups. Some believe; some don't believe. There are clever ways of being stupid, just as there are dumb ways of being stupid.

Usually, people who present an intellectual or academic objection to the Christian faith are concealing a much more basic problem in their hearts — the problem that *they simply refuse to believe*. The basic reason why men and women will not accept the authority of the King is not in their brains, but in their hearts. It's not that they don't understand; it's the problem of their stubborn *will*. As Christians trying to reach people, we need to realize that. This delegation already have the answers they need. They have spent the past two years investigating Jesus — Mark has told us this. All the evidence to identify Jesus accurately is there, and they refuse to see it! Today, many unbelievers stand in the temple courts with that hostile delegation. They long for people's respect, and fear they will lose it. They want to be accepted — what a powerful driver that is! — and so they will not entertain the claims of King Jesus.

3. The faith that submits

Jesus' questioning is a sharp knife into their hearts. The members of this delegation know exactly what he will ask them if they give their endorsement of John (11:31). But this is the chance Jesus is giving them — they still have the opportunity to believe! Even at this late stage, when his death is at most four days away, if any of these solemn gentlemen would break ranks and accept Jesus' claims, and put his faith in him, the Lord would welcome him. The faith that submits to the King is not just a mind that is convinced, though that certainly helps along the way. This faith means believing and trusting in Jesus Christ, accepting his absolute authority over our life, our plans, our destiny, our will.

Accepted or rejected?

There is a well-known story associated with the *Mona Lisa*. Two women have come into Paris from the countryside and visit the Louvre to view the famous painting. As they stand there in front of it, one says to the other, 'I don't like it. Whatever is all the fuss about?' The guard simply says, 'Madame, the *Mona Lisa* has stood the test of time. When you stand before her, it is not she who is being judged. It is *you.*' What he means, of course, is that you have no right to judge the *Mona Lisa*. Its place among the world's greatest works of art is not in doubt. If you say it's nothing special, if you pass judgement on it, you are saying nothing about the painting. You are simply demonstrating your own ignorance. Your verdict on the *Mona Lisa* says nothing about her, but everything about you!

When Jesus tells the parable of the tenants in Mark 12:1-12, this is precisely his point. It's the story of people who pass judgement on him, reject him and will eventually kill him. The message is that their verdict on Jesus Christ says nothing about him, but it says everything about them. While they think they are deciding his fate, the reality is that their judgement actually decides their own. The same is true today. What we decide to do with Jesus Christ makes him no greater or less, but our decision makes all the difference in the world for us. In this parable, Jesus gives the answer to the authority question which he refused to give in verse 33. He gives the answer on his own terms and in a way which the leaders don't like one little bit, because his answer makes it clear that people who pass judgement on him are actually passing judgement on themselves.

Again, let's get into the story and explore what Jesus says, before we come back and look at what the parable means. Immediately after his confrontation over the authority issue, with the official delegation still standing there, we read that Jesus begins to teach the people in parables. A man plants a vineyard, protects it with a wall and a watchtower to keep away intruders, and prepares for the harvest by putting in a winepress as well (12:1). Clearly, this is the landowner. His next step is to select tenants who will look after his vineyard while he goes off on his travels. Their job is to produce the best possible crop; their rent will take the form of a proportion of that crop.

All this is very true to the customs of the time. In the Israel of the first century, especially in Galilee, much of the land has been consolidated into large estates owned by absentee landlords. Tenant farmers are then employed to look after the land and produce crops for the benefit of the faraway landowners. Examples have been discovered of contracts just like this. We also know that wine is one of the region's major exports at this time, and that under these conditions, disputes could easily arise between the tenants and the landowners — which is just what happens next in Jesus' story. The time comes for the first harvest and a servant arrives to demand the owner's share of the crop, as per contract (12:2). But the tenants have other ideas: verses 3-5 recount their escalating rebellion. In the end, the land-owner has just one representative left to send. This one is not a servant; he's his son. But when the tenants see him, they spot their chance at once (12:6-8).

The story may sound odd, but it makes good sense in the light of the customs and the law of the time. If a piece of land has no identifiable owner, under certain circumstances it can be lawfully claimed by anyone — with priority given to whoever stakes their claim first. When these tenants see the son approaching, they make the not unreasonable assumption that his father must have died and the son is coming to take possession. If they can kill the son, they can make a legal claim to the land — and this they do. So the son is now dead but, unfortunately for the tenants, the father is not. The owner arrives, the tenants are executed and the vineyard is handed over to others who can be trusted to keep the agreement he has made with them. This is the story Jesus tells, and he gives it a very pointed ending. We will come back to that, but we notice straight away that he has obviously upset his audience, to put it mildly!

This parable is rather different from those in chapter 4. The story is more detailed than most other parables; it is closer to allegory than the others, by which I mean that many points in the parable correspond directly to things in the real world. But, more importantly, this one is clearly directed against a specific group of people, and whereas the earlier parables were designed to *divide* the hearers — Jesus says explicitly in 4:11-12 that he uses parables to divide his audience into those who can and cannot understand — with this parable, the meaning is unmistakable and obvious, so that even the most obtuse cannot miss it. Throughout his Gospel Mark has shown us, step by step, how Jesus gradually reveals himself more and more openly. Slowly, slowly, the veil of mystery is being lifted. Now very close to his death, Jesus is speaking of himself more clearly than at any time before, yet still with a residual element of mystery. Jesus is revealing exactly what he wants to reveal about himself, where he comes from and where he gets his authority, but he is doing it in a way which shows that it's his hearers who are the ones under judgement. If we look back at the parable, we can highlight four facets of his own story which Jesus explains to us here.

1. Jesus completes the line of the prophets

Jesus' original hearers have one big advantage over us when it comes to understanding the parable. The moment Jesus begins to speak about a vineyard and its owner (12:1), they know exactly what he is referring to, because the very same picture is used in Isaiah 5:1-7. There is a vineyard planted, with a wall (Isa. 5:5), a watchtower and a winepress (Isa. 5:2). Earlier in Mark 11 we saw that the fig tree was a popular image for Israel. Now here is one which is used even more often than the fig tree. Isaiah says his picture of the vineyard represents the people of Israel, and its owner and planter clearly is God himself. So, as they hear Jesus' opening words, they know immediately what he is talking about. This parable, evidently, has much in common with Jesus cursing the fig tree. The slant is slightly different now, and it's different from Isaiah 5 as well, because Jesus' focus is not on the vineyard, but on the people in charge of it. The target of this parable is not the people as a whole, but the nation's *leaders* — who are standing here in front of him.

Having begun with a picture from the prophets, Jesus next begins to tell their story. So far we have God, the owner of the vineyard, and the national leaders, the rebellious tenants. The next cast members in the story are the servants who come for the rent, and they are the prophets, the men God sent to Israel to call them to righteousness, to collect the fruit of good and godly living that he was looking for. In the parable, the owner sends what sounds like a ridiculous number of different servants on this fruitless quest, but that large number fits very well when we realize that Jesus is talking about the prophets, who kept appearing over a period of many centuries. The prophets came with God's authority into the life of the nation, to demand what was due to him. In every case the nation failed to produce the fruit, and in most cases the prophets themselves had a very rough reception. Some of them were killed; many others were threatened with death. **'Some of them they beat, others they killed'**, says Jesus (12:5). The prophets appeared in a long line, and right at the end of the line came Jesus Christ, the beloved Son (12:6). It is Jesus Christ who completes the line of the prophets. Jesus himself was a prophet, a man who spoke God's words faithfully, perfectly and with divine authority. What this parable shows us clearly is that Jesus is the end of the line. No one who follows him can speak with that same unchallengeable authority; no one who follows him has that unique ministry.

2. Jesus stands unique and alone

Look again at verses 6-7. Jesus is more than a prophet. Verse 6 very pointedly describes him as **'a son, whom he loved'**, a 'beloved son'. When the Gospels use that expression it has the sense of uniqueness — his *only* son. Already in Mark's

Gospel it has been heard twice — once at Jesus' baptism (1:11) and again on the mountain of transfiguration (9:7), both times in a direct affirmation by God that Jesus Christ is his beloved Son. In the parable he is clearly set apart from all the others, from all the prophets who have come before him and from anyone else in the human race — the Lord Jesus stands alone as God's unique, beloved Son. The prophets spoke with God's authority and had a divine right to be heard. The people would be judged for disobeying them. But Jesus is on a different level altogether. He is not some spokesman for God, carrying a message in a briefcase. He *is* the message. He *is* the word, the *final* word (Heb. 1:1-2). If we want to know about God, if we want to hear from God, we need to listen to his Son Jesus Christ.

3. Jesus suffers rejection and death

Read again verses 7-8. Jesus is now looking into the very near future. He knows how it will go. The tenants give the son no more respect than they gave the servants — quite the reverse. They now see their opportunity to take full possession of the vineyard. Here Jesus faces the 'tenants' of the nation. They see him as a threat to be disposed of. If only they can get rid of him, they think, they will be safe, unthreatened, securely in possession. So they will reject him, kill him and throw him out. In the parable this means the humiliation of being casually killed and his body thrown over the wall of the vineyard and left to rot. In real life it will be the humiliation of a shameful death, crucifixion, which was the most disgraceful of deaths as well as the most agonizing, and death outside the city walls. In the background there is also a reference to the way that the bodies of sacrificed animals were taken outside the camp and burned — the idea that what goes on outside is unclean (Heb. 13:11-12). So this detail that Jesus inserts in the parable suggests that his own death will be unclean, that it will be tied up with the sins of the people, and that is because Jesus himself is going to die as the final sacrifice, with the sins of a world of evil on his back. As Jesus tells this parable, he is face to face with the leaders who will actually make it happen. He is describing his own death to the people who are just about to engineer it.

4. Jesus crowns God's plans

But now look at verses 9-11. The parable is finished and the verdict has been given; the evil tenants have met their just deserts. To drive his point home, Jesus chooses to quote from Psalm 118:22-23 — the psalm which was sung to him by the excited crowd two days ago. In fact, these verses come from almost immediately before those words about 'Blessed is he who comes in the name of the Lord'. That choice in itself is certain to infuriate the authorities. These verses originally refer to building Solomon's Temple. The thought is of a stone on the building site that seems to be the wrong size, or the wrong shape, to be used anywhere in this great edifice, so it is rejected. But in the end this stone turns out to be just the piece they need to hold the whole structure together — the words mean literally 'the head of the corner', which can either refer to the 'capstone' or the 'cornerstone'; it doesn't really matter which. A rejected stone becomes the missing piece that holds the whole structure together. Jesus is saying, 'This is about the son in my story. This is about me.' So, yes, like the son in the story, Jesus suffers rejection and death. But God has made this rejected stone the keystone of his purposes, the crown of his plans. After his death, God publicly vindicates the Lord Jesus by raising him from the dead. The resurrection proves that his judges have brought judgement on themselves. Peter would declare this, speaking in the same city less than two months later (Acts 2:36).

Jesus dies, but he is raised from the dead, he is exalted to heaven and glorified, and he lives and reigns eternally with God the Father, the key and climax to God's purposes. For through him, God has rolled out his plan to bring salvation to all peoples. The vineyard has been taken away from the evil tenants and given to others, given to a worldwide people, Gentiles along with Jews, for the glory of the name of Jesus, with the result that at his name every knee will bow. **'The Lord has done this, and it is marvellous in our eyes'** — marvellous for Mark's first readers, the Gentiles in Rome, and marvellous for us, Gentiles of many races today, along with believing Jews.

The questions and demands of the Jewish leaders have blown up in their faces. In response to their probing about his authority, Jesus has shown them that he is the unique Son of the Father. He has declared to them that their own days as tenants are numbered and that, though they can kill him, God will vindicate him. As the story closes, we leave the leaders fuming. They know perfectly well that Jesus has told the parable against them. It's impossible for them to miss the point. For the third time since the Triumphal Entry, we read of their fear. It's only fear of the crowds that keeps them from arresting him publicly. So they disperse, and the scene is set for the secret arrest that will follow.

What we do with Jesus decides where our lives will go now and where we will spend eternity. The father in the parable says, **'They will respect my son.'** From the story, it looks as though he gets that wrong. But at the end of days, the time will come when every knee *will* bow and every tongue *will* confess that Jesus Christ is Lord (Phil. 2:10-11). God looks at the Lord Jesus and says, 'They *will* respect my Son.'

19.
The end of the old regime

Please read Mark 12:13-44

In 2009, Bernard Madoff was brought to trial. His name is almost laughably appropriate to what he was found to have done, for he literally 'made off' with billions of dollars of his investors' money. His scheme for ripping people off was not especially original; essentially, it works like this. You persuade a few people to invest their money and promise them a highly impressive rate of return. After a while, they can get their money back, and you pay them everything you have promised. Now the word spreads; very soon many more investors are piling in, eager to hand over their cash because you have proved you will honour your promise. As time goes by, you acquire a huge heap of people's money. The few who want to withdraw, you pay with the money from new investors — until the inevitable day when it all collapses, everyone demands their money back and there is hardly any money to be found. The whole scheme looks so appealing, so attractive, but in fact it's just a giant confidence trick.

Madoff's trial was a sensation; at last the long-hidden truth came to light. Thousands of people had lost money, including many who had seen their life savings wiped out, elderly and invalids who had handed over their entire pension funds and in some cases were now destitute. When it eventually came, Madoff's punishment was severe: a sentence of 150 years in prison, without parole. It was a relief to everyone when the judge declared that his reign of exploitation was at an end. There is really nothing amusing about hypocrisy like this.

In this next section of Mark's Gospel, Jesus concludes his public ministry, and he does so with what amounts to a sentence of death on the old religious regime. He confronts one group after another and declares them spiritually bankrupt. In the parable of the tenants (12:1-12), he has already established his authority to make such judgements; now he condemns the old regime for their hypocrisy and failure. Their days of misleading the people and turning the God-given law into an intolerable burden are at an end. This theme is the thread which ties together the succession of encounters which Jesus now has with his opponents, even though the issues — taxes, death and resurrection, love for God and one's neighbour, and so on — at first appear so different.

God or Caesar?

The shock of the parliamentary expenses scandal which struck recently in the UK continues to reverberate. It ended the careers of several ministers and dozens of other members of parliament, as well as the Speaker of the Commons himself. We discovered that a good-quality Stockholm duck house will cost you £1,645, not to mention what it costs to roll paddocks, clean out swimming pools and install chandeliers — all items which MPs had claimed as legitimate expenses. The expenses scandal was certainly a shock. Its main impact on our national life has been to make people think even worse of politicians. It has made it very hard for politicians to speak with any authority on issues of morality and integrity. All in all, we have become a more cynical people. We might be surprised to find that the Bible has something to say about this subject; but the New Testament was written in a world that knew all about corruption. The whole issue of paying taxes, and who you were paying them to, was far more edgy in those days than it is today. It was an explosive question, a question potentially of life and death, and that makes the incident recorded in verses 13-17 all the more significant. This story about paying taxes leads up to one of Jesus' best-known sayings, but it's also one of the most misunderstood.

As we begin, the top-level delegation from 11:27 have abandoned the attack and retreated. But they are not willing to leave it at that. In verse 13 we find them launching another attack, and the group the leaders now dispatch is an unusual combination. The **'Pharisees'** we know well by now. They are the great purists of the Jewish religion. For them, national salvation lies in a scrupulous observance of the law of Moses. Just to be helpful, they have added hundreds of extra rules and regulations around and on top of the law, in theory to make sure that no one breaks the law by mistake, but in practice making obedience an unbearable burden. The **'Herodians'** are much more obscure, and outside the New Testament they hardly get a mention. All we can gather is that they are some kind of political pressure group; they see Israel's best hope of survival in supporting the dynasty of the Herods. The various Herods may be a dodgy bunch, but at least, they think, 'if we can keep them between us and the Romans we have a chance of survival'. In fact in Judea, which includes Jerusalem, the Herods are no longer in power and the Romans are ruling directly through governor Pilate, whom the Jews cordially detest. It is an unusual combination of purists and pragmatists, but the authorities clearly see Jesus as such a serious threat by now that they are willing to try anything. Mark tells us explicitly that their aim is to catch Jesus, to trip him up in some unguarded statement.

They approach Jesus among the crowds in the temple and launch their attack with a most remarkable speech (12:14-15). It's obvious that they are simply trying to butter him up. There is a double irony in this speech. The first is that everything they say about Jesus is true! It is precisely his integrity and refusal to be intimidated that is making their lives so difficult — he simply will not be shifted from his mission. The irony is that they are pretending to praise him for what they find so infuriating! The second irony is that the character of Jesus that they accurately describe is so diametrically opposed to their own — especially the Herodians, who seem to have no principles whatsoever. By paying him these compliments, they hope to put Jesus off guard.

The question they ask is a very good one, and very cleverly selected. **'Caesar'**, by the way, is not a personal name; it's a title — emperor. The current Caesar is Tiberius. The repetition in the question makes it more probing. We get the sense that they are insisting on a simple, direct answer this time! In the debate about authority, Jesus asked a question that put his opponents on the spot (11:30). Now, Jesus' opponents are trying the same tactic on him. They are following his example by asking him a question where either answer, in this very public place, could spell suicide.

The danger in the question is that this tax is the Roman poll tax, levied at a flat rate on everyone who owns property. This tax, which has been in force for around twenty-five years, is paid directly to the Roman authorities and is therefore a concrete symbol of the occupation of their land. Every patriotic Jew loathes having to pay it. Beyond that, their attitudes differ. From what we know of the times, the Pharisees resent it as a humiliation, but they pay up. The Herodians will support it because doing so keeps the peace. The Zealots — the extremists who are working themselves up to rise in revolt against Roman rule — refuse point-blank to pay the tax. Among Jesus' supporters from Galilee, some of whom are no doubt within earshot at this moment, there are plenty of Zealots.

It is a *political* trap. Jesus has a choice. He can say it is right to pay, and thus alienate many of his supporters by looking like a collaborator. Or he can say, 'No' — an announcement the authorities will be very interested to hear, and his enemies will make sure they hear it very soon! There is a Roman fortress (the Antonia, on the northern side of the temple) about a hundred yards away as they speak.

Unfortunately for them, Jesus is more than a match for their strategy (12:15). He can see straight through their attempt to catch him off guard. No doubt their hearts sink as not only does Jesus not fall into their trap, but he refuses again to give an instant answer! The **'denarius'** he calls for is a common Roman coin — the only coin acceptable for paying the Roman tax. That Jesus himself doesn't seem to have one in his possession probably reflects his own poverty, but someone rummages around and finds one, and they gather round to look at it (12:16) — a silver coin, with a picture of the Emperor Tiberius on one side. The coin presents him as the son of the god Augustus and the goddess Livia — the Emperor Augustus and Livia his wife were indeed the parents of Tiberius, but the Romans are hailing them as gods and Tiberius is well on the way to godhood himself. The coin gives him the title *Pontifex Maximus*, 'supreme high priest' — all very worrying for any Jew who is committed to worshipping the one, *true* God, Yahweh. Finally Jesus gives his answer (12:17), the short saying that is so familiar. What does it mean? Let's examine the two parts of Jesus' reply here.

1. Giving to Caesar

We need to be clear about what this does *not* mean, for this little sentence has given rise to a lot of confusion. It does not mean, as some have suggested, 'All these coins belong to Caesar, so send them all back to him and let's get rid of this polluted Roman money.' Jesus never makes that kind of openly political statement. Neither does it mean, 'Get rid of the *authority* that *all* money represents and let's create a society without authority; let's have some kind of anarchy.' Occasionally you do find Christians who hold views of that type, but in fact there is no support for anarchy, Christian or otherwise, in the New Testament, and anyone who thinks anarchy is a good idea needs to go and live in Somalia or some similarly chaotic place for a year! Nor does Jesus mean that there are some things which belong to God and other things which belong to this world, as though not everything belongs to God, as though there are some things which are 'sacred' — God's special stuff — and some things which are 'secular' — *not* God's special stuff. No, the truth is that *everything* belongs to God. As Abraham Kuyper, the great Dutch theologian and politician, put it, 'There is not one inch of human existence about which Jesus Christ does not cry, "That is mine."' That is a beautiful summary of what the Bible teaches. So 'giving to Caesar', for a Christian, has to be part of 'giving to God'.

When Jesus talks of 'giving to Caesar', he is doing something very significant, if his hearers can understand it. He is telling them that he *hasn't* come to do what his supporters want him to do, to put the clock back to the glory days of the kings of Israel. He is not going to re-create an earthly theocracy, where God is the government, as in old Israel. Jesus is saying that the human government, even bad government, has a claim on them. Yes, the Roman government is hated and corrupt; yes, it gained its power through military might — but, for all that's wrong with them, they have a claim. So give to Caesar what is Caesar's. The simple answer to the question is, 'Yes. You should pay the tax.'

In saying this, Jesus lays the foundation for all subsequent New Testament teaching about how his people should relate to the state, especially in Romans 13:1-7. For us, rather obviously, this means we should pay our taxes, faithfully, fully and on time; we certainly should not try to dodge them. There have been times when people have refused to pay their taxes, or part of their taxes, for conscientious reasons; that has included some Christians. Often people have taken that stand with very clear and courageous motives. Some wanted to withhold their taxes over the 2003 Iraq war, for example. They said, 'This war is not to be waged in my name, and I will not contribute to it in any way.' I applaud their sincerity. But I have to say that Scripture gives very little support to this kind of idea. The New Testament gives little support to *any* form of civil disobedience by Christians, even in a rather passive sense such as non-payment of taxes. That doesn't mean that Christians should not protest or take action against evil and injustice, but it does mean that in most circumstances we should stay within the law — unless and until the law forbids us directly to do what God has commanded.

We should also recognize that, at least in Western countries today, we are far better off than the Jews of Jesus' day. How much of their taxes would go to pay for schools and hospitals, to pay for teachers, nurses and doctors? In case you are wondering, the answer is: none at all! Nearly all the taxes they paid, leaving aside the amounts siphoned off by corrupt officials like Zacchaeus (Luke 19:1-10), would go to pay for the armies of occupation, or the lifestyles of the provincial authorities, or to bribe the mob in Rome so that they wouldn't overthrow the government. But Jesus still tells them to pay! In fact, in this passage, Jesus is telling the Jews to pay taxes to the occupying authority which is about to crucify him!

That leads on to a more general point. It may shock us to say it, but we should be grateful for our government! In the UK, for example, we may feel cynical about the expenses scandal, but in how many countries in the world today would that abuse ever have come to light? As for ancient Rome, it's hard to imagine Pontius Pilate, or the Emperor Tiberius, even writing an expenses claim, let alone allowing the national press to quibble over a few million denarii here or there! If we have the privilege and blessing of living in a country where it still is a scandal, where it does make people resign, we should be grateful! We have great privileges that were denied to the early church and that are denied to most of our brothers and sisters in the world today — to live in a society where we can engage with the process of government and where we can make a difference. We must use these free-doms while we still have them — to argue our corner, to call for justice, to give praise where praise is due. Yes, our true citizenship is in heaven (Phil. 3:20), but as Christians we are also called to be good citizens here — above all, for the sake of the gospel. That is our priority. Let's not be cynical. Give to Caesar what is Caesar's.

2. Giving to God

We have already seen that Jesus is not dividing the world into two realms here — one that belongs to God and one that does not. It all belongs to God. 'Giving to Caesar' is subor-dinate to 'giving to God'. By putting it like this, Jesus is again making a revolutionary point. He is saying that earthly rulers can't claim unlimited power. That may seem obvious today, for those of us who have grown up in a democracy and have known no other way, but in those days — and in some places today — it is revolutionary! Tiberius has no right to make these claims on his coins. There is a higher authority before whom the world's biggest dictators, the greatest autocrats, must learn to bow. Even they will one day bow the knee to God and to his Son Jesus Christ. Far better for them to do it soon! And our own governments likewise are accountable to God for every step they take.

But when Jesus says, '**Give ... to God what is God's,**' in this company, it has a very pointed meaning. This is the sting in the tail; this is why his answer can't just be picked up and turned against him. Once again, he has turned the tables on his opponents. In chapter 11 we saw how Jesus cursed the fig tree. He went looking for fruit, but he found nothing but leaves. The tree put on a good show but produced nothing of use. The meaning is that the nation has not given to God what is rightfully his. In chapter 12 Jesus told the parable of the tenants and the vineyard. The owner sends his servants to collect the fruit, but nothing is forthcoming. The meaning is that the nation's *leaders* have not given to God what is rightfully his. Now Jesus says it right out and in public: 'Give to God what is God's.' It's like a final thrust to the parable of the tenants. Jesus is saying, 'It's all very well playing games with me about paying tax or not paying tax. But this is what you people have missed. You haven't given God what he wants from you.' That is the worst sentence God can declare over anyone. This is judgement. This is fatal. No wonder they are '**amazed**'. Here once more there is an opportunity to respond. Here once more, they are face to face with the one who will be their Saviour, yet all they are doing is looking for evidence that will kill him. If only they believed their own speech! Yes, Jesus truly is the man of integrity, teaching God's way in accordance with the truth. But to them it means nothing. The same message comes to us: 'Give to God what is God's.' What is God's, what belongs to God, is everything. He claims every inch of this

earth for his own, and he claims us, all that we have, and all
that we are.

Near or far?

In verses 18-34, Jesus speaks of the certainty we have as his
people. He speaks of the relationship we have with God: the
Lord's unbreakable commitment to us and our wholehearted
response to the Lord. He shows us that we have a solid and
certain hope that goes beyond death, because we have a God
who is unshakeably faithful and true. All this arises out of
yet more questioning, directed to Jesus first by the Sadducees
and then by a teacher of the law — one man who is near to
the kingdom, Jesus says, and a group who are far outside it.

First, in verse 18, come *the Sadducees*. Unlike some of
the other delegations, they don't come as part of a combined
plan of attack, and that's not surprising, because the Sadducees are fierce opponents of the Pharisees and the Jewish
mainstream. Our knowledge of the Sadducees is limited.
Everything we know comes from their opponents and,
because they were so closely associated with the temple, they
more or less disappeared when it was destroyed in AD 70.
We do know they are stricter than the Pharisees in their
interpretation of the law. They are very keen on preserving
the life of the temple and keeping the status quo, even if that
means collaborating with the Romans. They are theologically conservative in the sense that they reject what they see
as later or new-fangled ideas: they don't like the extra
traditions which the Pharisees have added to the law and,
crucially, they reject the resurrection. So in this story they
are taking advantage of the atmosphere of controversy
around Jesus to challenge him on this thorny issue of their
own.

To do this, they invent a very silly story. It's based on a law which you can find in Deuteronomy 25:5-10, which said that if a man dies without children, his brother must marry the widow and have children by her, so that the family line is carried on. The reason for the law is that in old Israel — an agricultural, land-based society — ownership of the land was vital and family lines had to be preserved. But the Sadducees see their chance to produce a knock-down proof that the resurrection is a daft idea (12:19-23). **'Seven'** is a good number for making the story sound proverbial and serious — which it isn't! In turn, each brother marries the same woman but dies without any children being born. So, last of all, this much-married lady arrives in heaven, and there are all seven husbands — what does she do?

Jesus, frankly, is not impressed by their argument. In his reply — and this time it's a very straight reply! — he begins and ends by telling them they are totally misguided. But it's Jesus' robust response to the Sadducees that encourages the next questioner to join the fray (12:28). Most of the teachers of the law, or scribes, are Pharisees; Matthew's parallel account confirms that this man is one of them (Matt. 22:34-40). We could have worked that out, because Mark tells us here that he approves of Jesus' answer to the Sadducees. The Pharisees believe in the resurrection; by this time, most Jews do. We know of a prayer that was routinely used at burials: 'God will cause you to arise. Blessed be he who keeps his word and raises the dead.' Now one of them comes up with a question of his own.

Again, the question is based on the law of Moses, but this time the questioner does not come across as a cynic. This man is sincere. He wants to know which of all God's commandments is the most important. It's a popular debating point, and it will be interesting to see what kind of answer Jesus produces. Jesus gives a very clear answer (12:29-31). Yes, there *is* one command that dominates all the others. It encapsulates the first half of the Ten Commandments (12:29-30). Jesus quotes directly from Deuteronomy 6:4-5. He quotes what is called the Shema, after its first word in Hebrew, **'Hear'**. It's used morning and evening every day by pious Jews as a prayer and a confession of faith. The commandment which takes second place is found in Leviticus: **'Love your neighbour as yourself'**, summing up the second half of the Ten Commandments (12:31). Love for God, love for your fellow man — that's what matters, Jesus says. His questioner, the teacher, agrees (12:32-33). **'Well said,'** he responds. This time Jesus does *not* dismiss him as mistaken. He sees that the man has tuned in to what he has told him: he has **'answered wisely'** (12:34). In fact, he says, **'You are not far from the kingdom of God.'**

We might think this man would feel flattered — but that's because we are so used to thinking that Jesus is great and the Pharisees are villains. But this teacher of the law is like a university professor; he is a career expert based in the nation's highest seat of learning, and to him Jesus is something like a promising student from some northern backwater. To him, this is Cambridge professor addressing rustic yokel! So how does the professor feel when the student replies, 'Not bad. That's quite a promising answer'? The teacher thinks he has just marked Jesus' exam paper, but in truth, it's the other way round! Jesus has put this man squarely in his place. That is why no one dares to ask him any more questions. Jesus has seen off the high priests, the elders, the Sadducees and the Pharisees; none of them can lay a finger on him. From now on, *he* asks the questions!

So much for the hostile Sadducees — *far* from the kingdom — and the friendly Pharisee — *near* to the kingdom. Through these two encounters, if we look again more closely, we shall see that Jesus has shown us what knowing God is all about. Beyond and above the questioning and banter, the manoeuvring and debating, this is what it means to be in a relationship with the living God. The encounter with the Sadducees shows us one side of the picture; the encounter with the teacher shows us the other.

First, we see God's side: *an unbreakable commitment.* Notice how Jesus responds to the Sadducees in verses 24-27. In verse 24 he tells them, 'You don't know what God is able to do, and you don't know what God has said he will do.' Now he deals with the issue of marriage, although it is not really the main point. In general, the Jews, if they believe in the resurrection, assume that human relationships will be picked up in the new world exactly where we left off in this world. Jesus says, 'That's not how it is' — which means that the Sadducees' silly story is exactly that. There will be no marriage in the new world, and Jesus clearly is talking about the new heavens and new earth, when we have resurrection bodies. When he says we shall be like the angels (12:25), don't take that too far: Jesus simply means that just as angels don't have marriages, neither will we. Probably he is hinting at the fact that the Sadducees don't have much of a belief in angels either (see Acts 23:8).

The way that we react to that news may depend on whether we have been blissfully married for fifty years, or have a less than happy marriage, or are single, but all such reactions miss the point. In fact, if there were marriages in the new world, they would all be perfect, like everything else there! The point is that we shall be in a better relationship than any marriage, even the best imaginable, because we will be in a relationship with Christ that surpasses anything we can begin to grasp. Hear the marriage song of heaven in Revelation 19:6-9. If we belong to him, that song is for us.

However, for this passage, that is not the main issue! The main issue is the resurrection. Look again at verses 26-27. I have often puzzled over this saying; maybe you have too. How does this reference to Abraham, Isaac and Jacob prove

anything about the resurrection? They hadn't been resur-
rected, had they? Most commentators fail to come up with
any satisfactory explanation — or at least, they don't convince me! Usually they say one of two things. Either Jesus is
using some kind of strange, rabbinic argumentation that
doesn't really work for us, or else he is forced to use a text
from Moses, even though it doesn't really prove the resurrection, because this is the only part of the Old Testament that
the Sadducees accept. There are much clearer texts elsewhere in the Old Testament, it is said, but Jesus doesn't use
them because the Sadducees won't believe them. In fact,
there is no good evidence for the idea that the Sadducees
accepted only the Pentateuch, the five books of Moses
(though they did accord it higher status than the other
books). It probably started with some confusion with the
Samaritans, who did accept only the Pentateuch. So to find
the real reason that Jesus refers to these words, and the
glorious truth they reveal, let's go to the place Jesus is
quoting from.

The story comes from Exodus 3 — Moses at the burning
bush. Out in the desert, the Lord summons Moses from out
of the fire. Moses approaches and the Lord speaks (Exod.
3:5-6). Now read the two verses which follow. The context is
about God remembering his promises to his people and
coming to deliver them from their desperate predicament as
slaves in Egypt. In that setting, God introduces himself as the
God of the patriarchs — Abraham, Isaac and Jacob. God is
saying, 'Just as I was the rescuer and protector of your
ancestors, so I will be your rescuer and protector here and
now.' God made a covenant with those men of old. He gave
them promises. He looked after them year after year, and he
will do just the same for Moses. In every trial, in every
struggle, God will be there. But how much is that promise
really worth? After all, the trials of this life are only a faint
shadow of the greatest trial, the greatest enemy of all —

death itself. What kind of God would he be, if when we arrived at this one supreme trial, he said, 'Sorry, I can't help you here'? He would be **'the God of the dead'**! He would be a God who broke his promise to be faithful to his people. When God says, **'I am the God of Abraham, the God of Isaac, and the God of Jacob'**, it has to mean, 'I was faithful to them all the way through, in life and in death. They are not just ancient history or honoured memory to me; their story goes on. Moses, I will be the same for you, in life and in death.' This is the Lord's certain promise of resurrection. Today, as he is our God too, he will be the same for us, in life and in death — through the trials of this life and through the greatest trial of all which lies at life's end. There is a resurrection; there is a hope — because our God is faithful, because he does *not* drop us at the toughest times. **'He is not the God of the dead, but of the living.'** The Sadducees don't grasp this. Like some of our own opponents today, their minds simply cannot embrace a God as great as ours. But our God has made an unbreakable commitment to his children — unbreakable by anything in life and unbreakable by death. He will take us through, and one day will come our resurrection to new life in a new and perfect world.

Now to our side of the relationship: *a wholehearted response.* Look again at how Jesus answers the teacher of the law in verses 29-31. Many people say they love God, but they don't all mean the same thing. The key point to notice here is that our love for God springs from who this God is. Jesus begins with a statement about him: even before the command to love, there is a call to understand. **'The Lord is one.'** That also means that God is *unique.* He is the only God. We are not in a position, as some religions claim, where we can pick our favourite god and worship that one. No, there is *one* God with almighty power in this universe, only one who holds sway, who is sovereign, who has created us, and to whom we must answer.

This God has made the first move. The Lord is **'our God'**, **'your God'** (12:29,30). Back in the days of Israel's desert wanderings, when these words were first spoken, Israel was already God's own people because he had called them to himself, brought them into relationship and declared his unbreakable commitment to them. That grace came first; that was how he became '*your* God'. You see how much of this is about God and what he has done, and how little is about us. In response to such a great and unique God, in response to his first move reaching out to us, this is what our love for him must look like. It's an extreme love, whole-hearted, single-minded, full-strength.

Of course love is a feeling, but the love which God calls for is vastly more. It pulls and draws on every fibre of our being. Nothing less is enough for such a God. It's a love that transforms our *attitudes*, because we want to please him and be like him. Loving God means *not* loving money, not pursuing a comfortable life just because it seems the easy thing to do. It's a love that changes our *decisions*, because we are determined that our lives will count for his glory. Our life choices, our career choices, our relationship and marriage choices, will be made deliberately for the love of God, as we delight in him for all that he is. It's a love that takes us into places that we would never otherwise go — for God's glory and for the love of our neighbour. A love like this, so strong and uncompromising, can't come from us. It can be in us only if God himself has put it here in the first place!

This teacher of the law seems to have all the right answers, even to knowing that these commands to love matter more than the sacrifices that God has told his people to perform (12:33). The prophets knew that, but even so it takes some saying when you are standing within earshot of the great altar of sacrifice — that love for God and man matters more than what is going on just over there. But still Jesus will only say, **'You are not far from the kingdom of God.'**

He is still not *in* it. Why? It is because there is only one way in to the kingdom of God. The only way in to the kingdom is knowing Jesus himself. This teacher of the law has a lot of right answers, but so far he still does not have Jesus. Here is a warning to us. Getting in to the kingdom means far more than knowing the right answers. You may have been brought up in church and be first with all the answers. But even then, you may only be 'not far' from the kingdom. 'Not far' is still on the outside. Are you near? Are you far? Or have you come inside?

Reality or hypocrisy?

In the final section of the chapter (12:35-44), Jesus takes direct aim at the Bernard Madoffs of the spiritual realm. He shows us the difference between the fakes and the genuine article. This passage gives us the very end of Jesus' public ministry, plus a follow-up session with his disciples. Then he will leave the temple for the last time.

The setting is still the temple courts. Now Jesus goes onto the offensive, posing a difficult question which is aimed at the teachers of the law (12:35). From what we know, these teachers are held in high honour. People rise to their feet as they pass by. In the synagogue a special seat is reserved for them, in full view of the congregation. They favour long white robes which mark them out from the colours that the ordinary people wear. Everything about them breathes respectability, seriousness, gravitas. Even so, there is a hint that not everyone takes the scribes as seriously as they take themselves. When Jesus throws out his question, which no one is willing to pick up and answer, we find in verse 37 that the crowds are quite happy to see these experts being given a hard time, and Jesus has just proved he can run rings round them. Meanwhile, receiving no answer to his question, Jesus now proceeds to lay into these scribes (12:38-40). He is saying that these people are not all they seem. Behind the fine façade there is a very ugly reality. At the end of it all, they are going to be judged. In Mark's Gospel, significantly, that warning of judgement is the *very last* public statement that Jesus makes.

The final part of this story takes place in a slightly different location. Jesus moves on from the Court of the Gentiles, the outermost courtyard of the temple compound, to the next courtyard further in, the Court of Women. Any Jew can go this far, but no Gentile, if he values his life, is permitted to enter. It's here in the Court of Women that the offering boxes are placed, fixed to the walls, thirteen of them in all, with trumpet-shaped funnels into which you throw your money. If you give a lot, it will make a nice loud clatter as it falls into the box. Here Jesus sits and watches what happens (12:41-42). He sees plenty of people who are obviously well off, walking by and throwing in their contributions — impressively large amounts, in some cases. But then someone else appears: a poor widow — her poverty at least will be obvious from her dress — and her contribution to temple funds makes no impressive sound. A barely audible clink is all that ensues as she puts in two tiny coins. The coin is the *lepton* — one of the smallest copper coins in existence, each worth less than one-hundredth of the denarius mentioned in verse 15. Mark tells his readers that together these coins are worth a *quadrans*; that may not mean much to us, but it does confirm that he is almost certainly writing for people in Rome, because the *quadrans* is a Roman coin that is only used in the *western* Empire, and not in places like Palestine.[1] By what he says to his disciples in verses 43-44, Jesus tells us that this woman is the genuine article.

What does this story show us about reality and hypocrisy? Let's start with Jesus. The first truth this passage shows us is that *Jesus is the ultimate reality*. This takes us into verses

35-37 and Jesus' tricky question. The Jews and their teachers understand that God is going to send a Messiah, a Christ — a specially designated leader who will rescue his people and reign over them as king. He will be a descendant in direct line from the great King David. That is the great national hope and, whichever of the various parties they belong to, and even though they won't all see it in the same way, it's a hope that all the Jews share. It's a hope that springs directly from the pages of the Old Testament, for example in Jeremiah 23:5-6 and Isaiah 9:6-7. Jesus' question is this: 'How can the teachers say that this Christ is going to be David's descendant when David himself describes him as his "Lord"?' The reference is to Psalm 110, written by David, inspired by the Holy Spirit of God and understood by everyone to be talking about the coming Messiah-King. Let's clarify the quotation. In English the first line sounds confusing, but in the original Hebrew it was crystal clear. The first **'Lord'** is *Yahweh*, the unique name for God himself. That's why in Psalm 110 itself the English translations put it in capital letters. The second 'Lord', **'my Lord'**, is *adonay*, which can refer to God but doesn't always. It means someone of superior status, someone higher than you. So, God speaks to 'my Lord' and says, 'Sit in this place of greatest honour and I will deal with your enemies. I will make you king.' So here is the point (12:37): David is calling this coming Messiah 'Lord'; but no one — certainly no one of the greatness and majesty of King David — would call his own descendant 'Lord'. The ancestor is the superior one. So, as we would say today, 'What's that all about, then?'

No one knows. No one can answer, because what Jesus has just shown them is that the coming Christ has to be more than merely man. He has proved it from a psalm they *know* is about the Messiah. He can't just be a human king, because he is David's 'Lord'. They can't answer the question, but we can. We know what this means: what Jesus at this point is only hinting at — that he himself is the Christ, that, yes, he is the Son of David, and that he is far more than mere man. That is why, speaking by the Holy Spirit, David looks ahead and calls Jesus Christ 'my Lord'. That is why Psalm 110 becomes the New Testament's favourite Old Testament Scripture, quoted more times than any other — because here we see the glory and majesty of Jesus revealed ahead of time. As Psalm 110 goes on to say, he will judge nations. The ends of the earth will acknowledge this Christ; they will *all* acknowledge him as Lord and King and God, and they will meet him as their Judge. The Old Testament contains the seeds of all these great truths; in the New, the seeds spring to life in Christ as he is revealed as the final, supreme and glorious revelation of God to humanity. This is what gives him the right to judge. In fact this is the final answer to the question in 11:28 about his authority. In a sense, he has been answering that question ever since. Jesus is the ultimate reality, and this is what gives him the right to say what he says next.

Secondly, then, *Jesus condemns the fakes* (12:38-40). Not every teacher of the law is necessarily like this. Presumably the one we met in verse 28 was not; but as a group, this is what they look like. They are fakes. Their lives are one big lie. Jesus gives four hallmarks of hypocrisy. The first is *an obsession with appearance*. They are proud of their flowing robes which mark them out for all to see. Everything Jesus describes in verses 38-39 takes place in public, where every-one can observe. They are obsessed with looking right and keeping up appearances! The second hallmark of hypocrisy is *a passion for status*. Those greetings in public places will be made with titles of honour: they relish being addressed as 'Rabbi', 'Master teacher'. They always have a close eye on the seating plan and that special place that is rightfully theirs. Being first on the guest list of the rich and famous is what matters. Hallmark number three is *a false spirituality*. They can pray long and impressive prayers. Jesus is not saying there is anything wrong with long prayers; what he condemns is that they do it all for show. It's all false. They do it all to conceal what they are really up to, because hallmark number four is this: *a ruthless greed.* **'They devour widows' houses.'** The scribes are not allowed to make money from their activities; they are supported by people's giving. In theory, they might be very poor, but from what Jesus says, not many of them are. To look after a scribe is felt to be a very worthy activity. So the temptation is there for the scribes relentlessly to sponge on people's hospitality. There is a widow, left with some property and a few savings. She wants to do what is right, so she invites a scribe round for dinner from time to time. Before she knows what has happened, he has done a Madoff and taken her for all she has got. All this when widows are singled out in the law as people who need special attention and care!

Behind this respectable veneer, says Jesus, this apparent spirituality, this swanning around in fine clothes, this honour and distinction — behind all this, there is no reality: no heart for God, no love for people, not even any true reverence for his Word which they make so much of. It's one big lie, and Jesus condemns them (12:40). As we have seen, Jesus has every right to say that. He is the Judge.

Now it's at this point that the spotlight turns on us. You may say, 'I don't see much of this going on in my church. I don't see too many people sitting in special seats or showing off their long robes!' Maybe not, but hypocrisy takes many forms. The truth is that many people have been put off the Christian faith, prevented even from coming to church, by the nauseating hypocrisy they find inside. Perhaps you yourself have been disgusted by the yawning gap between what some Christians say and the way that they live. If you really believe that there is none of this hypocrisy in your own life, then you have my permission to close the book now.

Otherwise, come with me and let's revisit what Jesus says here.

An obsession with appearance? That's you, if you care as much about how *people* see you as about how *the Lord* does. It may be your clothes — it may actually be that you go to church on Sunday to be looked at — but more likely it's about keeping up a good front, letting everyone think you are what you are not. It doesn't take flowing white robes to do that. *A passion for status?* Here is a challenge for leaders, especially anyone who gets a buzz from being admired, from being well known, either within the church or beyond. There are too many Christian leaders who clearly care more about status than they do about service. *A false spirituality?* How easy it is to pretend that we are doing well when in fact our spiritual life is in tatters, we rarely open the Bible and we never pray outside church services! We disguise our emptiness with spiritual language, just as a Madoff concealed his empty scheme with high-flown financial jargon. We avoid the challenge that might come if people knew what we were really like. And *a ruthless greed?* Perhaps we are not exploiting the poor as obviously as that — or at least, not the ones we will ever meet. But there are Christians who really care only about money, about when they can move into a bigger house, or buy a newer and shinier car — as if it mattered — and if that means their family suffers, or they have no time to serve God, so be it. Jesus says that fakes will be judged. Let these words search our hearts.

Finally in this story, *Jesus approves the genuine.* Remember what happens in verses 41-42. How would the world judge this scene? In business, what counts for most? A big order or a small order? A large income or a small income? It doesn't need an answer. In church, surely a big gift must automatically be worth more. Yet that is not what Jesus says (12:43-44). Whatever might be true in the world at large, says Jesus, in the eyes of God this widow with her few pennies has given more than all the big guys. They had plenty to give, and they gave some of it. But she gave her everything — all she had. Literally, she gave out of her lack. This woman is the genuine article. Clearly, there is a challenge for us here too. If you give sacrificially to the Lord's work, to the point where it makes a difference to your lifestyle, Jesus sees it. Just as he sat and watched the people's giving on that day in the temple, so he sees each of us today. As for those who don't give, God's Word shows us clearly that giving money to the Lord's work is a basic part of following Jesus. Not giving 'what you can afford' — that's what these wealthy people were doing; not giving from what's left over at the end of the month. It's an adventure of faith to see what God will do when you give him full access to your money — when your wallet finally gets converted! Serious giving is a blessing to the giver, just as much as the receiver, and you will never be the loser.

There is an even deeper challenge here also. This woman, this genuine, wholehearted lover of God, didn't give a proportion. She gave everything. If she could, she would have squeezed herself into the collection box. That's what this story really calls us to do. Jesus calls his disciples to an all-or-nothing faith, to trust the Lord for everything, without exception.

20.
The final crisis

Please read Mark 13:1-37

Not long ago I had the exciting experience of a trip to Wembley Stadium for the Championship football play-off final. It was a great day out, watching Bristol City playing for the privilege of entering the Premier League. Even though we lost, it was a good day, because for the first time I saw the new stadium. It's a truly amazing venue. You behold it for the first time as you emerge from the Underground station. You reach the top of the steps and look out, and you simply stop and stare. In fact, so many people stop and stare at that point that the police are stationed there specially to keep you moving! Already you can see the famous arch towering over the skyline and the great, multi-coloured crowds streaming up Wembley Way and up the ramps beyond. And now you follow them, processing up to the iconic statue of Bobby Moore and in through the doors in the glass curtain walls. Up you climb, up to the very top, until at last you emerge inside the gigantic, unbroken oval of the stadium itself, rapidly filling up with the cheering multitudes, 90,000 strong. Wembley Stadium is a stunning building — and so it should be, given what it cost! But if someone had told me that day that, shortly, the entire edifice would be totally demolished, violently razed to the ground so that not a trace remained, I would have been shocked. I would have been appalled. I would have supposed that some desperate crisis must be in store to make that happen, that London itself must be in for some devastating fate.

If you can imagine that, then perhaps you can grasp, just a little, how Jesus' friends feel at the start of Mark 13. It is not a state-of-the-art football stadium they are worried about, but a building far more impressive and whose meaning is a thousand times greater. Along with Jesus, they are just leaving the temple in Jerusalem, the beating heart of the Jewish religion. To them the temple is like Wembley Stadium, the Houses of Parliament and Westminster Abbey all rolled into one — and more besides. This place is the heart of their nation. Now Jesus calmly tells his horrified disciples that all this is to be obliterated, razed to the ground. In what follows, Jesus explains to his people what the years ahead will be like. What lies in store for the world is not just a single disaster, but years of crisis extending all the way through to the day when he returns to this earth. That means this is a message for us as well. For Christians, every time is a time of crisis. The question Jesus answers for us here is how we are to live through the crisis. The message of Mark 13 is serious and downbeat, reminding us forcibly that following Jesus is not a game or a hobby, but a matter of life and death.

Let's see how this chapter fits in to Mark's Gospel. Chapter 12 ended with a warning against the hypocrisy of the religious leadership. Overall, chapters 11 and 12 spell out the judgement of the King on the old regime — the temple worship and all that it stands for. That is why chapter 13 fits in here so well. Jesus now moves beyond declaring judgement on the temple and the old order: here we find him explaining exactly how that judgement will fall. This chapter forms a bridge between Jesus' public ministry, which has just concluded, and his passion and death, which bring in the new age. But we also have to notice how different this chapter is from the rest of Mark. The rest of this Gospel is basically a very simple story. It's not difficult to understand what is going on. This chapter is different! At times it seems like a little bit of Revelation dropped into the middle of a Gospel — in fact it is often known as the 'Little Apocalypse'. Parts of it have aroused a good deal of controversy; it's not entirely straightforward!

Jesus and the Twelve are leaving the temple and, as they look around, they are struck once more by the magnificence of the buildings (13:1). We know from the eyewitness accounts that this is a stunning building. It dominates the whole city; it's covered with marble and gold; it's one of the wonders of the world. Herod the Great used the top Roman engineers; archaeologists today have confirmed the quality of Herodian building, wherever it's found. From Josephus we know that the standard size of the stones in the temple walls was over ten metres (over thirty-two feet) long and five metres (over sixteen feet) wide. The Jews may detest the Herods, but they are fiercely proud of their temple. This is an impressive building — and now one of the disciples invites Jesus to join him in admiration.

Jesus' reply is hardly encouraging (13:2). Not surprisingly, the disciples are speechless. Not until they reach the slopes of the Mount of Olives, on their way out of town for the night, do four of them pluck up the courage to ask Jesus what on earth he is talking about. As they sit there, just across the Kidron Valley from the city, they have a breathtaking view of the temple and, as the sun sets, glinting off its towers and pinnacles, they put their question (13:3-4). In what follows, we need to understand that for the disciples, if the temple is destroyed in this way, that can only mean that their whole nation is destroyed; and if their nation is destroyed, that must mean that God is coming in judgement, with what the prophets called 'the Day of the Lord', the end of the age. Their question embraces not just a building, but the fate of the whole world. By now they have learned to take Jesus' words very seriously. They no longer have any doubt that if Jesus says it, it will happen.

Jesus' reply occupies the rest of the chapter. What he says is of shattering importance, not only for the disciples of those days, but for us, the disciples of today. Jesus is making it clear that this age is indeed going to end, and it will end with his return in glory, and he tells us how to be ready. But in this chapter he describes not one, but two great events that lie in their future. One is the destruction of the temple, of Jerusalem; the other is his own return at the end of the age. To the disciples, those two events must surely coincide, but Jesus tells them they are not the same and must not be confused.

First, in verses 5-13, Jesus warns them what the future looks like for his followers. Then, in verses 14-23, he warns them specifically what will happen when Jerusalem is destroyed and how they must be prepared. Finally, in verses 24-37, he talks about his own glorious return.

Living through the crisis

In verses 5-23 Jesus is saying, 'From now until I return to the earth, it's going to be tough. It will be one extended time of crisis for you, my people. In the middle of that, there will be this great cataclysm when God comes in judgement on this city. But don't jump the gun, because that's not the end.'

We will look first at the judgement on Jerusalem: this is the subject of verses 14-23. This is not the end of the age, but it will be so terrible that, for those involved, it will seem just like it.

We begin with the warning in verse 14. Frankly, this sounds highly mysterious! In fact, Mark is being deliberately

obscure, probably for security reasons — that's why he adds
this phrase, **'let the reader understand'**. The **'abomination
that causes desolation'** is a reference to the prophet Daniel
(specifically Dan. 9:27; 11:31; 12:11), where God warns
Daniel about an invader who will commit an outrage in the
temple, desecrating the sanctuary. That prophecy was fulfilled by a Hitler-like tyrant, an evil madman named Antio-
chus Epiphanes, around 167 BC. He built an altar to the god
Zeus in the temple sanctuary and sacrificed pigs on it. Jesus'
point is that that desecration, that abomination, is going to
happen again, only this time it will be even worse: 'When
you see it happen, then get out of town! Run for the hills.'
Verses 15-23 expand on that warning: Stop for nothing;
don't even go home to get your stuff. It will be worse still for
pregnant or nursing mothers. It will be worse if it's winter
because the roads will be impassable: pray it doesn't happen
then! Terrible times are coming — so bad that if they continued for very long, death would come to everyone in the land.
But even in those terrible times, Jesus says, God is still in
control (13:20). He will make sure that he protects his
people. The church will survive the disaster. 'There will be
people out to distract you, false leaders trying to lead you
astray' (13:22), 'but don't be put off. Don't lose sight of me
and what I have told you. I have warned you: be ready, be on
guard' (13:23). This is the first great crisis.

History tells us that all this came to pass in the years AD
66 to 70, within forty years of Jesus speaking these words.
The Jews rebelled against Rome. For a while it even looked
as though they might prevail. But then the Romans hit back,
and meanwhile the Jewish factions began to fight one another. The party called the Zealots took over the temple and,
as the Roman legions approached the city, and the threat of
destruction grew nearer and nearer, they permitted all sorts
of outrages within the temple precincts. They allowed
criminals to wander into the Holy of Holies; there was

murder in the temple courts; finally they enthroned a clown as high priest.[1] Perhaps that is the specific event that Jesus refers to in verse 14. We can't be sure. History also tells us that many people saw the disaster that was looming and fled the city while they had the chance. The church in Jerusalem remembered Jesus' warning and fled to the hills, to Pella across the Jordan, and they were kept safe. Meanwhile, the Romans arrived. They laid siege to Jerusalem, and in that siege the most appalling events took place. Hunger stalked the city. There is an account of a mother who killed, roasted and ate her own child. The defenders fought among themselves. Finally, with the temple in flames, the Romans broke into the city. The priests continued the routine of sacrifice until the last possible moment, when the sanctuary was destroyed. The remaining defenders were slaughtered and then, at the command of the new emperor Titus, the magnificent temple was levelled to the ground, never to rise again. The generation that rejected the Lord Jesus was judged. The old regime of priesthood and sacrifice was gone for good, fulfilled in the ultimate sacrifice of Jesus himself. Jesus says, **'I have told you everything ahead of time'** (13:23). His word can be trusted. We have the proof.

There would be this first great, dreadful crisis. Jesus warns them about it, and for us today the fall of Jerusalem lies in the distant past. However, as we look now at verses 5-13, we see that Jesus describes the whole of this age, from his first coming to his second, as a time of great crisis. So how do we live through it?

First, we live through the crisis by *keeping our focus* (13:5-8). The disciples have just asked Jesus, 'When is it going to happen, and what will it look like?' But Jesus is not concerned, as so many people are today, with giving calendar dates or drawing up charts of the last days. Jesus is not interested in satisfying our curiosity. He is interested in preparing us to face the days we live in. The days ahead will be difficult; it will be easy for us to get distracted. There will be wars: if you are not in the middle of one you will certainly hear about them in other places. There will be conflicts between one nation and another and famines and earth-quakes. It's very painful, but it's normal. The message is: there is no golden age just round the corner. At times in history — such as the opening of the twentieth century — people in the West, including many Christians, foolishly believed there would be. Today we ought to know better. It's a false hope. Until Christ returns, one disaster, one difficulty, will succeed another.

Jesus says, 'This will be a time of false religious hopes as well' (13:6). 'People will appear making all kinds of claims to be able to save the world; they will claim to do what only I can do.' The point of his words is not to give us information, but to help us to keep our focus. 'Watch out that you are *not* deceived!' With all the turmoil around you in the world, with all the claims of false religion, as powerful as it may seem — don't take your eye off the ball. Don't be distracted by *anything* from following Christ. In particular, says Jesus in verses 7-8, don't imagine that the end of the world has arrived just because these disasters are happening. These are just the warnings of what lies ahead. Labour pains certainly hurt, and they tell you the birth is coming soon, but labour pains are *not* the birth. You must be faithful to the end.

Secondly, we live through the crisis by *facing suffering* (13:9-13). 'If times are going to be hard for the people of the world in general,' Jesus says, 'it will be even harder for you, my friends. The world will not love you because you follow me, and it will certainly not like the message you bring them *about* me.' Jesus is saying, 'This is going to be normal life for Christians.' Today, around the world, Christians are persecuted on a massive scale, not because they have done anything wrong, but simply because they follow Christ. In every single Muslim majority country in the world today, the people of Jesus are persecuted, and in many other places too. Sometimes that opposition comes from the closest and most painful quarter (13:12) — from your own family, bitter and full of hatred just because of your allegiance to Christ. I have friends who know just what that means. Jesus says, Believer, disciple, the way to live through the crisis is not to keep your head down, nor to stay where it's safe, but to face suffering wherever you are called to go. 'If it comes to it and you are standing in court,' says Jesus in verse 11, 'don't worry because I will be there with you. My Spirit will be with you, and he will give you the words to say, even if the sentence hanging over you is death.' If we are disciples of Jesus, we need to count the cost. Discipleship, according to the Bible, is cross-shaped. Are we ready to face suffering for the Name?

Thirdly, we live through the crisis *by spreading the gospel* (13:9-11 again). When you are dragged in front of the authorities, Jesus says in verse 9, it is not so that you can persuade them to let you off, but as a *witness* to them, that there, in the place of greatest danger, you will still speak of Jesus Christ. Verse 11 paints the same picture: 'The words you need to speak are not to protect yourself, but to honour me.' That is the agenda; that is always our agenda: to point men and women to the Saviour.

Jesus has been speaking these words in part to prevent his people from becoming obsessed about the end of the world and to get us to concentrate on living faithfully while the world goes to rack and ruin. But here in verse 10 he gives one clear and glorious sign of the end. What will bring about the end of the age? Melting ice caps? A giant meteor strike? Nuclear war? No, the end will come when God looks down and sees that his church has finished the task he gave us — to carry the good news of Jesus to the ends of the earth. It must happen! When every last people group has been reached, in some lost valley or in a hidden corner of some vast city, when the name of Jesus has been spoken under every sky, the angels will get moving and the Son of God will return to the earth in glory.

Fourthly and lastly, we live through the crisis *by trusting God's purposes*. Verse 10 shows us God's great purpose for the church — that we will preach his salvation to every corner of the world. We need to be confident that God knows what he is doing. When the work is hard, and we face setbacks, or things don't turn out the way we planned and longed for and we haven't a clue why, we need to trust God's purposes. One day we shall see more than we do now. Whether we will ever understand fully, even when we stand in glory, I don't know. God's understanding will always be infinitely deeper than ours. What is certain is that the questions that trouble us now won't trouble us then; that we will praise him for doing every last thing which he has planned to do; and that it's best to learn to trust his purposes right now!

The closing note of this section in verse 13 is blunt yet comforting. If you belong to Jesus Christ, then his purpose is to bring you home. Standing firm is the proof of true salvation: if you belong to him, this will happen, as Jesus assures the suffering church in Smyrna (Rev. 2:10). And there will be one generation of his people whose faithfulness will culminate in the privilege of seeing and recognizing him as he comes in his glory.

Recognizing the King

If you had been standing on the streets of Manhattan around 8.30 on Tuesday morning, 11 September 2001; if you had heard, seen, felt and smelled the events of that morning, as one by one the aircraft swept in to strike the towers of the World Trade Center, and had witnessed the collapse that followed, you would have known in your heart that the world would never be the same again. Christ's return, which is described here in verses 24-31, will be more than that — an event that will not merely change history, but wind it up for good. It will be visible and unmistakable; like 9/11 it will come as a profound shock; but it is most definitely on its way. While the fall of the Twin Towers could be seen directly from just a few square miles in New York City, God will see to it that the return of his Son, King Jesus, is visible from every corner of the earth. With delight or with horror, every man and woman alive on earth that day will recognize the King. In this passage Jesus teaches his followers about his own return.

First, *Christ's return will be catastrophic* (13:24-25). Throughout this chapter, remember, Jesus is speaking of these two great climactic events, the temple's doom and his own return. The preceding verses are very clearly about the fall of the temple and Jerusalem; verse 23 has rounded that off as Jesus tells his friends that they are now safely fore-warned about what will happen then, and now verse 24 begins a new section. **'In those days'** is an expression the Old Testament often uses to describe the end times, the days of judgement. Verse 26 states explicitly that this is about his own coming. In verses 24-25 we find described the cosmic signs which will immediately precede his return — a prediction which reads very strangely to us. The first point to make is that these verses are worded in Old Testament language. The prophets often spoke about the Day of Judgement, what they called 'the Day of the Lord', in terms like this. In particular there are two references in the prophet Isaiah which we should look at: Isaiah 13:9-10 and Isaiah 34:4. Note how strikingly similar these prophecies sound. The question often asked is this: 'Are we meant to take these pictures literally? Will there really be these terrifying signs in the sky?' It's a good question, and a difficult one, which we can't ignore.

Some very respected commentators say that these prophecies are simply speaking of political upheavals. They are
metaphorical descriptions of the downfall of great nations, so
we shouldn't expect to see any 'signs in the sky' at all. They
point out that in Isaiah these prophecies are applied to
nations like Babylon which were overthrown thousands of
years ago — and the sun certainly didn't stop shining then,
neither did the stars fall! That is undoubtedly true but, in
spite of that, there are good reasons for believing that Jesus
does mean us to expect cosmic signs of his return.

One reason is the close connection with verse 26 where
Jesus speaks of what will be *seen*.

A second reason is that Jesus is probably drawing a
contrast with what he has just said in verse 22 — that at the
time of the great crisis in Jerusalem there will be *false*
Messiahs performing *false* signs and miracles to deceive
people. Now here, in verse 24, he is saying, 'When the *true*
Messiah appears — that is, when I return — there will be
these genuine signs, written in the sky for all to see.' That
contrast doesn't work if they are not visible signs.

A third reason is that the immediate context of those
references in Isaiah does not limit the prophecy in question
to Babylon, Edom, or any other nation. Isaiah has something
grander and more ultimate in mind as well. The Bible does
teach us that the story of the universe is bound up with the
story of mankind. When Adam and Eve fell, when they first
sinned, the impact was not confined to the human race. The
consequences of their sin rippled out throughout the world
and on through the whole of creation: nothing was un-
touched. Romans 8:19-22 teaches us that the whole of
creation is eagerly waiting for the freedom it will gain when
the human race is saved and restored. In view of that, it is not
surprising that when Christ returns to save his people and
judge the world, there should be disturbances on a cosmic
scale to accompany the event.[2] The day will come when God

'will shake not only the earth but also the heavens' (Heb. 12:26). When Christ returns in glory, the impact will be so great that even the sun, moon and stars will be affected. We don't know exactly how that will happen and we should not get hung up on this issue. We should remember that the Bible frequently uses the 'language of appearance'; it is certainly not interested in astronomical precision. What matters is what people on earth will *see* on that day. They will see the light draining from the sky — whether it's day or night when he comes. Darkness will fall. In that moment, they will all realize that something utterly catastrophic is beginning.

These verses are echoed in Revelation 6. The disciple John is one of the group of four sitting there with Jesus under the trees on the Mount of Olives; sixty years or so later the same John is given this vision of what the last days will look like. He has heard it from Jesus; now he sees it played out (Rev. 6:12-14). Now read the next two verses. The Lamb is the Lord Jesus. When King Jesus returns, everyone will know it. Everyone will recognize him — but for many it will be too late.

Secondly, *Christ's return will be majestic* (13:26-27). We know that **'Son of Man'** is one of Jesus' favourite ways of describing himself. On one level it simply means 'a human being'. But on another level it also means something far higher — especially when the Lord Jesus begins to speak of his own coming in glory, as he does here. That is because he is again drawing on Old Testament language, this time from Daniel 7:13-14. He comes **'in clouds'**, or 'with the clouds'; in the Bible that is always a picture that describes the glory and power of God appearing — what is called a theophany. But his Second Coming is not to be a private transaction between him and God the Father. It will be public and open — everyone will see it. When Jesus came to earth the first time, there was a dark, obscure village, a dirty manger and

some scruffy shepherds. There was a baby who grew up to
be a man, a man who walked the dusty streets and hillsides,
who was rejected, who suffered, who ultimately died a
horrible death in apparent defeat. There was no glory then,
no honour, no splendour. How different when he comes
again in **'great power and glory'**! Just as surely as those
planes could be seen in the skies over New York on that day
of disaster, so the coming of the Son of Man will be visible
to all. This is the triumph of the Son of Man; this is the vindication of the suffering Messiah; this is God saying, 'Behold
your King!'

In verse 27, we see that he sends out the angels and
gathers in his people. In the Old Testament, that is what *God*
says he will do (Deut. 30:4). The New Testament doesn't
often say directly that Jesus is God, but it frequently shows
us Jesus doing what only God can do; this is an example.
When Christ returns, he will gather his people together
around him. We will meet him, and we will celebrate —
what a day! Notice what has changed here. Up till now, the
focal point for God's people on earth has been the temple,
which Jesus is looking at as he speaks, but the days of the
temple are over. The gathering point for God's people will
be his Son, King Jesus. The ones who are gathered are the
elect — God's called and chosen people, all those who know
him and love him, from wherever they are, at earth's farthest
bounds, because in Christ we are one people, whatever our
race and background. Again this verse confronts us with a
stark reality. Those gathered and saved are his own people,
but those who don't know the Lord Jesus will be gathered
and judged. Christ's return for them will truly be a day of
disaster. On that day, they will recognize the King, but it will
be too late.

Thirdly, *Christ's return will be certain* (13:28-31). This
'lesson from the fig tree' is a simple country saying. In
chapter 11 the fig tree was used as a parable to represent the

nation of Israel; that's not the case here. You can get into all kinds of strange ideas if you try to read that meaning into this folk saying — and people have done that! The meaning here is perfectly simple. In the Middle East, most of the trees are evergreen, but the fig tree is not. In the winter, its branches are bare, and in fact they stay bare until late spring, when the sap starts flowing, the twigs soften and the leaves appear. When the fig tree comes to life, you *know* that it is almost summer. As Jesus speaks, in fact, it is that time of year, just before Passover. He is sitting on the Mount of Olives, well known for its fig trees as well as its olives. Around them there are fig trees bursting into green life again; Jesus says, 'When you see a fig tree like that, you know for sure that summer is just round the corner. So when you see the signs, you know that it's near, right at the door, as it were.'

Again, there is a difficulty to resolve here. Is Jesus still talking about his Second Coming, or has he gone back to the fall of Jerusalem? The difficulty arises from verse 30. The word for **'generation'** nearly always means literally that — the people who are present at any one time in history. Either Jesus is now talking about the fall of Jerusalem — about forty years away — or else he means something different like 'this race' or 'people like you'. This question is very difficult to answer with any certainty. We know that Jesus' main aim in this discourse is to prepare his people for whatever is to come. This whole of this intervening period, remember, is a time of crisis — right through to the Second Coming. Within that time, the fall of Jerusalem is one spectacularly terrible crisis. I think that when Jesus says this in verse 30, he is referring mainly to *that* great crisis, which would happen within one generation. He is answering the disciples' original question (13:4). But at the same time he is warning us that at *every* point, we must recognize the signs of the times — like the leaves coming out on the trees in spring — and understand what they are pointing to. There would very soon be signs that pointed to the Jewish War and the destruction of the temple; they must act on those signs. Later on there would be signs pointing to Christ's return, and *we* must act on those. In any case, the force of this passage for us is clear. All these things will happen; they are sure and inevitable (13:31). The message is that *nothing* in this world is permanent; *nothing* is for ever. Whether we are Christians or not, we must get hold of that vital truth. But Jesus is for ever. His *words* are for ever. They are true, reliable and certain.

Muslims, too, believe that Jesus the Messiah is coming back. They say he will return, announce that Mohammed really *was* the final prophet, destroy all the crosses and live and die an ordinary death as a man. This passage shows us how far wrong those ideas are. When the Lord Jesus comes back, he doesn't come quietly, nor does he point to anyone else. He doesn't speak like a prophet, saying, 'These are words which have been given me to say.' He says, **'My words will never pass away.'** Only God can say that! Jesus does what only God can do. He says he is coming back — and he is. We don't know when, but he is coming.

Preparing for the end

As the Lord Jesus continues to speak of his Second Coming, in the closing verses of Mark 13, the emphasis changes slightly. The main message in verses 32-37 is that we do not know the day he is coming — and for that reason, we must be ready all the time. Jesus is coming back, and we must be ready. This section is about preparing for the end. How do we do that?

Firstly, *we prepare by not guessing the date!* (13:32-33). It's not hard to grasp the basic message here. 'You don't know when I am going to come back,' says Jesus. We must not lose sight of that main thrust. However, there is a well-known difficulty in what Jesus says here — indeed it could be said that Mark 13:32 is one of the most difficult verses in the Bible. Jesus is saying, 'The only person who knows when I am returning is the *Father*. The *Son* does not know.' In other words, Jesus *himself* doesn't know. Now what does that say about Jesus? If Jesus is truly God, as we believe, surely he knows everything? How can he not know something as important as the date of his return? Both Muslims and Jehovah's Witnesses use this verse to claim that Jesus is really something less than God, because he is saying that there is at least one piece of information which he does not possess. Could they be right?

The first point to make is that *this very passage clearly teaches the deity of Christ*. In verse 26, Jesus says that the Son of Man — that is, Christ himself — will come in the clouds with power and glory. That statement, using that language, clearly and unambiguously implies that he is God. 'Coming with the clouds' in the Bible describes the appearance of God himself. Again in verse 31, Jesus declares that *his words* will never pass away. He doesn't say, as a mere prophet would, 'The words of *God* won't pass away,' but, '*My* words won't pass away.' So it is inadmissible to take the very next verse to mean that Jesus is less than fully God.

The way we have to understand verse 32 is to remember that *Jesus Christ is both fully God and fully man*. He has two natures — a divine nature and a human nature — in one person. Look at 4:35-41. They are in the boat, a violent storm blows up and the disciples are panicking. What do we find Jesus doing here? In verse 38 he is fast asleep in the back of the boat. Then in verse 39 he stands up and tells the wind and waves to be quiet — and instantly they do. In his *divine* nature, Jesus Christ is the Lord of creation who silences a storm. In his *human* nature, Jesus is the man who has had a tiring day and falls asleep on a cushion. He is the man who is

God, God who has become man — one person with two natures. It's difficult to understand, yes, but this is the truth the Bible bears witness to.

In his human nature, Jesus had to learn in the same way that we do. The New Testament tells us that he learned as he grew up (Luke 2:52). He learned the things that every child has to learn, and he learned what *suffering* meant (Heb. 5:8, another verse that people struggle with). In his finite human nature, Christ does not have all knowledge — humanity is limited. But in his divine nature, he is omniscient. He knows all things. Here in 13:32, Jesus means that in his human nature he does *not* know the day and hour of his return. In his divine nature, however, he *does*. But, if we can put it this way, he is choosing not to 'access' that knowledge because he wants to emphasize that these matters are for God, and the authority of the Father, and not for men to investigate. By the way, when he says **'Son'** here, it's likely we should understand that to mean 'Son of *Man*', emphasizing his humanity, rather than 'Son of *God*', emphasizing his deity.

However, here is the main point of verses 32-33: if even the angels don't know when Christ is returning — the angels who dwell in the very presence of God, the angels whose understanding is clear and unclouded by sin — there is no way that we can figure it out! If even the Son is content to leave it to the Father, we should be too! We don't know when he is coming back. That ought to be clear enough, but it hasn't deterred some people from making predictions, counting off signs and telling us when the date is going to be — whether that is the Jehovah's Witnesses, or some Christians who tell us with great confidence that such and such a world event is a sure sign of the imminent return of Christ. To pick a few random examples from recent decades: the Six Day War in Israel in 1967, the expansion of the Common Market or European Union in the 1970s and 80s, and the Chernobyl accident of 1986 have all been picked up by end-time enthusiasts as specific, biblically defined signs of the last days. We should be very wary of any such predictions.

Now, we may well suspect that the time of Christ's return is very soon. When we look at what is happening in the world and the various unprecedented crises and disasters, we may well find it impossible to believe that the world can continue on its present course for much longer, and that may well be right. We are to live as though it could happen at any moment — because it might. Even then, we should remember that people have thought that many times before in history; clearly they were wrong. The unmistakable signs of Jesus' coming will appear only just before the end, when it will be too late to prepare. Scripture simply does not give us the information to predict a date. It's not hidden there in code — however long you spend looking, you won't find it. Aren't Jesus words here clear enough? We don't prepare for the end by guessing the date!

Secondly, on the other hand, *we don't prepare for the end by ignoring the fact* (13:34-36). Jesus illustrates his warning about the time with a little parable (13:34). Here is a wealthy householder with a number of servants. He is going away, but at some point he will return. As he leaves, he gives each of his servants a job to do, and he gives the doorkeeper special responsibility to watch out for his return. Clearly, the householder is Jesus himself. That is the picture; verses 35-36 then apply the message directly. Now the servants in this household have a number of options — some better, some worse — but the one thing they must not do is to pretend that the master is never coming back. Verse 35 says you don't know *when* he is coming, but the parable assumes with absolute certainty that he *is*. That message has sounded throughout this chapter (see again 13:7,26-27,32), and now it is heard again in verse 35. It might be evening, midnight, just before first light, or at sunrise — the four watches of the night in Roman thought — but it will come! The most blind,

and frankly the most stupid, response anyone can make to
the news of Christ's return is simply to refuse to believe it.

It isn't surprising if someone who does not believe in
Jesus Christ at all will not accept the fact of his return. But in
these words Jesus demands that we reckon with him. He
demands that we understand that he is not just a figure from
history that we can leave safely in the past, or in the pages of
a book. He calls us to recognize him as the King who is
coming back to claim his throne, and he calls us to listen,
obey and be ready — to prepare for the end. We also have to
say that it is not only non-Christians who live as though
Christ is never coming back. How do our lifestyles show that
we expect the Lord to return at any time? How does it show
up in our priorities, in our ambitions, in the way that we
spend our money? When he returns, and we see his face, we
will leave behind the toys of this life without a second
glance. So why should they mean so much to us now?

Thirdly, *we prepare for the end*, quite simply, *by doing
the job*. Let's revisit the picture in verse 34. In this illustration the householder, the Lord Jesus, gives to each servant
his appointed task, so that they will all be ready for his
return. Who are these servants? This message comes first to
church leaders. The 'doorkeeper' probably refers especially
to pastors and church leaders who have the specific responsibility for guarding God's people who are under their care,
protecting the 'house' from marauders, from anyone who
might break in and cause mayhem — to change the picture,
it's the role of the shepherd with the sheep. That is how
leaders, in particular, prepare for the end. The Lord Jesus has
charged us to do this; it is what he wants to find us doing
whenever he comes back to the house.

Jesus, however, is careful to make sure that his words are
not just for the leaders. As he speaks, he has an audience of
only four, but look at verse 37. This message is for all God's
people. We are all to watch out for Christ's return — the

word used in these closing verses is a strong one (Greek *gregoreo*): it means more than the 'look out' of earlier in the chapter. It means, 'stay alert, keep awake, don't be taken off guard'. The way that we keep watch is to get on with the job he has given us to do, **'each with his assigned task'** (13:34) — whatever that may be, whatever our assigned ministry may be in whatever place he has put us. We should not expect that serving Christ faithfully will be easy. We have seen in this chapter, in verse 10, how Jesus talks about the gospel coming to every nation on earth before he returns. That is exciting, and it is moving, but the gospel for all nations is not just a vision about missionaries or peoples far away. It is a vision to galvanize us in our ministry wherever we are. The Lord Jesus is coming back. We don't know when, and we can't guess the date, but we certainly must not ignore the fact. We must be prepared for the end. The message is urgent: **'What I say to you, I say to everyone: "Watch!"'**

Part VI.
Jesus' passion and vindication (14:1 – 16:8)

21.
The scene is set

Please read Mark 14:1-26

Throughout chapters 11 to 13, since Jesus has arrived in Jerusalem, the tension has been rising. The sense of menace has grown as Jesus' opponents manoeuvre to trap him and as he himself looks ahead to the conflicts and suffering that his people must face. Here in chapter 14, we reach the point where those threats turn to action. The climax is now very near. In this section we combine two stories which set the scene for that climax: in verses 1-11 we are *preparing* for his death, and in verses 12-26 we are *picturing* it.

Preparing for his death

Financial advisers are fond of telling us that we should be very, very careful with our money. They make statements like, 'The market value and surrender value of traded endowments can go up as well as down,' and 'Past performance is not necessarily a guide to future performance.' In the wake of the financial disasters of recent years, that has become a more familiar message than ever. But the message from God's Word is exactly the opposite! The Bible encourages us not to be cautious with our money, but to be reckless.

The woman in the story in verses 1-11 does not calculate. She does not consult a financial adviser! She is joyfully free — and, to the horror of the onlookers, the Lord Jesus praises her.

The first point to notice about this story is that Mark is doing what we have seen before — he is bracketing, or sandwiching, one story inside another. At the beginning and end of the passage (14:1-2,10-11), he tells us about the plot that will lead to Jesus' death. At the beginning, the authorities are *looking* for a way to kill him. At the end, Judas *gives* them a way to kill him. The story in the middle, the filling in the sandwich (14:3-9), explains why Judas finally decides to do that. Understanding this structure explains something which otherwise looks like a mistake. John's Gospel (John 12:1-3) clearly places the story about the woman just before the Triumphal Entry — that is, several days earlier. But Mark is telling her story in flashback to explain why Judas becomes a traitor.

As chapter 14 begins, the Passover and the Feast of Unleavened Bread, which follows straight on from Passover, are just two days away. The chief priests and scribes are now desperate to get their hands on Jesus, but while that might sound easy, they have a problem. The city is crammed with people. Its population increases by at least a factor of five at this festival time — so catching Jesus in some quiet corner is next to impossible. If they try to seize him in public, there will almost certainly be a riot. They didn't dare to voice any criticism of John the Baptist (11:32) even though John had been dead for a year or so. A public arrest of Jesus, who is daily delighting the crowds by making the leaders look like fools, would be suicidal. Every night he seems to melt away into the countryside, so they need a stealthy way, a secret way, of getting hold of him (14:1).

Mark leaves that plot hanging in the air while he cuts back to the scene in Bethany a few days before. Jesus has evidently made this home in Bethany his base. Verse 3 tells us it belongs to one **'Simon the leper'**. John's Gospel tells us it's the home of Mary, Martha and Lazarus — possibly this Simon is the father of those three, perhaps living alone somewhere because of his leprosy. Into this scene, in the middle of dinner, into the busy, crowded room, comes the woman whom Mark does not name although John tells us that she is Mary, Martha's sister.[1] What she does is extraordinary (14:3). It's not that anointing someone at a banquet is surprising — that is how a special guest is honoured — but it's the wild extravagance of her action that is so eye-catching. In her hands she has a small jar, sealed to keep the contents fresh. Inside the jar is a phenomenally costly perfume. She breaks the neck of the jar and pours the entire contents onto Jesus' head. Conversation stops. All eyes turn. The fragrance of the perfume fills the room, then the whole house. Some can identify it; some probably have to be told. The whispers begin. 'It's *nard*.'[2] 'Do you know what that costs?' 'It comes all the way from India — takes a year just to get here.' 'What a waste!' 'Do you know what the orphanage down the road could have done with that money?' (14:4-5). The value of the perfume is such that it is probably a family heirloom. Ordinary people don't have this amount of money at their disposal. Being poor themselves, the onlookers probably view her actions as a personal affront.

Now the woman stands condemned for her profligate foolishness. 'What a waste!' 'Stupid woman!' Perhaps now she begins to wonder whether they are right. But Jesus sees it differently (14:6-8). He tells them to leave her alone. Note how kindly he shields her from embarrassment and makes it clear that he is *not* embarrassed. **'She did what she could,'** does *not* imply that she is rather pathetic but should be allowed to make this somewhat futile gesture! He knows that she has poured the perfume out of love for him. It is a beautiful thing she has done. She doesn't understand that in a

week or so he will be buried, that his dead body will be
entombed and that perfume and spices point to that death. No
doubt she can sense that some great crisis is approaching, but
only he understands what that is, as he always has done.
How appropriate, though, that at this time his body should be
anointed! Unwittingly, she is preparing for his death.

Jesus does not mean, of course, that it is wrong to help the
poor. Occasionally people have misread verse 7 to mean that.
Rather he is quoting the law of Moses in Deuteronomy
15:11, which says that if everything is as it ought to be, there
shouldn't be any poor, but in actual fact there *will* be, so
make sure that you take good care of them. Jesus is recalling
that passage and telling them, 'Yes, you should certainly take
care of the poor at *all* times — but what this woman has
done is to seize the moment when I am here in person.' Then
in verse 9 he goes even further. The tale of this woman's
extravagant love and sacrifice will be woven into the story of
his *own* death and sacrifice, so that wherever the gospel goes,
her story will go too. There is a nice twist to this as well. The
first people to share the gospel message and to tell her story
will be the very disciples who are grumbling about what she
has just done!

Having told us the story of the woman, Mark returns to
the 'outside' story, the story of the plot against Jesus
(14:10-11). We now know what tipped Judas over the edge.
He may well have had other reasons; probably he has become increasingly disillusioned over many months; but
certainly if Jesus can praise a foolish woman who throws
money away while publicly carpeting his own followers,
then it's time for him to go! For Judas, money talks, so, as
soon as the opportunity arises, he seeks out the authorities —
who, not surprisingly, are thrilled at their good luck — and
arranges that he will betray the Lord Jesus. All he needs is
the right moment. He won't have long to wait. Meanwhile
the tension hangs in the air!

You see what Mark has done here. The story on the *outside* is about the plot. The story on the *inside* gives us Judas' reasons. On the *outside*, they are preparing for Jesus' death in one way. They are preparing to kill him! On the *inside*, the woman prepares for Jesus' death in another way, by anointing his body for burial. They spend money to arrange his betrayal; she spends money to anoint him. They act secretly for fear of people's reaction; she acts openly and *faces* people's reaction. The skilful way Mark tells the story simply highlights this amazing and wonderful act of devotion. And the more he highlights her actions, the more pointed the story is for us. This story raises some very searching questions.

The first question is a simple one. As we hear this story, what is our honest response? Which of the characters in the dining room represents you? Do we have some sympathy with these glowering onlookers who disapprove of the woman's recklessness? I'm frightened by the suggestion of my own heart that perhaps these people had a point. Or does the woman's story make your heart leap at the thought of doing something so wonderful for the Lord Jesus? That is how it should be, of course. Yes, there is a time and a place for calculation — for remembering that prices can go down as well as up and for doing your sums very carefully! — but that time is not when you are making your commitment to Jesus. The measure of his commitment to us will be demonstrated within a week of this story, at the cross which fully reveals the reckless lengths of his extravagant love for us. How do our hearts respond?

That leads on to the second question. What do we value the most? Do we value money, or do we value Jesus the most? This woman's answer, her scale of values, was clear. The perfume was probably the most precious thing she had ever owned, but, with Jesus before her, she broke it and poured it out, and it was gone. Life would not be so secure from now on. That jar was her savings account. Our lives and actions reflect what is most important to us. If someone were to study our lives, what would they conclude? If they looked at the evidence of the books by your bed, or the history button on your web browser, what story would it tell? Or suppose — more searching still — that they could read even your thoughts and dreams, what story would be revealed? Or, to put it another way, have you ever done anything extravagant for the Lord — anything reckless, where there was a real cost to you, a cost that made life risky and uncomfortable? Sadly, there are some who would reply, 'Well, I used to be like that. When I was younger, I used to give to the Lord freely and trust him to look after me. I used to tell him, "Lord I will go anywhere, give anything to serve you." I used to love him like that. But not any more. Now I'm older, and I'm more sensible, and if I'm honest I'm more cynical.' If you are honest enough to admit that, you need to understand that it doesn't have to be that way. We don't have to accept the kind of Christian life that will always play it safe, that needs to see before it will believe — the attitude that would always put the jar of perfume back in the cupboard and shut the door.

But there are others who will read this who have shown by your actions that it's the Lord Jesus you value the most. You have given up your security, or left behind the people you loved, or given to the point of breaking your own lifestyle — and not to win points or to earn favour, but because you *loved* him. There have been times when people have questioned or mocked what you have done. They have told you it was pointless; they have asked, 'Why this waste?' Perhaps there have even been times when you have wondered whether they were right. But the Lord says, 'You have done a beautiful thing for me. You have done what you could.'

Picturing his death

Now at last the Passover festival arrives. Mark 14:12-26 tells
the story of how Jesus takes this old, familiar feast, shocks
everyone and seemingly hijacks the whole celebration.
Passover recalls the day, 1,500 years earlier, when the Lord
God rescued his people from captivity in Egypt and led them
out towards the promised land. Every year his people com-
memorate that night — God has told them to do that, and he
has told them how, and, while there are many of his commands that they don't follow, this one they certainly do, en
masse. It's a national event. It's a night to remember what
God has done, the freedom he brought them so long ago. It's
a night of anticipation for what they are longing that God
should do again. It's a night of excitement. It's all about
events of long ago — and here is Jesus saying, 'It's about
me, here and now, *today*.' Even more shocking is the fact
that the heart of Passover is a death, and Jesus is saying that
the death pictured by Passover is his own.

The time is now very short. Everything is in place for
Jesus' arrest and death, and this story pictures his death,
which is less than twenty-four hours away. It's safe to
assume that the story starts in Bethany, just outside Jerusalem, where Jesus has had his base for the week. In verse 12,
we have reached Passover time, the first day of the festival,
when the lambs are sacrificed — recalling the slaughtered
lambs whose blood was smeared around the doorposts on
that first Passover night. It's quite natural that the disciples
should ask Jesus where he plans to celebrate the feast: all
Jews have to do it. But it's not quite as simple as that. The
law is very clear that there is only one place you can slaugh-
ter and eat the Passover lamb (Deut. 16:2,7) — and that one
place is Jerusalem. So, like many other pilgrims at this time,
Jesus needs to locate a dining room within the city boundary.
Hence Jesus' plan in verses 13-15. It is likely that Jesus has

arranged this — he has had plenty of time to do so as he has passed in and out of the city over the last few days. He sends two of his friends ahead, probably for security reasons — he knows he is a target, whereas they will not be easily recognized. For the same reason, a signal has been arranged, probably a prearranged rendezvous. Jesus has a sympathetic contact in Jerusalem — a secret disciple, even — who owns an appropriate house with a room big enough for a party of thirteen. He arranges for a servant to intercept Jesus' advance party, and the signal is that he is carrying a water jar. For a man to carry a water jar is unusual — like it or not, that is women's work! The beauty of this scheme is that they don't even have to speak to the servant — the disciples simply follow him to the house, where clearly Jesus is known and expected.

It's possible that this house belongs to Mark's own family, which is the house where we read of the church meeting in Acts 12. In any event, the room is already set up and the disciples have only to prepare for the feast itself. It all turns out exactly as Jesus has explained (14:16). The two of them now busy themselves with the preparations. There will be the unleavened bread and the wine, the bitter herbs which recall the bitterness of slavery, and the special sauce whose ingredients also connect with captivity and freedom. Finally, they will arrange for the Passover lamb, which must be slaughtered after sunset, just as it was all those years ago. It is Thursday night: by Jewish reckoning, according to which the new day begins at sunset, it is the fifteenth day of the month Nisan, and before this day is out, the Lord Jesus will himself be dead. Evening has come, then; Jesus arrives at the house with the rest of the party. It's normal for the Passover meal to run far into the night, and right across Jerusalem, many thousands of other households are eating exactly the same meal, the various dishes in precisely the same order. At each stage the head of the house explains exactly what it all means. At the beginning and end of the meal they sing Psalms 113 to 118 — known as the *Hallel* psalms. Stage after stage of the meal is accompanied by words of blessing to God and prayers that they will enjoy many further feasts in peace, that the city will be built up in safety, and blessing him for his great works of the past.

It's near the start of the meal that Jesus drops the first bombshell (14:18-20). Although the most famous paintings of the Last Supper, like the one by Leonardo da Vinci, show the party sitting upright, they would in reality be reclining on sofas or on carpets. Jesus looks around and solemnly declares that there is an enemy in their midst. From their reaction, it is clear that the disciples haven't a clue who he means. Interestingly, Mark does not name Judas in this story. Mark is most concerned to highlight the fact that Jesus is betrayed by someone who is so close to him — one who for three years has been part of this closely-knit group will turn out to be a double agent. Jesus' words in verse 20 deliberately echo Psalm 41:9, the song of the righteous sufferer. They are at the point where bread is dipped into the special sauce and shared together — eating together is always meaningful for Jews, but this is a moment of supreme fellowship — and one who shares that bread is now to betray him.

The second bombshell soon follows. The leader would lift up the unleavened bread and bless it with the words: 'Praised be you, O Lord, Sovereign of the world, who causes bread to come forth from the earth.' He would break it and it would be passed round the room for each person to receive. But this time it's different (14:22). Suddenly, this is no longer about 1,500 years ago. Jesus says, 'This is about *me*!' Can you feel the shock? 'This bread which is broken is *myself* — it is myself which I am giving to you.'[3] Then at the end of the meal, as Passover comes to an end, a final cup is shared. The leader takes a cup of red wine, gives thanks over it and

passes it round. But Jesus does something different
(14:23-24). If the broken bread hinted at violence, this time
there is no mistaking the meaning. Jesus will die, violently
and soon. This would be specially striking because of the
stringent prohibitions in the Jewish law on eating or drinking
blood (Lev. 7:26-27; 17:10-14 — note especially in Lev.
17:11 the connection with atonement). We don't know — for
the Gospel writers don't tell us — quite how the disciples
react to all this. But for men who have taken part in this meal
so many times, from when they were little children through
to adulthood, gathered round the Passover table year after
year until they know all the words off by heart, it can't fail to
shock them to the core.

Now the Passover meal is over. The usual hymn is sung,
the second half of the Hallel psalms, and the group make
their way out into the darkness of the streets. It's around
midnight, perhaps later — too late to return to Bethany, so,
like many others, they prepare to camp out among the trees
on the slopes of the Mount of Olives (14:26).

The story of the Last Supper presents Jesus' death in four
important ways.

Firstly, *Jesus' death fulfils God's plans*. Look at how
Jesus speaks of his betrayal in verse 21: literally Jesus says,
'departs'. He knows that his approaching death is all in
God's plan: it is **'as it is written'**. The Lord Jesus knows the
prophets: all that is written about the suffering, dying Servant
in Isaiah, those mysterious words in Zechariah 12:10 about
looking 'on the one they have pierced', Psalm 22 with its
depiction of horrible suffering. He knows those words have
been written about him. Jesus goes to his death deliberately,
freely, voluntarily, knowing that he is doing the will of God
as he does so.

Still, that does not make it any better for the one who
betrays him (14:21). In other words, the betrayer of the Lord
Jesus is going to hell. He is fully responsible for what he is

doing, and he will face the consequences. Judas was tempted by Satan, but he can't blame Satan. He was carried away by the world's ideas of power and wealth, but he can't blame the people who influenced him. His betrayal of Jesus is part of God's plan, but he can't blame God. We, like Judas, stand responsible for our own sin and failure. We too are account-able for every action we take. Yes, there is a mystery here. There is God's sovereignty, whereby he brings about every-thing according to his own will. In this case he is doing something wonderful through an act of human evil: even the betrayal is part of his plan, yet the man involved is still responsible for his actions. His free will is absolutely genu-ine; so is ours.

It is this assurance that God is in charge that allows Jesus to go to the cross with confidence. The final words of the hymn they sing as they leave, the last words of Jesus as he heads out into the darkness, are from Psalm 118:28-29. Empty words, we might think, under the circumstances. But they are not! Jesus can sing those words with meaning because he knows his Father is in control. See how Psalm 41, which he has virtually quoted in speaking of his betrayal, continues in verses 11-12. This is the confidence that Jesus has as he approaches the cross. For us too, knowing that our Father is in control is what allows us to face times of pain and suffering with the confidence that we are in God's hands and he will bring us through.

Secondly, *Jesus' death takes our place* (14:23-24). There can be no doubt what this means. The red wine, the mention of the blood and the covenant, the Passover setting — Jesus is identifying himself with the Passover lamb. On that final night in Egypt, every Israelite household slaughtered a lamb. Its blood was brushed around the doorposts of the house. When God's angel came past, he *passed over* every home like that, and wherever there was no blood, the angel slew the family's eldest son. The death of each lamb substituted

for the death of one son. Inescapably, the Passover speaks of
a substitution. Now Jesus is saying, 'The true Passover lamb
is me. Those lambs are just a picture: the reality is before
you tonight. I am the one who takes your place so that you
can be set free. This is my blood!' **'My blood'**, he says in
verse 24, is **'poured out for many'**, reminding us of 10:45.
Both these verses echo Isaiah 53:12 where the prophet
speaks of the Servant who will bear the sin of 'many'. Jesus
dies as our substitute.

Thirdly, *the death of Jesus proves God's commitment*
(14:24). This, says Jesus, is covenant blood. The **'covenant'**
is God's commitment to us. In the covenant with Moses,
God commits himself to forgive sins and accept his people
on the basis of blood sacrifices. In the blood of Jesus, that
covenant is renewed. In the blood of Jesus, in fact, those
sacrifices are brought to an end. This is the only way that a
holy God could ever make a covenant with sinful people like
us — through the blood of the perfect sacrifice, his Son, the
Lord Jesus. So Jesus' death shows us God's total, unbreakable commitment to us — that he did not even spare his own
Son, but gave him up for us all (Rom. 8:32). This is the
ultimate act of commitment. Do we recognize the depth of
God's commitment to us and how unreservedly he has
expressed it?

Fourthly, *Jesus' death points to glory* (14:25). They have
drunk together the Passover cups of wine and water. Now
Jesus says, 'That's it. I won't taste this again here on earth.'
This speaks of the imminence of his death, but he also looks
far beyond, for he says, 'There is a time when I will drink
this again. When the kingdom I have begun here has arrived
in full, then I will celebrate once more. The day will come
when I will again share a feast with my friends.' Once more,
this shows that Jesus knows ahead of time exactly what is
going to happen. But these words of his take us on to the end
of the age, when he returns to the earth in glory and majesty.

Then will come what the Jews called the Messianic banquet, and what the New Testament calls the wedding supper of the Lamb, when the Lamb of God, the Lord Jesus Christ, claims his bride the church (Rev. 19:6-9). If we belong to him, this blessing is for us. Our names are already written on the invitations. The place of that feast will not be the earthly city of Jerusalem, where Jesus ate with his friends that night and where very soon he would be condemned to die. The place will be the New Jerusalem, where the Lord Jesus lives with his people for evermore, without interruption by death or by anything else, as Revelation 21 promises us. Every time we share the Lord's Supper together at the communion table, we remember the death of the Lord Jesus, and we look ahead to the day of glory, when he comes again and we celebrate anew, *with* him, in the kingdom of God.

22.
Countdown to the cross

Please read Mark 14:27-72

It is a night that Peter will never forget, and it all begins with the walk to Gethsemane. All week the feeling of danger, the sense of threat, has been growing. Now, while those strange words at the Passover table are still ringing in their ears, Jesus leads them out of the city to camp under the trees. Outside the city gates, they splash their way through the Kidron stream and make their way towards the Mount of Olives. Numbers of others are doing the same — there just isn't room for all the festival crowds to stay within the city. Finally, at the foot of the hill, perhaps twenty minutes' walk out of the city, they arrive at Gethsemane, so called because of the olive press there. An unforgettable night is about to take another dramatic turn.

Battle in the garden

The story in verses 27-42 forms the bridge from the Last Supper into the passion narratives which follow; the shadow of the cross falls starkly across it. Gethsemane is a double battleground, for there are *two* battles being fought here this night. One is lost; the other is won. One shows us human weakness and failure; the other shows us struggle and victory. Between them, the two battles give us a glimpse of the phenomenal price that was paid to save us and the depths from which God has rescued us. This story shows us the person and heart of Christ laid bare, and it holds up a mirror to warn us of our own failure and weakness.

1. The battle that is lost

Look at verses 27-28. The expression **'fall away'** means that they will find Jesus such an embarrassment, such a problem, that they would rather have nothing to do with him. This conversation probably takes place en route from the upper room in Jerusalem to the garden, the olive grove of Gethsemane. Jesus is warning them of the severe danger that lies ahead of them. The prophecy he quotes comes from Zechariah 13:7, and although some of the language is difficult, the prophet is clearly speaking about God's purposes to bring salvation to his people, cleansing from sin and the rescue of a remnant; and, in the middle of it all, God's shepherd, the one who stands close to God himself, is struck down and his followers are all scattered. Peter doesn't grasp all of this, but he has certainly picked up the words 'fall away' and **'scattered'**, and he knows who the shepherd is. He insists, **'Even if all fall away, I will not'** (14:29). In verse 31 his rebuttal becomes even stronger and more definitive. Peter envisages a choice between martyrdom and denial and is absolutely clear that whenever the challenge comes, he will be up for it — and he will win it! How typical of Peter to be so supremely confident, so brash! But the others are no different. Jesus' solemn warning that by next morning Peter at least will have disowned him three times makes no impression whatsoever. All this throws into sharp relief the disastrous failure which follows.

The walk to the garden, known as Gethsemane because of the presence of an olive press, is soon over. Judas having departed (Mark does not say when), Jesus now leaves eight of his disciples behind and takes his inner circle, the group of three, a little further, before leaving them too with clear instructions to stay awake and pray (14:34,38).

The command to **'watch'** echoes what he said a day or two before, about being prepared for the crisis that is coming (13:37). Some people read this story as if Jesus is asking the disciples to pray for *him* — as if he wants their company and their support. But that cannot be the case. Jesus is looking elsewhere for his strength; sadly, he knows he cannot rely on them. No, they need to pray for *themselves* because the challenge they seem so keen to bring on is now fast approaching. The fact that Jesus shows such care for them in the midst of his own agony is wonderful in itself. But instead of watching and praying, there in the dark at the foot of the olive trees, the three men immediately drop off to sleep. After all, it has been a long day, they are surrounded by the scent of the olive trees and they are used to sleeping in the open! They get another chance (14:37), and *again* they drop off to sleep. What Jesus says in verse 38 makes both the coming threat and the needed response explicit. They are about to face a deep temptation. In their human strength, the weakness of their flesh, they are simply not up to it. The only answer is to pray and so to gain strength from God, the strength of his Spirit — and they don't do it. Failure is now guaranteed. The battle has been lost, because they have not prayed. As he returns to them we hear a strange echo of the day of his transfiguration (9:6): the inner circle of three are lost for words (14:40). When Jesus comes back the third time and again has to wake them, it's too late. The moment has arrived, and they are lost.

Here are three men who have been so sure, so confident that they can face anything, but when it comes to it they are sunk by the deadly combination of human pride and human weakness. Mark wants to warn his first readers, facing the immediate and terrifying dangers of persecution in Rome, that this is what will happen to them if they don't watch and pray. The same is true for us. If we try to face the spiritual battles of this life in our own strength, we too will be sunk. Our human pride and human weakness will lead us to defeat, just as they did for the disciples. We have to understand that, as Christians, our life is a series of spiritual battles which we cannot face in our human strength.

The rest of chapter 14 will show how the consequences played out for Peter and his friends, but from this moment it is all too predictable — and so it will be for us. Whatever the next temptation will be for you or me — to cheat on expenses or to cheat on your spouse, to gossip about our friends, to look at those websites, whether the danger for you is pornography or your passion for the perfect home, which is idolatry — understand that every one of these battles is a *spiritual* battle, and if you do not pray, then you will not win. There will be spiritual challenges, danger, temptations, that you cannot avoid but will have to face. How will you face them? The answer is amazingly simple — watch and pray!

2. The war that is won

While the disciples are losing their battle, the Lord Jesus is fighting his own, and while they fail to pray, he really prays! The disciples have never seen him like this, overwhelmed as if he is drowning under the weight of sorrow (14:34) as he goes ahead to fight alone. Verses 35-36 show us what he faces. What is it that makes Jesus recoil in horror like this, makes him plead with the Father that he should be spared? Is it the physical horror of the cross? Is it the thought of the agony of crucifixion? No, it is something worse. Jesus speaks deliberately of the **'cup'** (14:36). In the Old Testament, the

'cup' comes to have a very specific meaning and because it is
so important that we are clear about this, we will look at a
number of references. In Psalm 75:7-8, the psalmist is clearly
talking about the 'cup' as judgement. In Jeremiah 25:15-18,
and on through the rest of the chapter, the prophet speaks of a
cup of judgement taken from the hand of God. A similar
picture is found in Isaiah 51:17. There are many similar
references in the psalms, in Ezekiel and in the other prophets.
The 'cup' in all these places, the cup which must be drunk,
stands for the wrath of God which is poured out on people
who are godless and disobedient. The image is used in the
New Testament as well — if anything with even greater
clarity — in Revelation 14:9-10 and 16:19.

The language is vivid, fearful — extreme, we might say.
But we have to stress the reality of the wrath of God because
many today do not understand it, or else deny it. This is what
the Bible teaches us about God's response to our sin — our
sin which is an outrage against him. What we call God's
wrath is his perfect, pure, just, steady and unending hostility
to sin. His wrath means condemnation, eternal punishment,
deadly separation and outer darkness. All who stand in
rebellion against this holy God are destined to face this
wrath, to drink this cup. There in the garden, this is what
Jesus now sees ahead of him. He knows he is going to the
cross, and he knows why. He knows that he will face the
wrath of God poured out on him, personally and directly, in
place of millions of those whose penalty he is paying. He
will become our substitute, to spare us from the wrath so that
we will be free. He knows it — and he needs no word
pictures to describe what it will be like. For us, God's wrath
is unimaginable, but the Lord Jesus knows it vividly, from
the inside. Of course, it is not as though he is realizing this
for the first time. But here, in the quiet of the garden, with
the arrest squad already forming up in the city nearby, it
strikes him like a thunderbolt — and with it the temptation to

find another way. This is his battle — no, this is the *war*. At
the very start of his ministry Satan tempted him to abandon
his mission (1:12-13).[1] Later on, when Peter finally grasped
that Jesus really was the Messiah, he tried to cut Jesus off
when he began to talk about the cross — and Jesus rebuked
Peter himself as Satan (8:33). The temptation to avoid the
cross is real, and now that temptation has come flooding
back — temptation to escape, to avoid the horror of the
wrath — and again he must fight it off. It is here in Gethsemane that the issue must be settled.

We might want to ask, however, if Jesus is really God,
why should this be such a struggle? Doesn't he have all the
infinite strength and resources of God at his disposal? In this
passage, more clearly than perhaps anywhere else in Scripture, we see the full identity of Jesus Christ laid bare. Look
again at verse 36. Jesus' battle in the garden is a struggle of
two wills, the will of his human nature struggling with the
divine will. Here we see him in his humanity and in his deity.
This is Jesus who is fully man — the Jesus who, as we read
in verses 33-34, feels overwhelmed with sorrow to the verge
of death, who throws himself to the ground in horror and
distress, who has to pray to communicate with his heavenly
Father. And it is the *same* Jesus, the *same* person, who is
fully God, fully divine: the Jesus who in verses 27-28 demonstrates complete knowledge of what lies ahead, including
the fact that he will rise again and even where he will go to
meet them after he is risen. (By the way, that also proves that
he could easily have avoided arrest that night — all he
needed to do was to go off in a different direction — but of
course he did not.) The Lord Jesus Christ — one person, two
natures — is here revealed. Yes, this is beyond our understanding. It is another mystery, the greatest miracle of them
all, that in Christ God has become a man and still remained
God, and that here, in sorrow and distress, almost crushed by
the horror that is ahead, the human will can struggle with the

will of God within this one person of the Christ — and yet remain sinless. In the words of the old hymn:

> View him prostrate in the garden;
> On the *ground* your *Maker* lies!

So in view of all this, how does the Lord Jesus win his war? The answer, again, is astonishingly simple — he *prays*! He enters the presence of the Father and he prays (14:36). The word **'*Abba*'** is not a baby or childish word, but an intimate, personal way of addressing your own father. He prays repeatedly; he prays intensely with his entire being. This is a struggle that goes down to the heart of his very identity. Jesus knows the will of God — of course he does; since the dawn of time he has known that this hour would come. He knows the will of God, and he wrestles and fights, but he submits — and wins the war. So by the time the arresting party arrive, all is well (14:41-42). The words he uses suggest the meaning: 'It's settled.' The business is concluded. As the sounds in the distance draw nearer and his betrayer approaches, he stands ready for all that he must face. The work has still to be finished — the cross still lies ahead, and it will still be appalling. But the crucial fight has now been won and Jesus goes forward to the cross with unshakeable resolve. Long, long ago, a *rebellion* in a garden brought in the reign of death. There was disobedience; there was a falling away; there was death. But now in another garden, *submission* brings in the reign of life — for us! What a hope!

Betraying the King

As I write, the war against the Taliban in Afghanistan rages on. One of the horrors of this particular war is that the enemy is working in so many different ways. There is what we might call the ordinary business of war: the combat with men who will stand and fight, who can be seen and who occupy ground. But there is also the terrible threat of the improvised explosive devices left buried by the roadside. Then there have been times when the enemy has struck from the inside, when someone the Allied troops believed was one of theirs has turned against them, and these attacks have been the most deadly of all.

An enemy who can strike in different ways, at different times, from in front, from far away and from the inside — does this remind you of anything? If you are a Christian, it should, because the Christian fight, the fight of faith, is just the same. Our enemy too appears and attacks in many different forms. If that comparison seems absurd, then I suggest that you are probably not in this battle. You probably don't know what it means to fight in the spiritual war, which is intense, personal, costly and painful, and where the stakes are in fact even higher. The next section of Mark 14 reminds us that we Christians face an enemy who comes at us in different ways and in many different guises. When we first read this story in verses 43-54, naturally we immediately focus on Judas and his attack of insider betrayal — it grabs our attention because it is so outrageous — but as we look more closely we can see that around that central theme there are other opponents too whom Jesus and we, his followers, have to face. This passage stands, in fact, as a briefing for battle, for anyone who is an active soldier of Christ, and it lays down a challenge for those who are not.

Jesus needs no special knowledge to announce in verse 42 who is about to arrive: they can be heard tramping up the hill through the trees. In verse 43 they appear — the arrest squad, with Judas showing them the way. He has probably allowed just enough time to be confident that everyone in the disciples' camp will have fallen asleep — and he is not far wrong; if it were not for Jesus, they certainly would be! These are not Roman soldiers (as they are sometimes depicted); at this point the Roman overlords have no interest in Jesus — that will come later. These are the armed temple police, probably with members of another small armed force which the Jewish authorities use to operate beyond the temple. They have been sent by a combination of the three groups who between them make up the Jewish ruling council. Those men have not turned out in person, of course, but we will meet them soon enough. It is the same combination who came to challenge Jesus about his authority in 11:27 (see comments there).

But because this armed squad may not recognize Jesus in the dark under the trees, Judas has explained that he will go and kiss Jesus (14:44), and when they see him do that, they are to make the arrest. The kiss is a perfectly normal way for a student to greet his rabbi — which is the word Judas uses here. So the signal is given and the fateful arrest is made (14:45). After all this time plotting and planning, finally the troublemaker is in their grasp (14:46). There is one feeble gesture of resistance (14:47). The way Mark tells this — the Greek says it's 'a certain one of the bystanders' — makes it clear that he knows the culprit's name: in fact John tells us that this is none other than Mark's own informant, Simon Peter (John 18:10). Perhaps we could have guessed that! It is a panicked move by a man who, not surprisingly for a fisherman, has no expertise with a sword, and it does no good. Jesus himself responds with *words*. He protests that they have no need to come armed as if for riot control (14:48-49). What **'Scriptures'** does he mean? There are many prophecies in the Old Testament which point clearly to the death of Jesus. One he has already referred to in verse 27 — Zechariah 13:7. There are also two verses in Isaiah 53 which Jesus probably has in mind. Isaiah 53:8 can be understood as referring to his arrest and trial; Isaiah 53:12 refers to his being treated as a criminal. All these scriptures and many more will be fulfilled in the events of the coming hours. By the purpose of God, written in eternity, Jesus Christ will be deserted, tried and convicted; he will be crucified for our sin and will rise again in triumph and to glory. In verse 50, Zechariah 13:7 is fulfilled exactly.

In verses 51-52, Mark presents an intriguing little episode. Who is this unexpected character, and whatever is he doing in the story? Mark's Gospel is the only one that includes him, and that is always significant. We can deduce that he got dressed in a tearing hurry, because he has nothing on under his garment; and that he is fairly well off, because he is wearing linen. The most likely explanation is that this young man is none other than Mark himself, our author. We know Mark's family lived in Jerusalem; it was a meeting place of the early church (Acts 12:12). Tradition has always held that it's the same house where Jesus has just shared the Passover with his disciples. So perhaps Mark has done what Hollywood film directors sometimes do and given himself a cameo role in his own production, in which case Mark is actually an eyewitness of this episode!

But as Mark, or whoever it is, disappears to find some clothes, and everyone else has scattered, at least for now, Jesus is taken away under arrest to face his trial (14:53). The scene has shifted back to Jerusalem, where the whole ruling body — the Sanhedrin — has assembled at the house of Caiaphas the high priest.[2] From the speed with which they gather, it's likely they have been warned that they will be needed. Here Jesus will face trial at the hands of the rulers of his nation, and meanwhile Peter, with what motive we don't really know, has caught up with the procession, goes into the courtyard, sits down by the fire and waits to see what will happen (14:54).

As we focus on the scene of Jesus' arrest, most prominent are the three different kinds of enemies he has to face and the way that he responds to them. Mark has continually told us that if we are to follow the Lord Jesus, we must be like him, and that includes facing the opposition that he had to face (8:34; 9:49; 10:29-30,43-45). To be a disciple is to follow Christ on the way of the cross. In fact, there is a sense in which the whole of Mark's Gospel is a briefing for our battle.

There are three kinds of enemy, then:

1. The violent

Look at the second part of verse 43. Here are the combat troops of Jesus' sworn enemies, the chief priests, the elders and the scribes. They have always detested him; their agenda is simple: destroy him. This is full-frontal opposition. See how Jesus responds in verses 48-49. They have come armed for battle, prepared for a riot; Jesus says, 'There's no need. That's not my way.' Now, there is a view that non-violence, pacifism, is the core of Jesus' message. This view would even say that the struggle that Jesus faces and wins in Geth-semane is against the temptation to take up arms, to launch a violent rebellion against the power of Rome, as others would do a generation later. There is a long and honourable tradi-tion which defends that view — it's the Anabaptist and Mennonite tradition, exemplified by John Howard Yoder in his book *The Politics of Jesus*; I respect the integrity of it, but it's not what Scripture actually says. Jesus' aim was not to turn the world upside down by preaching pacifism. This is what Jesus is saying: 'Look, your swords and clubs, your violent attitude, are wasted on me. You could have picked me up when I was teaching in the temple — I was peaceful then, and, look, I'm peaceful now.' He refuses to retaliate. He makes no attempt to call his followers to arms, and he has no time for the futile gesture with the sword. That is not how Jesus fights. We too will face enemies who want to destroy us. In the West, the violence will not usually be physical; elsewhere in the world it may well be. The agenda of these enemies is to destroy the church, to bring an end to Christianity; they combine intellectual argument with a deep contempt for anyone who takes the spiritual realm seriously, and they genuinely believe that Christians in particular are not merely deluded but also dangerous. These people are the chief priests and scribes of secularism. But also among these enemies — and what an odd combination this makes! — are the powerful world religions, and especially today the power of militant Islam.

The temptation is to respond with either hatred or fear. They appear so threatening and so very strong. We hear news about our brothers and sisters suffering in Iran, Egypt or Somalia — church buildings burned down, families broken up, stories of arrest and even death — and we begin to hate the persecutors. We hear some insulting dismissal of the gospel on TV, or read it in print, or we find it in a lecture in our university, and we feel weak and afraid. But look back at your Bible. Jesus is not fearful, and he does not hate, and neither must we. The answer to such violent hatred is love. We can hate atheism, but we are to love the militant atheist. We can hate Islam, but we must love every Muslim. Recently I spent some time with a Muslim friend: we went out for lunch and then to his mosque — a building that until very recently was a gospel hall. I sat there and imagined the services of worship that must have taken place through the years, the prayers that were prayed, the sermons that were preached. It hurts me to know that the Christian witness is no more. But the answer is not to rage, nor to keep quiet. The answer is to love. We keep on loving, through the power of the Spirit who can enable us to love anyone. We are to love people all the way into the kingdom — even if they are people who hate and despise us. Isn't that what Jesus did?

2. The cynics

Look at 14:44-45. Notice the massive irony as Judas names Jesus as his master teacher and gives him the kiss of respect in the very act of betrayal! What has brought Judas to this point? He has spent the past three years with Jesus. Jesus chose him to be a member of his select band, involved him in the ministry — he was even part of the Twelve's mission to preach, heal and drive out demons (6:7-13). This is what seems to have happened. As the months have passed, Judas has become hardened. Perhaps he is frustrated that he never makes it to the inner circle around Jesus, and he is jealous. Probably he feels that Jesus is missing the opportunities for power and influence that his popularity with the crowds has offered him. We know from John 12:6 that he has begun to help himself to the disciples' communal funds. Eventually, as we saw at the beginning of chapter 14, Judas has had enough. Jesus' approval of the woman who wastes her life savings on perfume to pour over his head pushes Judas over the edge. He goes to the authorities and offers to betray him.

Again, there have been attempts to recast Judas as a sincere follower who simply wants to force Jesus' hand. The idea is that Jesus' mission is coming to nothing and so Judas tries to bounce him into taking on the authorities head-on — in which case Judas would be horrified at what happens next. Unfortunately, there is no evidence for that point of view, and a great deal of evidence that Judas is exactly what he appears — a cynical traitor. His actions shock us, but he is no worse than we have been.

We too will face enemies like this. They may not directly betray us like Judas, but there will be people we think of as one of us, who in reality have sold out to the world. Over time they have been hardened. Other priorities appeal to them more than knowing Christ — their bank account, their image, their plans, or just being like everybody else — so their spiritual life becomes a burden and then it dies, and they become cynics. We must watch out for the warning signs even in ourselves. This is the person who for no good reason drops out of ministry because they no longer see the point, or who begins to say, 'You can't tell me — I've heard it all before'; who pours cold water on every new idea and smiles knowingly at any hint of spiritual enthusiasm. Such people are very hard. Judas himself spent three years with Jesus himself, and look how *he* ended up. It seems impossible, but it happened. You might meet a cynic in church or know one in your workplace. 'Yes,' this person says, 'I used to believe all that God stuff until I was about ten; then I grew out of it.' When we meet such people, we must do what Jesus did. Jesus extended the hand of loving welcome to Judas for three years. Maybe they are like this because some devastating experience has embittered them — they need our love all the more. We warn them as Jesus did in 14:21. We keep showing them what spiritual reality looks like. We keep reminding them, calling them back. Look at Jesus; look at the cross.

3. The deserters

Mark may have included the little story in 14:50-52 as a cameo appearance, but he certainly wants it to emphasize that Jesus was abandoned by everyone — not just his core of disciples, but even the casual onlooker as well! At this point, Jesus stands utterly alone and unsupported. These deserters are not really enemies, of course; they are friends who fail — though we could ask, 'With friends like these, who needs enemies?' If they stay, they face arrest along with Jesus, possibly a trial, perhaps even death. Obviously, they are afraid. In the Christian battle, and in our church life, there will be times when we will lose people in the same way, as they simply abandon the fight. Sometimes we will be tempted to do the same ourselves. When the going gets tough, the tough may get going — but many of us simply want to quit. It may be in the workplace, your school or your office, or with your friends in the pub, where the atmosphere is so virulently godless and un-Christian that all you want to do is to keep your head down and avoid any risk of being abused for your faith. You abandon the fight.

What does Jesus do for his failing followers, these deserters? Remember, he knew this was going to happen, yet still he loved them. He urged them to watch and pray, so that they would be prepared. He warned them, carefully and in detail, in verses 27-28. Mark doesn't tell us the story of how Jesus restored the disciples afterwards, but he does quote Jesus' words, 'After I have risen I will be in Galilee' — in other words, 'I want you to join me there! You may fail me — indeed, you will — but I haven't given up on you.' If you are reading this as a deserter, and you are hiding or running away, there is still hope. If you have run away, you can repent and come back. You know what happened to Peter and the others later on — that night they deserted, but a few weeks later it would be such a different story. That can be you!

Have you heard the call to battle? Some will attack us; many will fail us; at times we shall surely fail ourselves. But there is a battle to be fought, and we need to be ready. Our Lord Jesus calls us to war, and he is faithful.

God on trial

In April 1964 Nelson Mandela was on trial in South Africa, accused of sabotage and treason against the white-ruled apartheid state. There was no disputing that he led an organization that was struggling to overturn the government, though much of the evidence put forward by the prosecution was demonstrably false. Mandela was sentenced to life imprisonment with hard labour; the authorities hoped he could be quietly forgotten. But the world was changing. Slowly the apartheid government was forced to shift its position. Finally, on 11 February 1990, Nelson Mandela was dramatically released. The event was broadcast live around the world; it was a public vindication — one of that small number of moments in world history which everyone who witnessed it will remember. Four years later, Mandela's vindication was completed as he was elected president in his country's first ever multi-racial elections. It had taken decades, but the reversal in fortunes was now complete: from *victim* to *victor*; from *enemy* of the state to *head* of state; from condemned *criminal* to chief *lawmaker*!

Now take that dramatic reversal and multiply by a thousand: make the one who is accused perfect; make the injustice absolute; make the final authority worldwide and universal — and you have a faint glimpse of what happened to Jesus Christ. Here in verses 55-65 he stands in court, the accused: for all his dignity, he is weak, vulnerable, abused — and yet this is the Christ who today is exalted in glory, seated in heaven at the Father's right hand and who will one day soon return in majesty as the Judge of all the earth.

Peter is warming himself by the fire; Mark will return to his story in verses 66-72. Meanwhile, Jesus himself faces trial. The court that has been hastily summoned for this all-night sitting is the Sanhedrin, the ruling council of the Jewish nation. The three groups that comprise the council are listed in verse 53: **'the chief priests'** — that is, high priest Caiaphas and a small selection of other senior men; the scribes, or **'teachers of the law'**; and the **'elders'**, who represent the elite families of Jerusalem and the surrounding region. From what the Jewish documents tell us, we know that the Sanhedrin consists of seventy members in addition to the high priest, though only a third of that number is needed for a quorum. They sit in a large semi-circle, with clerks to keep records, and when they are acting as a court there are seats in the middle for the accused and the witnesses. In this court there are no barristers; the witnesses themselves act as prosecutors.

To make full sense of this story, we need to understand what is on the council's mind. If they are going to dispose of Jesus, as they are so keen to do, they must achieve two goals. First, they must make some charge stick that the Jews will accept. Jesus is popular with some sections of the crowds; so it's essential that they prove his guilt *in Jewish terms*. That means proving that he has broken the Jewish law, the Torah. But there is still a second challenge. Although the Romans allow the Sanhedrin to operate, along with other Jewish institutions, the right to impose capital punishment has been removed — to the intense resentment of the Jews. That means they will also have to prove some *political* crime which will persuade the Roman authorities to have Jesus executed. The Jewish leaders dare not risk Governor Pilate taking the line that Gallio would later take in Corinth (Acts 18:14-16).

So here they are, in the early hours of the morning, sitting down to try a case. It is highly irregular for the court to sit at night, so much so that some commentators have argued either that the trial is illegal, or that it can only represent a preliminary hearing. However, given that most of our information about the Sanhedrin's operations is deduced from later information in the Talmud, I think it's impossible to be sure about this. Other scholars have gone further, taking the opportunity to deny the historicity of the account altogether in an attempt to remove blame from the Jewish nation and preclude anti-Semitism. It has even been claimed that the Sanhedrin are trying to rescue Jesus from the Romans, whereas the reverse is the case. The reason they are sitting at night is simple: they are in a tearing hurry. At last they have their opportunity to convict Jesus and finish with him; they dare not let this long-awaited chance slip away. It's Passover — a superb time to execute someone because, with all the crowds around, it will maximize the deterrent value. And there is one very practical reason for rushing the case through: they will need to catch Pilate before he goes off duty — and, like other Roman officials, he starts work at daybreak and packs up by lunchtime.

The really irregular feature of this trial, in fact, is what we read in verses 55-56. A court is meant to be impartial; this one patently isn't. It is in fact a desperate quest for credible evidence. It's not just the august members of the court who have been hastily roused for this sitting; the witnesses have all been collected as well. There is plenty of evidence available; the problem is that none of it is any good.

The rules on this are very clear (see Deut. 19:15). If two witnesses differ in even one minor detail, their evidence has to be entirely dismissed. In fact it would be virtually impossible to bring any genuine charges, because Jesus has lived perfectly according to the true Jewish law all his life. But perhaps help is at hand: in verses 57-59 a new charge is introduced. Jesus did say something vaguely like this. Mark doesn't record it, in fact, but John does (John 2:19), so we know Jesus never said that he would destroy anything himself. All the same, it makes a handy accusation. However, to the dismay of the court, they cannot get an agreed story here either.

By now, Caiaphas has had enough. Caiaphas, we know, is a wily character: in a time when high priests last only an average of four years, he manages nineteen. He refuses to give up on this dysfunctional trial. Thus far, Jesus himself has said nothing, so the high priest rises from his seat and demands a response (14:60). But still Jesus says nothing (14:61). These nonsensical allegations don't deserve a response, and so it is that he fulfils the prophecy of Isaiah 53:7. Faced with this silence, Caiaphas decides that he will have to take on the interrogation himself, directly. So, standing over the accused, he demands to know, '**Are you**

the Christ [Messiah]**, the Son of the Blessed One?'** This
time, faced with a direct and worthwhile question, Jesus
finally responds in the words of verse 62. This is the crux of
the trial. These are the key words, and in what follows we
can see that the court now has the evidence they so desperately need. But exactly what is Jesus claiming for himself?
The high priest has asked him whether he claims two titles:
first, the *Christ*, or *Messiah*; second, the *Son of the Blessed
One*, which is another way of saying, 'Son of God'. The high
priest certainly doesn't mean what we would mean by that
— 'Are you the Second Person of the Trinity?' No, for him
and for all Jews of his time, 'Son of God' would mean
someone who has a unique and exalted relationship with
God, but someone who is still just a man. So Caiaphas is not
asking two different questions — to him, the Christ and the
Son of God are really one and the same title.

Jesus accepts both these titles. But now he goes further:
verse 62 claims more. Jesus is putting together two of the
greatest Old Testament prophecies about judgement and how
God will bring it about; to understand this, we need to look at
them both. The first is in Psalm 110:1. In Jesus' day, everyone knows that this is a Messianic psalm — one that points to
the promised Messiah. Jesus has recently quoted this very
verse to prove that the coming Messiah must be something
more than a mere man, more than the Son of David (see
comments on 12:35-37). The second prophecy is Daniel
7:13-14. The Son of Man figure comes into the presence of
God, receives an eternal kingdom and is given authority over
the whole earth; what is more, he comes with the **'clouds'**,
which in Old Testament language always stands for the
majestic appearance of God himself. In the face of the rulers
of his own nation, in the face of the high priest himself, Jesus
combines these two pictures of majestic authority into one
and applies them to himself: 'I stand before you today as a
prisoner accused. But I tell you, *yes*, I am the Christ. *Yes*, I

am Son of God. I am the Son of Man who will wield the very
authority and judgement of God over the world. I am the
"Lord" who sits at God's right hand, and when I come in
divine majesty you will see it for yourselves.'

It is an electrifying claim, and now they have him
(14:63-64). Blasphemy can be established here on two
grounds: to claim to be Messiah is not blasphemy as such,
but to claim it *here*, as a bound and helpless prisoner, makes
a mockery of God who has promised to send them a powerful deliverer: 'You claim *you* are the authorized agent of
Almighty God — look at you!' But still more than that, to
claim the divine authority and the majesty of God, the one
who will take eternal power and reign — that is most certainly blasphemy; hence the high priest's dramatically
indignant gesture. Blasphemy is a capital crime, without
question (Lev. 24:16). They are right, of course — unless,
that is, what Jesus says is true. But no one in this room is
pausing to consider that possibility! So the whole Sanhedrin
rubber-stamps the conviction. Jesus has been condemned; all
that remains is to persuade Pilate to pass the death sentence.

With the formal business out of the way, it is the august
members of this council who begin the physical onslaught
(14:65). Spitting is the age-old way of showing utter contempt, and if he is really Messiah, he should be able to tell
who hits him without looking. He can **'prophesy'** it. Then
the guards follow the lead of their masters and beat him up in
their turn. The appalling physical ordeal which Jesus must
endure has begun, and it will continue all the way to the
cross itself.

It is Caiaphas the priest who has the last word in the trial.
But who will *truly* have the last word? Jesus is now on his
way to execution. For any other prisoner, that would be the
end. The torment of the cross, the slow lingering agony of
death — that certainly lies ahead, but for him it is not the end!
After the cross comes the grave, and from the grave comes

resurrection, and after resurrection comes his ascension to glory, returning in triumph to the Father's side, seated at the right hand of the Mighty One (14:62). No, the cross will not be the end. Heaven first sees his triumph and vindication. Meanwhile, despite the best efforts of the same Sanhedrin, the church Jesus leaves behind refuses to die. Instead it grows and spreads: they expel its members from Jerusalem, but that just makes the flames spread further and faster.

Then the first judgement falls. The nation rises up in rebellion against the Romans, and in AD 70, within a generation of this scene, Jerusalem itself is overwhelmed and destroyed. Its proud walls are flattened; the temple burns and the ruins are razed to the ground; and the priests — the successors of Caiaphas and his colleagues? As the temple falls into blazing ruins around them, they pursue the routine of the sacrifices until the moment when they are slaughtered, struck down at the great altar. Jesus' words to Caiaphas are coming true.

Then one day the final judgement will fall. Finally, every eye will see him as he returns in glory to the earth, as he comes on the clouds of heaven and receives the eternal kingdom: from victim to victor; from enemy of the state to head of state; from condemned criminal to ultimate Judge!

We look at this world and we see the injustice. As God's people we are called to fight against injustice, but we know that injustice will remain as long as this age endures. We don't have to despair, because we know the Judge; we know that he is coming, and when he comes he will deal out perfect justice in every single case. We see injustices in the lives of people we know. Perhaps you yourself are the victim of some deep and painful wrong that has forced you to suffer. We think of our brothers and sisters around the world who are persecuted for their faith in the Lord Jesus — it's one of the biggest injustices of all. Even in heaven the souls are crying out for justice (Rev. 6:10). The Lord will bring it, and, as his own people, we are safe in the Judge's hands.

Failing the test

We now come to verses 66-72, a story that takes us to the depths of human failure. Who knows what is really in Peter's mind as he follows the procession into the courtyard of the high priest's house? Presumably, it is confusion above all. Picture the scene. As he sits down by the fire to keep warm, many others are waiting too. Some are the household staff; some are the personal attendants of the grandees who have swept upstairs to the council; some are witnesses, wanted for the trial. Probably there are a few of the temple staff as well. Peter will be glad he has dumped his sword! They have nothing to do but wait for the court to finish the job, so they do what they always do: stand around in groups and talk. Whenever it is quiet for a moment, they all hear the drone of voices from upstairs. From time to time another of the witnesses is called, and he climbs the stairs and a few minutes later comes down again and strolls off into the night.

It isn't long before one of the servant girls comes and peers at Peter (14:66-67). 'I know where I've seen you before! You were with that Nazarene guy, Jesus — right?' There is contempt in her voice. 'I haven't a clue what you're talking about', says Peter (14:68). After all, he won't do anyone any good by getting arrested. Just to make sure of that, he edges his way out into the gateway, where he can stand in the shadows. Faintly he hears the sound of first cockcrow.[3] For some reason it doesn't register. But even in the gateway he doesn't find much peace. He can see the group standing there, glancing over and talking among themselves — that same girl is there again, pointing and whispering; then one of them calls over: 'Hey! *You're* one of them — right?', gesturing up the steps towards the trial. Peter thinks, 'There's no point changing my tune now!' So again he denies it (14:69-70).

It satisfies them, perhaps, but not for long. The voices upstairs are louder now: someone is getting angry. Then it happens. Several of them come walking over. 'We've heard you talk. We know you're a Galilean — your accent is so obvious. We can tell you're one of them; we know you're a follower of his!' The voice is hostile now, sharp, dangerous. Panic sets in. It's not enough just to deny it, now. He has to curse and swear as well, to persuade them that he has nothing to do with the one he has known as Master and friend (14:70-71).

Then, as he pauses for breath, he hears it. In the yard opposite, the cock crows again, and in that second it all comes flooding back (14:72): 'I tell you the truth, Peter. Today — yes, tonight — before the cock crows twice you will deny me three times.' With that comes too the memory of his own boastful words: 'No, no! Even if I have to *die* with you, I will *never* disown you!' *Die*? When it came to the test, he hasn't even stood up to a servant girl! So, for the second time that night, Peter disappears from the scene, stumbling out of the gate, away from the questioners, away from the trial, away from the Lord, and collapses in tears.

The story of Peter's denial comes as a deadly warning of the power and reality of sin. It's a story that embarrasses us. Judas we can maybe write off as a traitor. But Peter is one of us. If he can fail so spectacularly, what is to stop us from doing the same? If we want to be able to stand firm, and *not* to fail the test, we need to learn the lessons of Peter's disaster. Mark has set the story out very carefully. He makes it clear that Peter's denial takes place while Jesus' trial is in progress: in verse 54 he leaves Peter sitting by the fire getting warm; he then cuts to the trial scene; and now from verse 66 he cuts back to Peter. More than that, not only does

Mark show us that these events are simultaneous, he also points up the contrast. For while Jesus stands with such integrity and dignity before the court, Peter abjectly fails the test. While Jesus remains in control of the situation even under trial, Peter totally loses control. And at the moment when Jesus is being mocked as they beat him — 'Prophesy!' — his own prophecy about Peter is coming true. Mark does not want us to miss the point. We, like Mark's first readers, need to understand what happens to Peter so that we will be warned and prepared. We will highlight four ways this story impacts on us.

1. It brings us face to face with sin

Look at how sin works in this passage: see what it does to Peter. He actually denies his Lord — Jesus, his friend, his Master (14:71). He insists he has nothing to do with Jesus Christ. It sounds appalling — and it is. Yet, ultimately, *all* sin is a denial of Christ. A Christian is someone who has laid all their sins on Jesus Christ and asked for forgiveness, who has said, 'Jesus is enough for me.' But when we sin, we are saying, 'Jesus is *not* enough. There is something I want more, something more attractive and appealing than Christ, and I want it.' So every sin we commit denies the Lord. We have two clever ways of dealing with our sin. Either we make excuses for it — as I am quite sure Peter was doing as he stood in that gateway — a reason why it's 'not that bad', or we call it something else. We call it a shortcoming, or a character flaw — anything but sin. But if we are serious about living the Christian life, we must learn to call sin by its name. I was challenged recently by something I read about 'respectable sins' — the sins we make excuses for and don't *call* sins. For example, impatience is a sin. Failing to trust the Lord is a sin. Envy of what others have is a sin. Speaking behind someone's back is a sin. Laziness is a sin. All those

may be respectable; some of them will be unseen by others
— but they are all sin, missing God's best for us. When we
do these sins, we are denying Christ.

The first time Peter is challenged, it would not be that
tough to give the right answer. Imagine it: 'You also were
with that Nazarene, Jesus,' she said. 'Yes, you're right', Peter
smiled back graciously. 'I *was* with him — and I still am.'
But the second time it was harder, because he had already put
himself in the place of denial, and now the challenge was
greater — not just one girl, but a group. The third time it was
harder again. Each time was a chance to obey the Lord, but
with each successive denial it grew harder to go back. Sin is
like that. It's progressive. Once you have compromised the
first time, it's so much harder to stop. You and I know that's
true. You start a new job and from day one you find yourself
being drawn in to the risqué banter, the gossip, or the office
politics. Because you let that happen on day one, by day ten
you feel hopelessly trapped. That's how sin works.

Of course, we believe there is grace for those who have
been trapped in sin, for those who have stepped over the line.
But we will never get hold of grace until we grasp the reality
and horror of sin, the sin that has blighted and infected every
part of our being. We reach the cross as guilty sinners,
profoundly and universally guilty. The Christian faith is not a
game of let's pretend — let's pretend our sin is just a weakness; let's pretend we are all OK really — the sort of words
that people in the world use all the time. In fact, of all the
world's great belief systems, ours is the only one that allows
us to be honest about how we really are — corrupt, sinful,
rebellious and enemies of the God who made us. We can be
honest about what we are because we have the only really
good news — the gospel of Jesus Christ our Saviour. But we
come as big sinners. Peter ends up in tears; have we ever
wept over our sin like this — not because we have been
found out and it's embarrassing, but because it has suddenly

burst upon us that we have denied the Christ who saved us? Do we know what real repentance means?

2. This story confronts us with our weakness

Remember what Peter said in verses 29-31. They were big, fine words, but they were useless. Jesus knew that Peter's words were empty. Now why does Mark give this story such prominence in his account of Christ's passion? After all, it is really a sideshow. Peter has an altercation with a few servants in the yard — so what? It makes no difference to the major theme, which is Christ's journey to the cross. But Mark is sending a very serious warning to his readers in Rome. He is warning them that one of their great heroes, Peter himself, had this disastrous fall, and if it happened to him then it can happen to any of us. Big words count for nothing. That is why Mark emphasizes this story — and all the other Gospel writers follow suit because they know it will be an issue for their readers as well. It is always tempting to take the easy way out and say, 'I don't know this man you're talking about.'

That leads on to the third point.

3. This story summons us to battle

Peter's battle, as we have seen, was lost before it even started (14:37-38). He *didn't* watch and pray — so he *did* fall into temptation. It followed as night follows day. Suppose Peter had watched and prayed, had stayed awake that dark hour among the olive trees, had armed himself with the Lord's strength for whatever lay ahead? Suppose, in fact, that he had done exactly what the Lord Jesus was doing. He would have stayed at Jesus' side, marched with him — he might even now be standing by him at his trial, or at least he could have given a straight answer to a servant girl! Sin is real and deadly; we are weak. So we need to be ready for the fight. Satan does not ask us if we are ready before he sends us temptation. He will attack when we are at our weakest — when it has already been a hard day, when we are feeling tired, when someone has just had a go at us — which is exactly what happens to Peter here. Then he will whisper to you, 'Do you know what would make you feel better? Go on, you deserve it.' Can we recognize his voice? Paul would write with masterly understatement, 'We are not unaware of his schemes' (2 Cor. 2:11). That must be true of us all. This story calls us to watch and pray. The Christian life is not a holiday; it's a war — a war fought with weapons of prayer and the Word of God — but the key message here is: Be *ready* for the battle, or you will be knocked *out* of the battle!

4. This story promises our hope

While Peter is so dismally failing his own test, the Lord Jesus is victorious in his. While Peter lost the battle in Gethsemane, the Lord Jesus was winning the war. This is our great hope. Against our record of sin and failure stands his perfect record of holiness and obedience. Every outbreak of anger, lying, hatred, sexual immorality, impatience is outmatched by his love, his integrity, his peace, his purity, his patience — fulfilling the law and being perfectly pleasing to God. At the cross, those two records are exchanged. He got my sin and took the penalty, bore the wrath, suffered the curse. I got his perfection, his obedience, his nobility — credited to me at the cross. That is why there is hope in this story. In verse 28, in the middle of that prophecy that they will abandon and deny him, Jesus reassures them that, when it's all over, he will see them again. They will meet again in Galilee. He is looking forward to it already! Because of the cross, there is restoration. Because of the cross, there is the promise of hope.

23.
Sentence executed

Please read Mark 15:1-32

As we come to Mark 15 and the account of Jesus' death, we have to begin with politics, for, humanly speaking, it is politics that send Jesus to the cross. If we are used to the relatively polite and well-ordered arrangements of the Western world, the politics of first-century Palestine will be very unfamiliar. It is hard, for example, to imagine the key players from Judea lining up for a live election debate: Pontius Pilate the Roman governor sharing the platform with Caiaphas the high priest and some leader of the Zealot nationalist party — all taking questions from a studio audience! Still, there are elements we might recognize. There are some unexpected cross-party alliances at work. When the pressure is on, just as in our own elections, people behave in unexpected ways!

Verdict decreed

We begin, then, with Jesus' appearance before Pilate in verses 1-15. It is early Friday morning (15:1). The Sanhedrin have reached their verdict, but they still have a problem. If there is to be an execution, the authorization for it can come only from the Roman authority, personified in the prefect, or governor, Pontius Pilate. They have to convince him to condemn Jesus to death. Because Pilate follows standard Roman practice of starting and finishing his working day very early, they need to catch him quickly. Pilate is not normally based here: his official residence is by the sea at Caesarea, and when he visits Jerusalem, as he will often have to do, he establishes a temporary headquarters here. The probable site is in Herod the Great's old palace on the western side of the city, rather than the Antonia fortress at the edge of the temple.[1] Pilate appears many times in the historical records, and what they tell us fills out the picture from the Gospels in a fascinating way. Pilate holds office for ten years. He is loyal to Rome and prefers to avoid trouble; he is willing to be flexible when it suits him; in fact, he is rather weak; and he despises the Jews, so whenever he gets the chance, he loves to humiliate them. On one famous occasion he needs money to pay for improving the water supply, so he goes and raids the temple treasury, which to him is perfectly normal practice. When the Jews protest, he has soldiers in disguise mingle with the crowd, and at an agreed signal they club large numbers of the protesters to death. Eventually Pilate is removed from office following a massacre of Samaritans. Such is the character of the man the Jewish authorities now have to deal with.

Pilate, we can assume, has been briefed; hence verse 2. Clearly, it is the Sanhedrin who have produced this accusation. It will do no good to tell Pilate that Jesus is a blasphemer, so they frame a different charge which he will have to investigate. **'King of the Jews'** is a sort of translation of the word 'Messiah' for the benefit of Gentiles. The key word is 'king', because that is a political term which Pilate is forced to take seriously. This expression, 'King of the Jews', now runs through the whole of the crucifixion narrative. Pilate interrogates Jesus with it; then he taunts the Jews with it; then he actually has it written on the cross (15:26); meanwhile in verse 18 the soldiers use it in savage mockery. The Jews themselves would never choose this expression. If they wanted to use the term 'king' at all, they would say 'King of Israel', as their leaders do in verse 32.

Jesus' answer to Pilate in verse 2 is difficult to translate exactly. We might express it: 'Yes, that's one way of putting it.' In other words, Jesus clearly accepts the title 'king', but he hints that he is not what Pilate understands as a king. John's Gospel gives us a long exchange between Jesus and Pilate on this point, where Jesus explains that his kingdom is not the sort that Pilate would recognize. Mark doesn't report that, but he does imply that Pilate is not quite satisfied with Jesus' first answer. But to all the accusations of the chief priests, Jesus, most unconventionally, has nothing to say at all (15:3-5). A man on trial for his life will normally either try desperately to plead his innocence, or else make a defiant speech, seizing his final moment in the spotlight. Jesus does neither, and at this point there is no doubt that Pilate would prefer to dismiss his case.

It seems, in fact, that Pilate may get his chance to do so. There is an established custom of releasing a prisoner at Passover — now — and it's not long before someone attempts to invoke it (15:6,8). 'Surely,' Pilate thinks, 'the crowd will get me off the hook by asking me to release this Jesus.' Pilate may be cynical; he may be weak; but he is not an idiot. It's not hard to work out that the Jewish leaders have a hidden agenda. Pilate can see that Jesus poses no danger to law and order; he can see that these chief priests simply want to dispose of him for reasons of their own (15:10). Pilate would really prefer not to oblige them, so he hopes the crowd will kindly help him out (15:9). Unfortunately for Pilate, the crowd don't want to play his game. They have another candidate in mind (15:7).

Defining this Barabbas depends on your point of view. The word Mark uses in verse 7, translated **'insurrectionists'** in the NIV, appears nowhere else in the New Testament, but some would call Barabbas a terrorist, and others a freedom fighter. It's a *political* question. The big political issue of these days is not, 'How can we reduce our budget deficit?', or even, 'How should we deal with immigration?' The big issue in Jerusalem is, 'How can our nation be truly free? What is the path to national salvation?' Everyone has their own view on this question. The Pharisees say that the way to national salvation is to obey the law of Moses in every tiny detail. The Sadducees say that the way to survive is to play the Romans' game, to collaborate with them; then at least they can keep the temple and the sacrifices, and some people can do quite well out of it. Out in the desert somewhere is another group called the Essenes, who don't appear in the New Testament itself; they say that all the others are corrupt and what is needed is to start again and build a new nation. Then there are the Zealots, whose answer is armed violence against the Romans, a violent revolt to expel the oppressors from their land. That is what politics looks like in first-century Israel.

Jesus has not lined up with any of these groups — a political act in itself — but Barabbas is a Zealot. One of Jesus' disciples, Simon, is a Zealot too; it is quite possible that they know each other. It turns out that the crowd, stirred up by their religious leaders, much prefer Barabbas to Jesus (15:11). It's ironic that the chief priests, who are Sadducees and collaborators, and therefore detest the Zealots, should agitate to get *Barabbas* released. As so often in politics, the fear of losing produces some strange alliances!

Three times Pilate asks the crowd; three times they respond. Pilate doesn't help his own cause here: he cannot resist having a dig at the Jews by referring to Jesus as their **'king'** (15:12). Of course they don't call him 'King of the

Jews' — and saying that they do is not calculated to win them over. The crowd's response is unequivocal (15:13,14). They might, perhaps, have called for a lesser penalty. There are less horrible methods of execution, but crucifying someone is the standard Roman way, especially out here in the provinces. And so, although to the end Pilate would prefer to set Jesus free, he adopts the line of least resistance and pacifies the crowd by decreeing the verdict of crucifixion (15:15).

This hideous flogging — using a leather scourge embedded with pieces of metal or bone — could sometimes be imposed as a penalty by itself, but often it was used as a prelude to crucifixion, making the degrading humiliation even more severe. With no limit prescribed, contemporary history tells us it was quite common for men to collapse and die from the effects of the flogging alone, never even surviving to be put on the cross. In Jesus' case, that doesn't happen; he survives the flogging and is still just able to walk.

So Mark presents the drama. We will examine it more closely by looking at some of the characters. We have seen enough already of Pilate, with his abuse of power, weakness and lack of principle.

First, then, we look at *the crowd* (15:8-14). In chapter 11 we read about the cheering crowds who joined Jesus on his triumphal entry into Jerusalem. Sometimes people will compare these two stories and remark on how fickle crowds can be, but these are different crowds. The crowd who followed him into Jerusalem were pilgrims coming up for the Passover; probably they are not even staying in the city, and they are most unlikely to be out on the streets at the crack of dawn. Most of *this* crowd have probably followed the Sanhedrin across the city; they will include the people who were taunting Peter as they waited for that first trial to conclude. Many of them probably work for the Jewish establishment. But, whoever they are, they have their sympathies. They don't particularly like Pilate and, given the chance, they are quite happy to shout for Barabbas. They might not be Zealots themselves, but it is a rare chance to put one over on the Romans. As for Jesus, most of them have seen him, and everyone has a view on him; they have no special reason to wish him harm, but they have to listen to what their lords and masters tell them. In short, like most crowds, they are very easily won over. They don't have much to go on themselves, so they borrow someone else's point of view.

One of Mark's goals in this book is to bring everyone to a verdict about Jesus. He gives us the facts; he lets the evidence speak for itself; and he calls us to make our own decision about Jesus Christ. Everyone must reach their own verdict, just as Pilate did so unwillingly in this story, and just as the crowd did, for all the wrong reasons. Many today follow the example of the crowd and simply borrow a ready-made opinion from someone else, swayed by a sound bite or inherited prejudice.

Secondly, look at *Jesus*. Mark, as we have noted several times, wants to show his readers how to prepare for suffering. He wants to warn them that if the Lord Jesus had to face injustice and hatred, the same would be true for them. He wants them to see how the Lord Jesus faced all that, so that when the time came for their own personal passion story, they would know how to stand firm. If we are Christians, we need to know that too. We have already seen what Jesus told his friends at Gethsemane: if you want to defeat temptation, watch and pray! But the challenges would not finish with that night. Remember what Jesus warned his disciples in 13:9. Until Christ returns, this is how it will always be. In many parts of the world Christians face just such treatment today. One day the same may happen to us in the West; meanwhile, we have our own battles to fight, and we must learn to be on our guard, to watch and pray and to follow the example of our Master.

It is worth recalling what Jesus has already been through before he faces Pilate. In the course of a totally sleepless night, he has struggled with the horror of death and the dread of God's wrath as he has wrestled in solitary prayer; he has been betrayed by an ally and deserted by his friends; he has faced volleys of unjust accusations by people who hate him; and then he has been beaten up — all in the last twelve hours. In other words, before this story even begins, he has encountered more trauma and provocation than we ever will.

Throughout his life, the Lord Jesus has obeyed the will of God actively. He has spoken, taught, healed, worked; now we find his obedience taking a different form. It is striking just how little Jesus now says or does. In fact, all the way through from his arrest to his death, Mark records only three times when Jesus speaks at all. Assaulted, he does not protest. Accused, he does not defend himself. He simply follows the path laid out for him. He makes no attempt to avoid the cross. He treads the path of a humble servant all the way to that dreadful death. How can he do that? Simply, he did what Peter and friends did not do. He watched and prayed. The victory was won at Gethsemane in solitary prayer among the trees. How do *we* stand firm when we are accused or persecuted? We watch and pray — ahead of time.

Thirdly, let's look at *Barabbas* (15:6-7,15). All the Gospel writers mention Barabbas, but while Mark's account of Jesus and Pilate is barely half the length of what we find in the other three Gospels, he tells us more about Barabbas than any of them do. Mark clearly wants us to think about this man. What does he want us to see? Whatever his precise motives, Barabbas is a murderer. In one of the frequent failed uprisings of those days, he has killed people — perhaps he even managed to kill a Roman soldier, or maybe it was just some Jewish collaborator. He is a big sinner, a certainty for crucifixion; he fully deserves what he is going to get. By rights, it should be Barabbas carrying his cross out to Golgotha with the other criminals that spring Friday morning. But instead, the soldier who comes and takes him from his cell does not drag him outside the city walls to the place of execution. Instead, he leads him to the gates of the fortress, pushes him outside and turns his back: 'Go on — you're *free*!' And that is what the cross of Jesus does. The cross substitutes an innocent victim for a guilty criminal, so that the guilty criminal walks free. Barabbas is you and me — the offenders, the criminals, the guilty ones, released from our cell, taken out into the light and set free. Like us, Barabbas deserves his sentence. Like us, Barabbas contributes nothing to his freedom except for his sin. As with us, the action takes place somewhere else while he reaps the benefit — just outside the city, where the innocent victim is nailed to the cross and takes the wrath of God on himself, and meanwhile we walk free.

There is, however, another character in this story. *God the Father* is unseen, but he is here. None of these events happens by accident, or by merely human decision. How could Jesus make that detailed prediction in 10:33-34? He knew it all in advance, because he knew the plan. Jesus knows who is in charge — the unseen hand of God the Father is behind all these events. Why does Jesus not die under flogging, as so many others did? It is because God has decreed that he shall die on the cross. Prophecy said that he must be lifted up, not die on the floor. Prophecy said that he must be hung on a tree, so he dies on a wooden cross — because it is in God's plan. Again, why are so many people implicated in the story of Jesus' death? There is a word which recurs time and again in this story — the Greek word *paradidomi*, which is sometimes translated 'betray', sometimes 'hand over' and sometimes 'turn over', but is really all the same word. Judas *hands over* Jesus to the chief priests (14:11). The chief priests *hand him over* to Pilate (15:1). Pilate *hands him over* to the soldiers to mock and crucify him (15:15). With every handing over, the guilt is spread around. So Judas is to blame; the chief priests are to blame; the crowd is to blame; Pilate is to blame; the soldiers are to blame; and we, each and every sinner, are to blame. God wants it made unmistakably clear that we are *all* to blame — and it is Jesus who can release us all.

True lies

History marches on. Governments rise and fall. Wars are won and lost. But, whatever historic moments this world may have seen, Christians know there was one supreme moment in time, a day when the earth witnessed its greatest drama of victory and defeat, one moment above all when history was made. In verses 16-32 we come at last to that moment. Christians know that there has never been a moment like this. When Jesus Christ went to the cross, that overused expression was literally true: the world would never be the same again.

As we look closely at this account of the cross, we notice at once how little Mark tells us about the physical ordeal that Jesus has to undergo. In this whole episode, Mark uses only a single word in verse 15 to describe the flogging and two words in verse 24 to tell us that they crucify him. We have to ask, why does Mark, this most gritty and hard-edged of all the Gospels, say little or nothing about the whips and the nails, the lacerations and the wounds, the long slow torture of death by crucifixion? There are two reasons.

One is that most of his first readers in Rome already know the dreadful details. It is recognized as the extreme punishment, understood to be so unspeakably awful that the great Cicero, a century earlier, said that 'Even the mere word, cross, must remain far not only from the lips of the citizens of Rome, but also from their thoughts, their eyes, their ears.' But on the other hand, crucifixion is also fairly common, particularly in times of turbulence and upheaval. The Roman authorities see it as quite normal to crucify many hundreds after rebellions, to deter people from ever again daring to oppose their rule. That will certainly happen forty years later, when the Jews rebel against Rome and the temple is destroyed.

The second reason is more important. Mark does not dwell on the physical horrors of the cross because he knows they are not the most important part of the picture. Although this is what we would naturally dwell on, there is something even greater and more significant going on. So while he does not forget or ignore the physical dimension, and throughout the story he gives us reminders of that aspect of Jesus' suffering, his focus is elsewhere. Mark's focus, this day of days, is on *the meaning of the cross*.

We begin in verse 16, still at the scene of Pilate's temporary headquarters in Jerusalem. These soldiers — the Greek word *speira* indicates several hundred men — have come up with Pilate from his official base in Caesarea; they are probably local Gentile recruits who have no more love for the Jews than Pilate himself. Jesus is now entrusted to their tender care and they see this as a bit of light relief from the routine of garrison life. They proceed to indulge themselves in abusing him (15:17-20). Why not? He is as good as dead now! They have heard that this prisoner is claiming to be King of the Jews, presumably one of those irritating rebels they keep having to hunt down. So they find a purple robe to wrap round him — it may be no more than someone's old cloak or blanket, but the point is that purple is the colour of empire — and from thorn twigs they create a wreath to crown him with. The crown of thorns is not intended as an instrument of torture, although it will certainly hurt him. It is a parody of the common portrayal of emperors, wearing what are known as radiate crowns with rays of light shining out from their heads to lend them the appearance of gods.

They give him a staff as a sceptre, but they use it to strike him as they spit on him. They kneel before him in pretended homage. It's a scene of grotesque abuse from beginning to end. This is what they do with 'kings'!

But soon it is time to go. They take Jesus outside the city to the place of execution. Following common practice, he has to carry his own cross, or at least, the cross-beam — it's part of the humiliation — through the streets for everyone to see and take note. But, weakened by the flogging, he simply cannot do it (15:21). Mark tells this as if at least one of the family of Simon is known to his first readers in Rome. None of the other Gospels mentions Alexander and Rufus, but Paul refers to a Rufus in Romans 16:13 and it could be the same man. If so, Mark would be saying, 'You know Rufus — well this is how his dad first met Jesus!'[2]

Now Jesus arrives at the place known as Golgotha, **'The Place of the Skull'**, which suggests the appearance of a bare, rounded hillock. His walk to the cross is just a few hundred yards. He is now offered an anaesthetic drink — not by the Romans, who have no interest in mitigating the ordeal, but probably, according to tradition, by women from Jerusalem as an act of mercy. We can only imagine what it must have taken for Jesus to refuse the offer. He is determined to endure everything in full and without aid.

Finally, around the middle of Friday morning, he is nailed to the cross and hung up to die.[3] Below his feet, the execution squad gamble for his clothes — normal practice according to military custom as far as they are concerned, but with a deeper meaning of which they know nothing, for this is prophecy being fulfilled. A thousand years ago David wrote the song of the innocent sufferer which we know as Psalm 22, a psalm which, as we shall later see, is fulfilled almost line by line in the death of Jesus: it is verse 18 that refers to the division of clothing. Here is another reminder that these horrible events are all in the plan of God — and Jesus knows.

Mark completes the crucifixion scene by telling us that the charge against Jesus is inscribed above his head: **'King of the Jews'**. The custom is for the charge to be written on a wooden board and paraded to the place of execution along with the criminal, before being fixed there for all to see. Jesus' cross is one of three that are hoisted up that morning. On either side there is a criminal, an outlaw (Greek, *lestes*, which is probably best translated by a word like 'bandit'), like Barabbas, who should by rights have occupied the third. Again there is an echo of Scripture, this time Isaiah 53:12, another passage which calls up the theme of innocent suffering, foretelling the Servant who suffers in the deliberate purposes of God. (By the way, some manuscripts of Mark include that verse from Isaiah at this point; the quotation was then labelled as verse 28 of this chapter.)

So Jesus hangs dying on the cross, in the company of rebels and surrounded by torrents of abuse, even from the two criminals. Luke's account implies that one of them changes his mind (Luke 23:40-43), but in Mark's stark narrative we read only of how the Lord Jesus is isolated and abused even in his dying hours. As we read verses 16-32, the spotlight falls most strongly on *the words that are said*, not by Jesus — for in Mark's account here he utters not a word — but by his enemies, one group after another: soldiers, passers-by, Jewish leaders, fellow-victims. Here is the really remarkable thing — all that they say is *true*. Even the lies are true! Jesus goes to his death as the target of volley after volley of hateful insults, yet they are taunts that are ironically accurate. It's with the words of three taunts that Mark points us to Jesus' true identity and mission.

The first of these taunts is **'King of the Jews'**, which, as we have seen, is a 'translation' of the Jewish idea of Messiah, or Christ, into terms that Pilate could understand. In

verse 32 both expressions, **'Christ'** and **'King of Israel'**, are
used in the same breath: they mean much the same. Now see
how it is used as a taunt against Jesus, beginning with verses
17-20. The soldiers have done Jesus up as a king; acclaiming
him as 'King of the Jews' is the whole point of their game.
To them it can mean only that he has set himself up in
defiance of their emperor — that he has dared to challenge
the might of imperial Rome. How pitiful an idea that is, now,
as they look on this bloodied, gasping, half-collapsing figure
who is entirely at their mercy — 'King of the Jews'! We find
the words again in verse 26, this time in the notice pinned
above Jesus' head. This time the taunt comes from Pilate,
directed not just at Jesus, but at the entire despised Jewish
nation, his message being: 'See what will happen if any of
you dares to rebel.' We hear it again in verse 32 from the
chief priests and scribes, two of the groups involved in Jesus'
trial who have now come out to gloat at their success.

'King of the Jews' from the soldiers, from Pilate, from the
Jewish leaders — none of them is serious; none of them
believes it is true. A king should lead an army; a Messiah
should reign in triumph. But, ironically, it *is* true! King of the
Jews is just what he is. After the long centuries of waiting,
after all the prophets have said about him, after four hundred
years of silence when God seemed to be doing nothing,
Messiah is here; their promised Christ has arrived. Astonishingly, their King is reigning from the cross — reigning with
a crown of thorns on his head. There is something significant
about those thorns — for how and when did thorns come into
the world? Remember what the Lord said to Adam, that day
of the first sin in the Garden of Eden (Gen 3:17-18). Ever
since, thorns have been part of our lives. Thorns are a sign of
the curse. They take us back to the Fall, back to our sin.
Now, as Jesus hangs on the cross that morning, he wears the
thorns — he wears the curse for us. He carries the curse that
affects the whole of humanity, descended from Adam and

poisoned by sin; he takes it to the cross and deals with the curse for us, for people of every nation and language, not just for the Jews. He wins a kingdom from all of mankind, no longer from Israel alone. King of the Jews; King of us all — it is true!

The second taunt is heard in verses 29-31: **'He saved others … but he can't save himself.'** Jesus has been crucified in a public place — deliberately so, for crucifixion was always intended to frighten and cow the local populace. Many of the passers-by are clearly hostile. They have accepted the line that Jesus is an enemy of the people, a threat to the peace. The chief priests and teachers of the law, meanwhile, have long hated him. They have longed for this day. They chortle to one another, 'He saved others' — that's intended as a reference to Jesus' healing ministry, which no one could dispute — 'but he can't save himself.'

If the first taunt was sarcastic, this one is absolutely straight. In their eyes, Jesus is helpless — of course he is — and his very helplessness is the final proof that he is a fraud. His claims are empty, and now they have proved it by getting him nailed to that cross, pinned to a wooden frame — what clearer picture of powerlessness could there be? But again, their taunt is true. Jesus *cannot* save himself. It was not possible for Jesus to save himself if he was to achieve his mission. Yes, he had the power to come down from the cross — the nails could not have held him back — but then he would not have done what he came to do. The truth of what he has come for is explained by Jesus' own words in 10:45. Jesus has to give his life, so he must stay on the cross until his life has departed. Jesus came to lay down his life for others, to save others — and not just to heal their bodies, but to save them completely, from the hell he is even now experiencing. As Jesus hears the words flung at him, he knows what he is doing and he knows that, beyond their understanding, their words are true. He saved others, but he could not save himself.

For the third taunt, look again at verses 29-30: **'you who are going to destroy the temple and build it in three days'** — on the face of it, a strange thing for anyone to say. It came up at his trial before the Sanhedrin in 14:57-58. That claim is now recycled by onlookers at the cross who have heard it passed on. Now we know this is not, in fact, what Jesus originally said. We know from John 2:19-21 that Jesus was not talking about destroying the great edifice of the temple; he was saying, 'If you destroy *this* "temple", my body, I will raise it up again in three days.'

Again, on the lips of his abusers, this taunt is a reminder of his weakness: 'You are going to tear down the temple, are you? I'm sorry — when was that going to start? It still looked pretty solid when I went past this morning!' It's just one more insult to throw, but in reality it's true! They are destroying the temple of his body — life is ebbing away with every tortured breath — but that is not the end of the story! The cross is not the end of the story! Without knowing it, those onlookers are reminding the Lord Jesus of the resurrection that is coming soon. I wonder if, in some unexpected and certainly unintentional way, this final taunt even brings him comfort. What their words really mean is that on the third day, he will be raised to life again! The taunting accusers will not have the last word, because beyond the cross is the empty tomb. The body destroyed will be raised again. This is not a day of defeat, whatever it might look like. This is victory.

Years before, at the start of his earthly ministry, Jesus was baptized (1:9-11). It was a baptism of repentance, but Jesus had no need to repent, not one single sin to turn away from, yet he was baptized with sinners, as one of us. Now, at the close of his ministry, Jesus is executed — a criminal's execution, though Jesus has never committed a single crime.

Yet he is crucified with sinners, numbered with the transgressors, dying our death, bearing our sin, wearing our curse. This is the true King of the Jews — the true King of all, who is reigning now, not from the cross, but from his heavenly throne, the Lord of history who will return in glory as high as his humiliation was deep. This is the Christ who could not save himself because his mission was to lay down his own life to save us. And this is the one who will be raised again, the temple destroyed but rebuilt in three days, for the cross is not the end.

24.
Mission accomplished

Please read Mark 15:33-47

All of a sudden people are looking at the sky. The crowd are no longer watching the figure on the central cross; they are staring upwards instead. Suddenly, incomprehensibly, with the sun shining overhead out of a clear blue sky, it's getting dark. No one can explain it. They have heard of eclipses, but you can't have an eclipse now — it's Passover; it's full moon. They look out across the countryside and see the valleys filling with shadows; they look back towards the nearby city and its buildings are barely visible. It's midday — and it's *dark*. Some scurry home; some stay to watch; some must simply remain on duty. The centurion at the foot of the cross casts worried glances about — after all, this darkness would make great cover for anyone trying to stage a rescue attempt. He has heard that this prisoner claimed to be a king. But there is no rescue attempt. Instead, the darkness simply continues. The centurion settles down again to wait.

At last the growing silence is broken. The prisoner speaks, or yells, words that the centurion does not understand, words of Aramaic, the common language of Palestine: **'*Eloi, Eloi, lama sabachthani?*'** The words confuse even the Jewish onlookers. Some imagine he is calling on the prophet

Elijah — there is that old tradition that Elijah pops up at times of need to pull innocent men out of impossible situations: 'Perhaps this crazy character thinks Elijah will come for him now! I wonder if he will say anything else bizarre; or — who knows? — Elijah might actually appear!' So they dip a sponge in a jar of sour wine, the soldiers' customary drink, and raise it to the prisoner's lips. This cross is higher than most; they have to jab the sponge on the end of a stick and reach up to his mouth. That should keep him going for a little longer.

To their surprise, the end is not long delayed. One more loud cry and, quite suddenly, the prisoner is dead. The body hangs limp and silent. The soldiers are baffled. They have seen dozens of crucifixions and this is simply not how it goes. Crucified men invariably sink in torment, gasping into unconsciousness. They do not give a powerful cry and then breathe their last!

Again the centurion wonders; he thinks back over all he has seen and heard during these past few hours; he looks round — and he realizes he can see the faces of the crowd again. The light has returned. He peers up at the face that gazes back with lifeless eyes, the mouth that has screamed none of the usual curses, the man who has accepted this hideous death with heroic dignity — who, in a place where no one has control or decision over anything, seems to have decided the exact moment to give up his life! He thinks about the darkness that has paralleled this man's dying and that has lifted as he dies, and he puts his thoughts into words: **'Surely this man was the Son of God!'**

Meanwhile, not far away in the city, the priests in the temple, scurrying round the precincts on Passover business, hear a sudden sound that first puzzles and then terrifies them. The great temple curtain which guards the way into the holy places of their religion has mysteriously torn; a single tear extends from top to bottom, and the two pieces can be seen hanging separately so that anyone can see inside. The barrier is down! Horrified, they run to tell the authorities. Immediate action is imperative. The dividing barrier must be kept intact!

Back at the execution scene, the crowd begins to disperse. A group of women have been watching the central cross, keeping their distance, supporting one another through what is a terrible ordeal for them — for they were devoted to this prisoner. This past couple of years they have done all they could to support him as he has moved around the country, and here they have stayed to watch. Three in particular are watching closely: two named Mary, and one named Salome — eyewitnesses who have heard and noted every detail, and who quite soon now will see something even more astonishing than this. But all they know for now is that the Jesus they knew and loved so much is dead, and no hope remains in their hearts as they gaze at the body on the cross.

This is the story of how Jesus dies, as Mark recounts it. Finally, he dies; his mission is accomplished. He has done what he came to do. But exactly what has he accomplished, and why does it matter? These are the two major questions which are answered in Mark 15:33-47.

Jesus under judgement

We turn first to verses 33-41 — to Jesus' death and what it achieves. Mark's narrative gives us five clear pointers.

First, *Jesus' mission took him to the depths* (15:34). This verse gives the only saying from the cross which Mark records, indeed the only words he mentions Jesus speaking between his opening exchange with Pilate and the moment of his death. So this is important! These are astounding words — especially in view of the claim that Jesus himself is God. It sounds at first like a cry of utter despair. We need to know that Jesus is quoting the opening words of Psalm 22, though he speaks in the common Aramaic and not the original Hebrew. Psalm 22 is the song of the innocent sufferer; it speaks of someone enduring torment and abuse that is totally undeserved and crying to God to rescue him. As Jesus hangs on the cross, he is living the experience described in this psalm. It is amazing to think that the Lord inspired David to write it so that a thousand years later he himself could speak it from the cross!

Psalm 22, however, is not entirely about suffering. If you read it, you will see that it ends on a high note of praise and assurance. Some have suggested, therefore, that Jesus' cry from the cross is really an expression of confidence that everything will be all right in the end. I believe that idea is mistaken, for Jesus' experience on the cross does not lead towards that confident conclusion; it actually leads *away* from it. Compare Mark's account with Psalm 22 and you will see what I mean. Jesus goes to the cross and the soldiers gamble for his clothes (15:24), corresponding to Psalm 22:18. Then Jesus is mocked (15:29-32), corresponding to Psalm 22:6-8 — notice how the details line up. Then comes this cry from the cross, the 'cry of dereliction' as it is known, in verse 34, corresponding to Psalm 22:1. It's as though Jesus is being taken back through the psalm to its opening verse, not *towards* the place of assurance, but *away from* it.[1] Jesus knows the whole psalm is about him, and of course he knows how joyfully the psalm ends, but his experience is telling him something quite different. We must not lessen the force of these words, or try to explain them away. Jesus knows that in this moment he is *abandoned* by his Father. From eternity past, not the tiniest suspicion of a difference has ever clouded the perfect unity of the Father and the Son, the bonds of dynamic love that unite them, yet now he is plunged into the horror of utter desertion.

Does this mean, then, that God is torn apart from God? Is the Trinity broken apart at the cross? Many have gone astray here, including prominent theologians,[2] but perhaps it's not surprising because this is so hard for us to fathom. The relationship between the persons of the Trinity — Father, Son and Spirit — is far beyond our comprehension and there is no analogy or illustration that can make it clear. What we can say is this. Jesus is one person in two natures — a divine nature and a human nature which makes him one of us, sharing our full humanity. This cry of dereliction expresses his suffering in his *humanity*. It is his humanity that suffers and dies. We cannot fully understand that and, given our finitude and fallenness, this should not surprise us. But what we can do is to gaze at the scene of the cross and wonder that God, the infinite Creator, put himself through all this for us. Jesus' prayer in Gethsemane reminds us of the astounding truth that he knew he was coming to this, yet still he set his face to endure it.

Secondly, *Jesus' mission placed him under judgement.* This explains his abandonment by the Father. Jesus knows he is innocent — not just of any crime worthy of execution, but of anything remotely sinful or wrong in his entire life. He identifies with the righteous sufferer of Psalm 22:9-10 who proclaims his obedience to God — and in the case of Jesus this is literally and absolutely true. He has been totally faithful, but instead of a reward, he gets condemnation. Here on the cross he finds himself under the judgement of God: the darkness that falls is a clear sign of that. The prophets often spoke of the Day of the Lord, the day when God would intervene in history, judge his enemies and save his people. Those who had rebelled against God would be judged and punished for their sins. Judgement means that every offender faces the consequences of what he or she has done — an utterly terrifying prospect, for judgement means God's wrath, his pure and perfect anger against human sin, poured out on the rebels. The prophets foretold that this Judgement Day would be accompanied by unmistakable signs, such as supernatural darkness (see, for instance, Amos 8:9). Darkness falling at midday is a sign of falling judgement. But it is not falling on the whole world — not now. Today judgement is falling on just one spot; it is focused down on a rocky outcrop outside the walls of Jerusalem, on that one agonized figure on the cross. That is why he is abandoned. The Father's fury is poured out on the Son.

This raises the question again: 'Why?' Why is Jesus, the perfect one, under judgement? Why is it falling on him? It is because, thirdly, *Jesus' mission paid for our sin*. The darkness of judgement and wrath which he endured was endured for us. Jesus is doing exactly what he explained in such simple words in 10:45, and this is the cost. The cost of the ransom is to take our judgement, our hell, to divert the wrath of God away from us and onto his own head. On the cross, Jesus takes our disastrous record of failure and rebellion onto himself. Jesus suffers in his humanity, as we have seen, but it is only because Jesus is also divine, only because of the infinite strength of his divine nature, that he can bear this unimaginable weight. The Father looks at him, the pure and innocent one, and sees there the guilt of a billion sinful lives, and he holds the Son to account for them all. In these agonizing hours, Jesus is a terrorist, a mass murderer, a rapist, a child abuser. He is an armed robber, a drug dealer, a gangster, and God's wrath is poured out on him for all of these. Has our sin appeared yet in the list? Jesus has stolen, blasphemed, bribed, walked out on responsibilities, cheated in exams, envied the rich, looked down on the poor. God's wrath is due for all of these too. Jesus has resented his parents, been infuriated by his children. He has left the truth half-said. He has talked behind people's backs, dodged taxes, fiddled expenses, snapped in impatience, said one thing and done another, held grudges, failed to offer a kind word when he had the chance. Surely we recognize these sins — and for all these too, Jesus bears the unspeakable wrath of God. He has become sin for us (2 Cor. 5:21).

Fourthly, *Jesus' mission was accomplished in full.* Mark does not give us the words of Jesus' final cry, as John does (John 19:30), but he does tell us *how Jesus died* (15:37). This is simply not how crucifixions end. If the victim has any strength left to cry out, he is not close to death. If he *is* close to death, he has no strength left for a cry. Mark makes it clear that Jesus chooses to lay down his life when the task is done, when the sacrifice is complete. Hour after hour he has hung there in the darkness. Wave after wave of God's wrath has engulfed him as the long record of our sin rolls on and on. It has seemed unending, but at last the moment comes. At last he has the sense of the burden beginning to lift, the horror abating; God's wrath is exhausted; the price is paid. He brings his mission to its conclusion; he completes the sacrifice by surrendering his life. Jesus dies. Fellowship with his Father is restored. On earth, the darkness lifts. Mission accomplished!

There is another sign that Jesus' mission was completed (15:38). There were in fact two curtains in the temple. The first hung at the entrance to the building, the entrance to the Holy Place which only the priests could enter. The second curtain was inside, dividing off the Holy Place from the innermost sanctum, the Most Holy Place, where only the high priest went, and that only once a year — understood to be the place where God's very presence dwelt at the heart of his people. The traditional view has been that it is this *inner* curtain that is torn at Jesus' death, showing that his death opens up the access for us all into the presence of God. It is true that his death achieves exactly that, and the book of Hebrews expands on that truth. But I think it is more likely that it is the *outer* curtain that is torn. Damage to the inner curtain could be very easily hushed up — it would only ever be seen by a handful of priests and no one outside need ever know. But a tear in the outer curtain — eighty feet (twenty-four metres) high and vividly coloured — could be seen by anyone in the temple courts, as long as the gates were open, and there is a Jewish tradition that something very strange *did* happen at the entrance to the temple building. Everything else in this passage is about public evidence of the meaning of Jesus' death — signs that can be seen and heard — and the outer curtain was far more public than the inner one.

At the end of our previous chapter, we noted a strange parallel between Jesus' death scene and his baptism in Mark 1. But there are other parallels as well. At both his baptism and the cross, there is a declaration that he is God's Son. At both baptism and cross, there is the image of something descending from above: the dove descends at his baptism; the tearing curtain at his death. And at Jesus' baptism, we read that the heavens were seen torn open as the Spirit descends and the voice of God speaks into the world. On the outer curtain of the temple there was a great woven tapestry, torn open as Jesus dies. And the tapestry depicted a picture of the night sky — the heavens! His earthly ministry began with a moment of God's intervention, rending the heavens; now it concludes in the same way![3]

Whichever curtain it was, the meaning is much the same — it's a message of salvation completed, the way opened, either into the temple for us all to serve as priests, or right into the presence of God. At the same time, it marks the end of the temple era. Now that Christ has died, now that our sin has been paid for in full, there is no need for sacrifices, for priests, for dividing walls, or for any barriers to the presence of God. Jesus has already told his followers that one day soon it will be utterly destroyed (13:2), and here is the first sign of it.

Fifth and last, *Jesus' mission proved him to the world* (15:39). We have seen what induced the centurion to say such words, but what did he mean by **'the Son of God'**? The

Greek allows either translation, 'Son of God' or 'a son of God'. In either case, the centurion does not and cannot mean 'he is the Second Person of the Trinity'; that concept would mean nothing to him. 'Son of God' to him would mean something like 'superhero', a 'man with godlike powers'. This exclamation may very possibly be the first step to a living faith in Jesus Christ, but it is no more than a step. Mark, however, intends more than that. Mark wants his readers to recognize a true statement in a far greater sense than the centurion could understand. Just as when Peter confessed, 'You are the Christ' (8:29), without really under-standing what that would mean, so the centurion declares, 'This man was Son of God' and Mark whispers to us, 'He said it!'

This is especially important for Mark's first readers in Rome. 'Son of God' is exactly what the emperors are begin-ning to call themselves. Mark is telling his persecuted readers that there, at the cross, the official representative of Rome called Jesus by his true name. The *emperor* is not the Son of God; Jesus Christ our Lord is Son of God. In this recognition by a Gentile, limited as it might be, unwitting as it might be, we see the beginning of the way Christ's death is preached across the world. With the death of Christ the dividing wall between Jew and Gentile is broken down; the great news of the gospel goes out to every nation, as Christ, who has taken the judgement of humanity, creates a single *new* humanity. Jesus is truly identified, at last, at the foot of the cross; his saving death will be proclaimed to every nation and people group on earth; and when that task is complete, the Lord Jesus will return — not in the humiliation of the cross, but in glory and as Judge.

For us, the most important thing by far is simply to see and to grasp what Jesus has done: to see how low he went, what he went through as he faced the judgement and bore the wrath. When we talk about salvation, God's rescue plan, this

is what we mean — that the Son of God himself, with depths
of love beyond our comprehension, should suffer in our
place so that we can have full and free access to a perfect
God.

As we look at Jesus suffering on the cross, we see too
what it means to trust God in impossible situations. When
Jesus is in the depths, when he knows that for this time the
Father has abandoned him, he still insists on saying, '*My
God*', and does not let go. Jesus, in a situation more appalling than anything we will ever face, cries out, but he cries
out to God. If your situation is impossible, if there are
questions neither you nor anyone else can answer, remember
that you are united to Christ, who plumbed the deepest
depths — and in the place of no answers, still trusted his
God.

Finally, we need to remember that if Christ died for us,
there is no guilt left for us to worry about — none at all! If
we are still plagued by guilt from our past, the answer is to
look at the cross and see what was done there. See the cost;
see the completeness — and understand that we have nothing
to add.

Death confirmed

In the Khanyar district of Srinagar in Kashmir stands a very
ordinary-looking building, single-storey, rectangular, on a
slightly raised platform with green railings at the front. Until
recently, it used to be open on request, but ever since it was
listed in the *Lonely Planet* travel guide, it has been much
harder to get into. Inside, there is the final resting place of a
Muslim holy man; another man who may be a Muslim saint,
though some say he was just the caretaker; a gravestone
covered in green cloth and a rock with mysterious markings,
said to have been made by feet that have been crucified.

This, according to some, is the true tomb of Jesus of Nazareth, or Yuz Asaf as he is known locally. According to the story, Jesus did not die on the cross. He survived the crucifixion, recovered from its effects and travelled to Kashmir, where he lived out the rest of his days and died a perfectly normal death. This building is the place of his burial. Until recently, most of the world had never heard of this idea, but that is changing. Its growing popularity, to quote a recent BBC article, is due to 'an eclectic combination of New Age Christians, unorthodox Muslims and fans of the Da Vinci code', all of whom prefer to believe that Jesus Christ did not really die on the cross.

This is in fact the official doctrine of the Ahmadiyyas, a Muslim sect regarded as heretical by other Muslims. Mainstream Muslims believe that Jesus did not go to the cross at all; he did not die — neither in Jerusalem nor anywhere else — but was taken straight up to heaven. They say that someone else, such as Simon of Cyrene, was made to look like Jesus and crucified instead, though exactly why God should want to perpetrate such a deception is not very clear. But, either way, Jesus did not die on the cross, and so the very basis of the Christian gospel is challenged and denied. In which case, the story of Christ's death on the cross may be very powerful, may be intensely moving, but it is not actually true; in fact it is deeply misleading. Some people today would say that doesn't matter. Perhaps the remains of Jesus *are* lying in an obscure building in Kashmir — so what? We shouldn't worry whether the Bible has got its story straight or not; as long as we believe it and it gives us hope and meaning, as long as it 'works' for us, that is all that counts. Is that right?

It is interesting that at this point in his story (15:42-47), Mark seems to pause for breath. He seems to be standing back in order to set out the evidence that these events really did happen; so, with Mark, having studied the story of the crucifixion itself, we will now stand back and look.

At this point, with Jesus dead, there comes a quieter interlude. Mark begins this section by reminding us of the time of day (15:42). Here is another pointer that he is writing mainly for Gentiles, who might need to be told that **'Preparation Day'** is Friday, the day before the Sabbath, which would begin at sunset. Joseph of Arimathea — a village about twenty miles north-west of Jerusalem — is introduced in verse 43 as a senior member of the Jewish council, the body that convicted Jesus the previous night. Almost certainly Joseph was absent from the meeting; there could be a wide variety of reasons for that, but clearly he was not part of the decision that sent Jesus to Pilate and the cross. That Joseph is **'waiting for the kingdom of God'** means that he is a faithful Jew who is longing for the day when God will intervene in the nation's history and bring in the new era foretold by the prophets. So Joseph is presented to us as a godly man, who has recognized that Jesus is at least a prophet, and perhaps something more, and who must be devastated that Jesus has been sent to the cross. His death has galvanized Joseph into action: at least, he resolves, Jesus shall have an honourable burial. Joseph will have in mind the law on burial found in Deuteronomy 21:22-23. It is imperative that Jesus be buried before the day is over.

The move that Joseph makes is risky. By going to ask for Jesus' body, he is associating himself with a man convicted for rebellion against Rome. Moreover, Governor Pilate is off-duty by this time of day and probably doesn't want to be disturbed. It's likely that Joseph has to use every bit of prestige and influence he can muster to gain access to Pilate and obtain a hearing for this remarkable request. So the word **'boldly'** is absolutely appropriate: Joseph is risking his life.

He faces a further problem too. Under Roman law, executed men lose all their rights, including the right to a decent burial. That is even more the case with a crime of high treason, like this. Normally the body would be left on the cross in public view to rot. History tells us that exceptions were occasionally made, but only at the discretion of the authorities, and there is no reason for Joseph to think that Pilate will co-operate. Why should he want to soften even slightly the terrible deterrent value of a crucifixion? What Joseph does not know, as he waits nervously for his hearing, is that Pilate has already concluded that Jesus poses no real threat to the state. He would have much preferred to let Jesus go, as verses 9-15 make clear. That explains why, most unexpectedly, Pilate will eventually agree to Joseph's request, but first he makes an important check (15:44-45). Crucified men might well survive for two or three days until they died of suffocation or thirst, but Jesus has lasted no more than about six hours. This is unusual.

Naturally, there can be no question of releasing the body if there is any possibility of life remaining. So Pilate does the sensible thing and calls in the professional. This would be very easy to do. All the locations in this story are very close together. Golgotha, where the crosses are standing and where two men are still dying, is probably no more than five minutes' walk away; in fact, depending on where in Herod's old palace this conversation takes place, it is even possible that they can see the cross of Jesus as they speak. The centurion confirms what he has observed so closely: unexpected it may be but, yes, Jesus is certainly dead. Death is confirmed. This account is perfectly consistent with verse 37, that just before he dies, Jesus is still strong enough to cry out, loudly, indicating that his physical strength is not exhausted, but he has laid down his life at the moment he chooses. The period of unconscious struggle that normally precedes death does not happen; indeed, in the purposes of God there would be no point in that.

Now Joseph has what he wants. Given his status, he will certainly have help available — John's Gospel confirms that he does — and he will need it, because time is running out. By now there can only be a couple of hours of daylight left: when the sun goes down, the Sabbath will begin and no work can be done. It is only Mark who tells us that Joseph has to buy the linen shroud now (15:46) — another indication that he did not expect Pilate to agree to his request! There is no time to perform the full rites of burial; that will have to wait until after the Sabbath. Carefully, they take the body of Jesus down from the cross. They will find time to wash the body; then it is wrapped in the linen and placed in a rock-hewn tomb nearby which Joseph has at his disposal.[4] With only such dignity as the rapidly sinking sun permits, the body of the Saviour is buried. In front of the entrance to the tomb they roll the stone which covers it. Several such tombs have been discovered by archaeologists. In a typical design, the stone is disc-shaped and rolls along a slightly tilted slot, so that it would be fairly easy to close the tomb, but much harder to roll the stone away again and open it.

At this point Mark gives us another supporting witness (15:47). While the male disciples are still lying low, the women are watching on. These are two of the same women listed in verse 40 as witnesses to the crucifixion. Having watched the burial, they will be in no doubt at all (as is sometimes alleged) which tomb contains the body of Jesus. They know that burial has been hasty and there is more work to do to prepare the body. So they make completely sure they know where it is, because they are planning to return. This is a detail no one would invent. In New Testament times, women are simply not regarded as reliable witnesses. In the mindset of these times, inserting a note about women as witnesses would not strengthen the evidence base; if anything it would weaken it. Mark tells us they are there, so they must be there. In God's purposes, the women are primary witnesses of all these events, and in making them primary witnesses, God is demonstrating that the testimony of women is worth exactly as much as the witness of men. We might wonder why the women seem so silent in this account. In a culture where extravagant and public wailing and mourning is the norm, why do they just stand and watch? The answer is simple: it's against the law to mourn the death of a condemned criminal. So they contain their pain; they simply watch and witness.

All this we know from Mark's account. Can we say any more, for instance, about exactly where these events took place? This is where archaeology helps us. We can be fairly sure, though not certain, that we know exactly where Jesus was crucified and where he was buried. Neither 'Gordon's Calvary' nor the 'Garden Tomb' are credible locations for these events; rather, both sites lie within the walls of what is now the Church of the Holy Sepulchre. The tomb at the focal point of that rather grotesque building is very likely the real tomb of Jesus, although not in its original form; and about fifty yards away to the east, an outcrop of rock is probably the remains of Golgotha, where the cross stood nearly two thousand years ago. The evidence for these sites is very strong: the area was indeed just outside the city walls in the time of Jesus, being enclosed about ten years later in the time of Herod Agrippa. It is known to have been a stone quarry in previous times, leaving just the kind of low cliffs into which tombs could easily be cut. Indeed, six other first-century tombs have been located in the immediate vicinity. As for the rocky outcrop identified as Golgotha, it was probably left unquarried because of its poor quality and would have formed a low hillock, a prominent landmark close to the path leading in to Jerusalem via the nearby Gennath Gate.[5] All the evidence points to these being the actual locations where Jesus died and was buried; they fit and satisfy the biblical data precisely; but we don't know for sure, and we don't need to know. It is enough to know that the account is true.

So why does it matter? We have seen so far that Mark's account makes sense, that it is consistent both internally and externally, and that it fits what we know from history and archaeology. We have also seen that Mark has gone to some lengths to set his story out as a sober historical account, fully backed up by witnesses and evidence. There are at least three reasons why it matters that all this is true.

First, it matters because *the Christian faith is grounded in history*. Some people say that the Christian message is all about some good ideas, or some profound teaching; that is all that matters. The ideas and the teaching don't depend on whether anything happened or not. But the early church knew that it mattered. Peter's speech to the crowd just six weeks later shows as much: he emphasizes the facts they know as the foundation for his message (Acts 2:22-23). In similar vein, see what Paul says in 1 Corinthians 15:3-8. Notice how he stresses the reality of the events, the named witnesses who saw them: these facts of history are 'of first importance', not just a useful bonus. Peter and Paul are quite clear that the Christian message stands or falls by the reality of these events. The early Christians lived and died for a faith that was grounded in history. Christianity was never just a philosophy, merely a set of ideas. That made it different from all the religions on offer at the time, which were about secret knowledge, mythology or mysterious ceremonies. The great scandal of the Christian faith — it's known as the 'scandal of particularity' — is the claim that at this *one* time, and in this *one* place, and in this *one* way, God intervened uniquely in the person of his Son, the Lord Jesus Christ, who suffered and died to set people free of their sin and restore their relationship with him. That is shocking, but it is the gospel.

It matters that this is true, secondly, because *there can only be one truth.* Today we talk about living in a time of postmodernity. This means that we can all tell our different stories; we can all hold our different beliefs — and they are all equally valid. No one's story can be privileged over anyone else's. My truth can be true for me, while at the same time your truth is true for you. In most areas of life we understand that this idea is ridiculous. If my car runs out of fuel and I need to fill it up, I might have a sincere belief that it will work best when I fill it with water. You might have an equally sincere belief that diesel is the best thing for it, but in fact, we would both be wrong, because my car won't run on either. The idea that our sincere beliefs about how to run my car are equally valid is understood to be absurd. Sincerity does not make nonsense into truth! And sincerity is not enough to determine whether our beliefs about the world, and about God and Jesus and life after death, are true either. Jesus did not both 'die' and 'not die' — one option must be true; the other option must be false. However sincerely you believe the false option, it is still false. If Jesus did really die, so much more follows. If Jesus died, as the Bible asserts on page after page, and as the historians of the time also agree, then it follows naturally that the Bible writers are also telling the truth in the way that they explain that death. One thing non-Christians cannot reasonably say is that Christians are fine with their beliefs, and at the same time so are their own. There can really only be one true truth.

The third reason is simple: *if this is the truth, then a response is required.* If Mark's account as we have it is true and reliable, and all we have seen about the cross and the tomb is much more than an inspiring story, it cannot be left as an episode of history. This is the message we have to proclaim, summoning people to recognize the reality of Jesus' death, what it has to mean for them, and their need to accept his sacrifice for themselves. We can be sure that our faith is no exercise in wishful thinking. The Gospel accounts are sure and certain; we can be absolutely confident of the foundations they give us. We can stand firm on the ground where the early Christians stood firm. If we know all that, then we are called to be witnesses — confident in our faith, bold in our proclamation. In this passage our model is the boldness of Joseph, who took his life in his hands as he approached the Roman governor; our model is the women, who watched and witnessed faithfully to what they knew — to the death of the Lord, and then to the glorious events they would see on the day after the Sabbath.

25.
Jesus is alive!

Please read Mark 16:1-8

Daylight spreads slowly across the sky. Away to the east, beyond the towers of the temple and the adjacent Roman fortress, the sun rises above the horizon as they make their way out of the city gate. Already at this early hour there are people moving about; here, business starts at daybreak. But the three women have business of their own. Last night, they pooled their limited funds to buy the spices needed to pre-pare a body for permanent burial. Just a couple of hundred yards beyond this gate, the body of someone very special awaits their attention. They have had to wait until now because of the Sabbath; everything stops for the Sabbath; only when yesterday evening came could they get hold of what they needed, and only now, Sunday morning, can they make their way to the tomb. The weather is warm; he has been dead for over thirty-six hours; they really can't wait any longer to honour their dead leader. All three of them watched him die on the cross, that moment of death on Friday after-noon, and two of them observed the hurried burial nearby. They saw Joseph and the others rolling the great stone down its slot; they heard the thud as it reached its resting place in front of the doorway. That, they know, will be their problem. As they walk the last few yards they are asking each other,

'How in the world are we going to roll the stone away
again?' They know these tombs are designed to be easy to
close but hard to open. They might have to enlist the help of
passers-by; they have to get in somehow. That thought
brings them to the old quarry where a number of tombs have
been cut in to the rock face. Here's the one; it's rather
grander than the others; Joseph of Arimathea is a wealthy
man, after all. The tomb has an outer chamber; beyond it lies
the burial chamber, sealed by the stone; but here comes the
shock.

As they enter the outer chamber and come face to face
with the tomb itself, to their utter amazement they see that
the stone has already been removed. It has been rolled right
back and, more shocking still, just inside there is someone
sitting and waiting for them. He doesn't seem at all surprised
to see them, but at the sight of him they are terrified. In
appearance he is a young man, robed all in white, but a white
that can be clearly seen even in the darkness of the tomb.

It's disturbing enough to find the tomb open and someone
sitting inside. But they are far beyond surprise; it is dread, it
is terror, that they feel, because they recognize this is no
ordinary young man. This is an angel of God; this is an
eruption of heavenly glory into their grey world. What can
the messenger of God be doing here, inside a grave? The
words he speaks in verses 6-7, words which will transform
their lives for ever, add further astonishment to their fear.
'Calm down; don't be so fearful', he says. 'I know why you
are here — you are looking for Jesus from Nazareth, the
crucified one. He has risen! He is not here! Look, this is
where they put the body: see, it's empty space! Now, here is
what you must do. Go and tell his disciples — Peter as well
— "He's going ahead of you into Galilee. You will see him
there, just as he told you before."'

The women need no second invitation to back out of the
tomb. The encounter with the angel, coupled with the

stunning news that he has given, leaves them trembling with fear. Their heads are spinning as they run back towards the city. They career down the streets now filling with people; heads are turned at the unusual sight of three women running full pelt along the road, but not a word do they utter until they have done what the angel told them to do.

Before we can begin to grasp the astonishing story of Jesus' resurrection, we need to enter into the experience of the women that early Sunday morning. We need to feel something of their fear and bewilderment as they encounter the angel and the sheer, overwhelming shock of the news that the one they loved has risen from the dead — hence my attempt to capture these feelings in the preceding paragraphs.

The other issue we need to face at the outset is a strange one: it concerns the point where Mark's Gospel actually ends! I have provided an additional note to explain this; for now I will simply say that I am convinced that Mark intended to finish his Gospel with what we call verse 8. We will return to the reason Mark chose to end like this shortly.

Now let's get back to the story. It is clear that Mark is still interested in confirming the facts of what happened at the resurrection, just as he was with Jesus' death and burial. The time, the day, the details of the preparation, the problem of removing the stone, the fact that it *is* removed, the repeated confirmation that the body of Jesus has gone, even the reference to meeting him in Galilee — all this demonstrates that Mark intends us to take the resurrection as sober, historical reality, rooted in real places, marked on a real calendar. There is no place here for the idea that the resurrection is merely some kind of metaphor, a picture representing new hope, or the disciples' determination to carry on the ministry and message of Jesus after his death. In fact after the crucifixion all the disciples are determined to do is to keep their heads down! But, in any case, that idea is completely alien to the New Testament accounts, all of

which are fully convinced that these events actually happened; our faith stands and falls by that.

The resurrection of Christ is such a real and pivotal event
that, ever after that, Sunday, resurrection day, became the
church's day of worship. We should note, by the way, that
the claim of the empty tomb was never denied by the enemies of the church. Within a few weeks the young church
will be preaching a message that is squarely based on the
facts of the case, at a time when it can easily be disproved if
their opponents can find any way of doing so.

Thus Mark clearly establishes the reality of the empty
tomb; he wants us to be sure that it actually happened. But
that is not enough. The belief that Jesus rose from the dead is
of no value unless we understand what it means. If you
simply believe that Jesus rose to life, amazing as that is, all
you have is a sort of happy ending to a sad story. They
crucified him — how tragic, how unjust, how horrible! But
he rose again — so that's OK! No, the facts of the resurrection are just the foundation; we need more. The women in
the story are terrified; the word Mark (and only Mark) uses
in verse 5 is very strong — not just because they have had a
shock, not even just because they have seen an angel, but
because they have witnessed God doing something spectacularly supernatural. This is God turning all human expectations upside down — there was not one person on earth
who expected Jesus to rise that Sunday morning. Anyone can
be executed, but not anyone can emerge from his grave a
couple of days later!

This is the same fear the disciples feel when they see
Jesus calm the storm (see 4:35-41) — remember, they are
more frightened *after* the storm than they are *in the middle of*
it when they think they are going to drown, because in that
moment they have seen a glimpse of God. It is the same fear
they feel on the Mountain of Transfiguration where they see
the Lord Jesus revealed for a moment in his divine glory (see

9:2-8), when they see him drive a horde of demons out of the man called Legion (5:1-20) and when he walks on the water (6:45-52). These were great wonders, but their overwhelming reaction every time they saw God revealed in Jesus was *fear*. Now these women feel it too. Unless you and I, reading this story, feel something of that disturbance ourselves, we have probably never grasped the meaning of the resurrection. This is no mere happy ending! I want to highlight two life-changing realities that this passage brings out.

Firstly, *death is defeated* (16:6-7). Jesus is alive! Notice that triple affirmation in verse 6. This is where he was — and *he is not here now*! Notice the way Peter is singled out for special mention, because Peter is the one who denied Jesus publicly while the Jewish high court had him on trial. We can imagine the sense of wonder in Peter's voice as he tells Mark the story and recalls the grace of Jesus that restored him. In 14:28, just where Jesus is telling his disciples that they will all desert him, he says he will meet them again — Peter as well, the chief failure. Yes, Jesus will meet him as well, and back in Galilee, where they have spent those years together, Peter will be restored. What a message — even after such a disaster, there is hope for failures like him, and for us!

So Jesus is alive! Death is defeated! But what does that mean? It gives further proof that his mission was truly accomplished. We have seen that demonstrated in the account of the way Jesus dies, but the resurrection is further proof. God declares that Jesus has triumphed by raising him to life. Over and over again, the early church stressed this in their preaching (see Acts 2:22-24; 3:13-15; 13:29-30; Rom. 1:4). The resurrection confirms that Jesus' death is not futile, it is not a half-finished job and it is not the end. But, more than that, it means that there is resurrection for us all. See what Paul says in 1 Corinthians 15:12-14,17-20. That expression 'first fruits' refers to harvesting crops. 'First fruits' are literally what you bring in first — and all the rest will follow behind. In other words, Jesus' resurrection is the proof that all the Bible's promises about eternal life are true. If God did it for Jesus, then he will do it for us. All of us who die will experience resurrection. We shall be raised to life for eternity, just as he was, in bodies that are equipped for eternity — bodies that will not show the wearing of the years, the decay and the pain that come from living in the bodies we know so well today.

There is resurrection for us all, but that is not necessarily good news. For believers, this story is one of immense comfort. Because he has gone through the grave and risen to renewed life, we too shall go through the grave and rise to new life. For everyone who belongs to Jesus Christ, we can *know* that our destiny is to live with him in eternity. This resurrection truth gives us all, young or old, near death or remote from it, the assurance that we need. But for unbelievers, those who are outside of Christ, the resurrection is actually a very *uncomfortable* truth, because it reminds us that our story does not end with physical death. This present life is not all there is. Beyond death lies resurrection and judgement for everybody. People may be able to ignore God in this life and to reach death taking no account of him at all, but death is not the end. The warning is that they too will be raised to life, will stand before the Judge and be called to account for the full record of their days on earth.

Secondly, however, *life is still messy*. The reason people wrote extra endings to Mark's Gospel — and there are at least three variations on the longer ending — is that it seems to come to such an untidy conclusion. But that is just the point. What does the angel emphasize to the women? **'He is not here'** (16:6). Yes, that certainly refers to Jesus' physical resurrection: he has gone from the tomb! But it is also Mark's way of saying that Jesus isn't going to be around any more. He is risen — and this account clearly states that he will indeed appear to the disciples — but they must learn to live with the fact that he won't always be here. They have to live with his absence — until the day when he returns along with a whole army of angels (13:26-27).

The four Gospels, as you probably know, all handle the resurrection story differently. The other three all record various appearances of Jesus after he is risen, to various places in different locations. But even those endings are not as neat and tidy as we might think. The conclusion to all four Gospels contains this note of uneasiness. In Matthew, false rumours are spread about the resurrection (Matt. 28:11-15) and, even as Jesus says his final farewell, some of the disciples are still doubting (Matt. 28:17). John concludes with the prediction of Peter's humiliating death (John 21:18-19), and Luke's Gospel is the prelude to Acts, where the early Christians after the resurrection face hostile courts, stoning, judicial execution, beatings, imprisonment and a host of other unpleasant experiences as a normal part of life. And this is Mark's way — typically brief, typically sharp, typically hard-edged, finishing his Gospel on a note of fear and bewilderment. (This is why you will hardly ever hear a sermon about the resurrection from Mark's Gospel!) The closing note is disturbing — because life here on earth is still going to be messy; the life we know now is full of loose ends. It's full of events and experiences that we don't understand and find hard to handle, where there is suffering and pain, and where we can be deeply injured, even by other Christians.

The resurrection is not a happy-ever-after story — not yet! The resurrection of Jesus is past; it stands in history as a supremely glorious truth, an established fact to give us hope and assurance. But our own resurrection still lies ahead. For Christians, the trials and struggles of this life are given to make us more like our Saviour, gradually to transform us into the image of Christ. Every difficulty, every painful relationship, every encounter with illness or old age, every exam failure, every conflict in your office or your school, is an opportunity for that to happen. So when life seems to be falling apart, it doesn't necessarily mean that you have gone wrong, and it certainly doesn't mean that he has lost control. God's purpose for us is not to make our path through life as easy as possible. He has a bigger agenda than that. His intention is to make us more like his Son, while we still live in a messy world.

For people who are not yet Christians, the struggles of this life are a *warning*, a loud trumpet blast calling for surrender. The harder the struggle, the louder the call. God is calling you to realize that you are not in control, that only he can be in control, and that you still have the chance to submit and come to him through Christ.

The message of the resurrection story is that life is still messy, but death is defeated! The resurrection has happened! It was real; Jesus was raised to life; the tomb was vacated; the angel was waiting for the women to arrive. The stone was rolled back, not for him to get out, but for them to come in and see the proof: he is not here, he has risen! It proved that Jesus' mission was fully accomplished. For believers, the resurrection is the certainty that we can look death in the face and know that our already-risen Saviour is waiting for us beyond the grave.

As we reach the end of Mark's Gospel, the question is simply: have you seen this crucified and risen Jesus for who he really is? Do you know him? Are we following him as he leads us through this painful, messy world, until the day when we see him face to face — either beyond the death he has defeated, or when he returns in glory as the Judge?

Additional note on the endings of Mark's Gospel

The question of where Mark's Gospel really ends is an issue which everyone who studies or preaches through Mark has to face, because, as you will see from your Bible, the printed text actually runs on to verse 20. Depending on which version of the Bible you are using, you will probably have an explanatory footnote that tells you that some of the early manuscripts include verses 9-20, while others do not.

For English readers brought up with the Authorized or King James Version (which simply includes verses 9-20 without explanation), it may be hard to accept that part of the familiar text may not be genuine. However, I am convinced (along with many others!) that Mark finished his Gospel at verse 8. There are several reasons for holding this view.

Firstly, even in English, verses 9-20 read like a deliberate tidying-up operation; in the Greek that impression is even stronger. There is no continuity between verse 8 and verse 9, and the style and the use of words is totally unlike that of Mark. It sounds very much as though some later writer has read the endings of the other Gospels, along with Acts, and produced what he thought was a tidier ending for Mark's Gospel. Read verses 9-20 with that thought in mind, and you will quickly see what I mean. You will find a brief survey of this passage after this note.

Probably many of us have felt that verse 8 does leave the story rather in mid-air. We feel that a Gospel should end more neatly, certainly not with a group of women running away from the empty tomb! Gospels, we feel, should end with appearances of the risen Christ, preferably involving a fishing trip, a walk in the countryside or a rendezvous on a mountain top. But since Mark invented the genre we call 'Gospel', it would be better to let him show us how a Gospel ought to end, and not the other way round!

Secondly, there is very good evidence that Mark's book circulated widely with an ending at verse 8; this evidence comes from several sources. The two oldest manuscripts we have (the codices known as *Vaticanus* and *Sinaiticus*) finish at verse 8, as is well known. What is less well known is that many of the oldest translations into other languages, such as Georgian, Ethiopic and Old Latin, also finish there. This indicates that the Gospel circulated widely in this form and tends to counteract the argument that the great majority of the Greek manuscripts (mostly produced much later than *Vaticanus* and *Sinaiticus*) include a longer ending. Moreover the early church historian Eusebius, writing in the fourth century, clearly believes that the genuine ending of the Gospel comes at verse 8, and even before that church fathers such as Clement of Alexandria and Origen seem to be unaware of any longer ending.

A further, minor, argument in favour of the ending at verse 8 is that it is consistent with the structural parallel with 14:1-11. These two passages begin and end the closing section of the Gospel: in the first, Jesus is anointed for his burial; in 16:1-8, he is not anointed at the actual place of his burial — because he is no longer there!

It has often been argued that Mark could not have finished with verse 8 as it stands, because it ends impossibly with the Greek word *gar* (meaning 'for'). However, it has now been shown that this is a legitimate way to end a sentence, and even a document, so this argument has lost its force. It is also worth noting again that verses 9-20 as printed in our Bibles do not constitute the only additional ending: a shorter one is also found — usually, but not always, in combination with the longer one; and the longer one has a major variant of its own.

All in all, I believe it is safe to say that what we call verses 9-20 were written by someone other than Mark, probably some decades later, and that in our study and our preaching we too should conclude at verse 8. Mark's reasons for finishing on this abrupt note are discussed in the main text. For more extensive discussion of the question of the endings, I suggest consulting a larger commentary, such as Lane or France. Hendriksen's treatment is also helpful.

Notes on the text of Mark 16:9-20

For the sake of completeness, I will include here a brief survey of the passage we know as Mark 16:9-20. I will do no more than note the other variant endings — the 'shorter ending' inserted between verses 9 and 10 in a number of manuscripts and the long extension which one manuscript includes after verse 14. These are universally agreed today to be spurious, although their presence does support the view that there was very early confusion about the form of the text of Mark 16.

Verses 9-11 tell us of Jesus' appearance to Mary Magdalene. The Greek does not include his name. These verses give a summary of the information in John 20:11-18, with the additional note that Mary had had seven demons expelled (Luke 8:2). The disciples' unbelief at this point is consistent with what we know of them from elsewhere (and see Luke 24:11). It would not be surprising if they were **'mourning and weeping'** (16:10), since we know that they had not grasped the repeated promise of the resurrection.

Verses 12-13 refer to the incident recorded at much greater length in Luke 24:13-35, where Jesus encounters Cleopas and another disciple on the way to Emmaus. The reference to Jesus being **'in a different form'** (16:12) is odd.

Presumably it refers to the pair's inability to recognize him, but Luke's explanation is simply that 'they were kept from recognizing him' (Luke 24:16). Verse 13 contains another seeming discrepancy. Luke's account describes a very different reception (Luke 24:33-35). If the two incidents are indeed the same, and Mark 16:13 is to be taken as reliable, the only possible explanation is that *part* of the disciple group were now believing, while the remainder were not.

Verse 14 describes the appearance of Jesus recorded in Luke 24:36-49 and John 20:19-23. Jesus' rebuke is framed in stronger terms than it is in Luke or John, perhaps suggesting that whoever wrote this ending wants to address people who are casting doubt on the truth of Jesus' bodily resurrection.

Verses 15-18 contain an extended version of the Great Commission (Matt. 28:18-20). The emphasis on baptism is true to New Testament teaching (Matt. 28:19; Acts 2:38); the second half of verse 16 confirms that baptism itself is not regarded as essential to salvation. Verses 17-18 give a list of five signs (Greek *semeion*, a word which Mark nowhere uses of miracles, though John frequently does) that will accompany believers. Of these, driving out demons and healing the sick occur frequently in the Gospels and in Acts. Speaking in tongues is not mentioned in the Gospels, but is prominent in Acts. Handling snakes safely is mentioned once in Acts 28:3-6, the story of Paul on Malta, though there is no suggestion that picking up the snake was deliberate! But drinking poison without harm is mentioned nowhere in the New Testament and credible records are very few. The early church historian Eusebius quotes the second-century author Papias as describing such an incident in the life of Justus Barsabbas (see Acts 1:23). Those who regard these verses as genuine will see that incident as a fulfilment of verse 18; those who do not may see it as explaining the invention of verse 18!

Finally, verses 19-20 tell the story of Jesus' ascension and its aftermath. Unlike Luke, verse 19 alludes to his glorification. Whereas the blunt ending at verse 8 may be thought too abrupt, this version certainly seems 'too good to be true'! Mark has been at pains to stress the suffering and trials which lie in store for Jesus' true disciples, but verse 20 reads like a deliberately happy ending. Of course, that is not the same as saying it is not true. The theology of verses 19-20 is entirely consistent with the New Testament. The question is whether their emphasis could possibly be true to Mark.

In conclusion, we may say that Mark 16:9-20 adds little information that the other Gospels do not already give us, with apparent discrepancies in verses 13 and 18 and a suspiciously neat ending in verses 19-20.

Notes

Introduction to Mark's Gospel
1. This structure is based on the one proposed by Chris Kelly in *Foundations,* Issue 59, Spring 2008, though I have changed all his headings! Unlike Kelly, I have followed most other writers in taking 1:1-13 as a separate prologue. The pattern of *inclusios* which forms the basis for the structure still works, however.
2. The phrase is from Richard Hays' *The moral vision of the New Testament.*

Chapter 1 — The good news begins
1. The most likely site for John's baptizing — though there are other contenders.

Chapter 2 — The mission is launched
1. According to the structure proposed in the introduction, this section of Mark's Gospel ('Authority and opposition'), runs from 1:14 to 6:30 and is bracketed by the two references to John's imprisonment.
2. See Jeremiah 16:16.

Chapter 3 — Who does he think he is?
1. Lane (*The Gospel of Mark,* NICNT, pp.96-8) has a helpful discussion of this problem.

Chapter 4 — Wanted: genuine followers
1. This is in fact the first example in the Gospel of *bracketing* — a device Mark uses to illustrate one story by means of another. There is a striking

example in chapter 11, where the cursing of the fig tree is an acted parable illustrating the downfall of the temple. In this case Mark is highlighting the fact that Jesus' own physical family understand him no better (at this point) than his religious adversaries.

2. The name literally means 'Lord of the Flies'; this is where William Golding found the name for his famous novel, the message of which is that evil dwells inside us all.

Chapter 5 — Wanted: ears that can hear
1. This is the difference between a parable and an allegory — an allegory contains many more 'connections' between the story and the real world which it represents. A popular example of an allegory is C.S. Lewis' *The Lion, the Witch and the Wardrobe*, where Aslan, the Emperor over the Sea, the witch, the children, the winter, the battles, Turkish Delight, and the good and evil creatures in the story, all correspond to characters or situations in the real world — and many of these are worked out further in the other books in the series. Having said that, a few of Jesus' parables are more like allegories. The best example of this is the parable of the tenants in Mark 12.

2. Arthur Fallowfield, played by Kenneth Williams in the comedy series *Beyond our Ken.*

3. For a useful fuller explanation, refer to Lane, *The Gospel of Mark,* pp.165-7.

Chapter 6 — Power to restore
1. According to Lane, contemporary remedies included carrying around the ash of an ostrich egg wrapped in a cloth, and drinking wine containing a powder made from rubber, alum and garden crocuses!

Chapter 7 — Tradition!
1. Actually the word *paradosis*, referring to something handed down, appears five times in the Greek text; the English translations generally use the word 'tradition' six times in verses 1-13.

2. A number of manuscripts, but not the two generally regarded as most reliable, include one of Jesus' popular sayings at this point: 'If anyone has ears to hear, let him hear.' Traditionally this was labelled as verse 16. Hence in the newer English translations there is no verse 16.

Chapter 11 — Catering for the nations
1. See Lane, *The Gospel of Mark,* p.269. On the arrangement I have chosen, 8:22-30 actually lie in the next major section; the fact is that these

verses are transitional and function both as the end of the present section and the start of the next one. Lane, who adopts a more geographically based structure for the Gospel, ends a section at 8:30.

2. Such rebukes can be found, for example, in Isaiah 6:9-10; Jeremiah 5:21 and Ezekiel 12:2.

Chapter 12 — The turning point
1. Greek, *apodokimazo.*

Chapter 13 — Glory revealed
1. Many Greek manuscripts do include the extra words, but the two early manuscripts which are widely regarded as the most reliable do not.

Chapter 15 — The demands of the kingdom
1. A full discussion of the grounds for divorce is well beyond the scope of this book. For a range of views see the following recent books: Stephen Clark's *Putting Asunder: Divorce and remarriage in biblical and pastoral perspective*; Jay Adams' *Marriage, divorce and remarriage in the Bible: A fresh look at what Scripture teaches*; Ralph Woodrow's *Divorce and Remarriage: What does the Bible really say?* and David Instone-Brewer's *Divorce and remarriage in the church.*

Chapter 16 — Following the real Jesus
1. Mark 10:45 is one of the few texts in the Gospels which provide explicit support for the element of substitution in the atonement. The Greek word translated **'for'** (*anti*) does not in itself require the meaning 'in place of', but the idea of a ransom payment does provide that note of substitution by an equivalent.

Chapter 17 — The judgement of the king
1. There is more to the cameo of the colt than first meets the eye. It is probably reasonable to see an allusion to Genesis 49:10-11 in the repeated reference to a *tied* colt. See Lane, *The Gospel of Mark,* p.395, for further details.

2. Some manuscripts include as verse 26: 'But if you do not forgive, neither will your Father who is in heaven forgive your sins.' These words don't appear in the oldest manuscripts, and it is most likely that they have been transferred from Matthew 6:15, where they follow a verse similar to Mark 11:25.

3. The quote is from T. W. Manson, quoted by Lane, *The Gospel of Mark,* p.399.

Chapter 19 — The end of the old regime

1. To be precise, a *quadrans* was worth one sixty-fourth of a denarius. The parallel passage in Luke does not include this explanation. The only other New Testament mention of the *quadrans* is in Matthew 5:26, but in that case it is not being used to explain the value of something else.

Chapter 20 — The final crisis

1. The enthronement by the Zealots of the clown named Phanni as high priest is recorded by Josephus in his *Jewish War*.

2. There is a view that the descriptions here — and those in Revelation 6:12-14 as well — are not only metaphorical, but don't even refer to the return of Christ. This view states that the 'coming' referred to in verse 26 is Christ's coming to God the Father to receive his kingdom, and that this took place with the destruction of Jerusalem and the temple in AD 70. In this way the reference to **'this generation'** in verse 30 can be easily understood to mean 'the people who are alive now'. This view is set out, for example, by Dick France in his commentary on Mark (see introduction) and in his commentaries on Matthew 24. It is also supported by N. T. Wright (*Jesus and the Victory of God*, pp.339-65). We don't have the space to tackle these issues in full here, but as far as this passage is concerned, the view fails to account for the emphasis on what will be *seen*, especially in verse 26.

Chapter 21 — The scene is set

1. Oddly, the fact that Mark does not name Mary here has been taken by some to imply the subjugation of women in the Gospel stories; hence the title of Elisabeth Schussler Fiorenza's feminist theology, *In memory of her*, which is taken from verse 9. The truth is that it accords with Mark's style to name few of his characters. Judas is not identified in the anointing narrative either, whereas John names both Mary and Judas.

2. The word translated **'pure'** in 14:3 is the Greek *pistikes*. Its meaning is uncertain: one interesting possibility is 'pistachio', in which case pistachio oil is the base of the perfume!

3. The words, **'This is my body'**, have been used to support the Roman Catholic doctrine of transubstantiation — that the bread literally becomes the body of Christ and that the mass (or Holy Communion) is a continuing sacrifice of Christ's body. Apart from the fact that, as he says this, his physical body is still in the room with them, the Catholic interpretation contradicts the very strong emphasis in the New Testament on the completeness of Christ's sacrifice. This is especially obvious in Hebrews

9 and 10, where it is stated no less than six times (Heb. 9:12,26,28; 10:10,12,14).

Chapter 22 — Countdown to the cross

1. Mark does not specify the content of the temptations, as Matthew and Luke do, but even in Mark the placing of the temptations between Jesus' baptism and the start of his ministry implies that this is what Satan is trying to do.

2. The site of the high priest's house where Jesus was tried before the Sanhedrin is not known for certain: there are rival claimants. Archaeology has, however, confirmed the wealth of a number of houses in Jerusalem at this time. The high priest's would certainly have been one of these.

3. Although the NIV omits the phrase, **'and the cock crowed'**, from verse 68, there is good evidence for its inclusion here (the ESV does include it). All but one of the key manuscripts include **'the second time'** in verse 72.

Chapter 23 — Sentence executed

1. Older books sometimes mention a stone pavement excavated at the Antonia fortress site, on which are carved markings relating to what is called the 'King Game'. But it is now known that this pavement is of later date and cannot be connected with the abuse suffered by Jesus in Mark 15:16-20.

2. The idea that Simon of Cyrene was substituted for Jesus is believed by many Muslims. The fact that he is identified as the father of two men who must have been known to the early church makes Simon a rather unlikely candidate for such a substitution. Surely his family would have missed him!

3. There is a well-known difficulty over the timing, since Mark says Jesus was crucified at **'the third hour'** (about 9 a.m.), whereas John indicates that he was sentenced 'about the sixth hour' (about midday, John 19:14). While Lane suggests that Mark 15:25 may be an insertion by a copyist who noticed that no timing was provided, noting that neither Matthew nor Luke include it, there is no manuscript evidence for this. Given that all the synoptists record that Jesus died around the ninth hour, and that all the Gospels agree that proceedings with Pilate began early in the morning, it would seem that it is John's timing that raises the greater difficulty. The best solution is probably the simplest: both Mark and John are working in approximations.

Chapter 24 — Mission accomplished

1. This line of thought was suggested by Paul Wells' chapter, 'The cry of dereliction: the beloved Son cursed and condemned', in *The Forgotten Christ*, ed. Stephen Clark, Inter-Varsity Press, 2007. As Wells puts it, when Jesus uttered this cry, he knew that he had 'reached the end of the line': there was no going forward or back, only going 'out' (p.113).

2. Jürgen Moltmann's *The Crucified God* is the best-known vehicle for this view in recent decades.

3. Fuller details of the amazing parallels between Jesus' baptism and his death can be found in the article, 'The heavenly veil torn: Mark's cosmic *inclusio*' in *Journal of Biblical Literature*, Vol. 110, No. 1 (Spring 1991), pp. 123-5.

4. These events clearly fulfil the prophecy of Isaiah 53:9.

5. The name of the Gennath Gate, referred to by Josephus, almost certainly comes from *ganoth*, meaning gardens. There is some archaeological evidence for the existence of the gardens mentioned in John 19:41 in this quarry.